Keming Yang

ANALYSING INTERSECTIONALITY

A Toolbox of Methods

S Sage

1 Oliver's Yard
55 City Road
London EC1Y 1SP

2455 Teller Road
Thousand Oaks, California 91320

Unit No 323-333, Third Floor, F-Block
International Trade Tower, Nehru Place
New Delhi 110 019

8 Marina View Suite 43-053
Asia Square Tower 1
Singapore 018960

Editor: Charlotte Bush
Editorial assistant: Rhiannon Holt
Production editor: Imogen Roome
Copyeditor: Neil Dowden
Proofreader: Leigh Smithson
Marketing manager: Ben Sherwood
Cover design: Shaun Mercier
Typeset by: KnowledgeWorks Global Ltd.

Library of Congress Control Number: 2023936528

British Library Cataloguing in Publication data

A catalogue record for this book is available from the British Library

ISBN 978-1-5297-8988-1
ISBN 978-1-5297-8987-4 (pbk)

CONTENTS

LIST OF FIGURES

LIST OF TABLES

ABOUT THE AUTHOR

Dr Keming Yang is currently an Associate Professor of Sociology at the University of Durham in the UK. He was born and grew up in the city of Tianjin, People's Republic of China. He studied sociology at Nankai University and worked there for 3 years before going to study for a PhD at Columbia University in the US. His first job after receiving the PhD was at the National University of Singapore. He then took a position at the University of Reading in the UK and moved to the current position at Durham. His first research area is the political and economic sociology of entrepreneurship in China, in which he published two books, *Entrepreneurship in China* and *Capitalists in Communist China*, and some articles. Since working at the University of Durham, he has been working on the issue of loneliness from a sociological perspective. He is the author of *Loneliness: A Social Problem* and many articles on this topic. He also has a research interest in research methods in the social sciences, and is the author of *Making Sense of Statistics in Social Research* and the editor of *Categorical Data Analysis*.

PREFACE

I used to think that anthropology, especially social anthropology, and sociology were almost the same, but then I observed a key difference between the two: anthropologists study 'others', whilst sociologists study 'themselves'. This is not always true and becomes less and less true over time – anthropologists have come back to their own countries and many sociologists study people far away from themselves both in time and in space.

There are times the observation is true, however. Although the word 'intersectionality' is in the title, this book, more precisely, is about how to analyse intersectionality by using existing research methods. As the reader will see in the first chapter, it was Black feminists who made the idea of intersectionality explicit when they were trying to highlight and defend the interests of Black women. I would recommend that readers who are looking for profound discussions on the meaning of intersectionality from critical theoretical perspectives (feminism, critical race theory, decolonization, etc.) turn to texts such as *Intersectionality in Feminist and Queer Movements: Confronting Privileges* (edited by Elizabeth Evans and Eléonore Lépinard, Routledge, 2019), *Critical Race Theory: An Introduction* (by Richard Delgado and Jean Stefancic, 3rd edition, NYU Press, 2017) and *Disability and Colonialism: (Dis)encounters and Anxious Intersectionalities* (edited by Karen Soldatic and Shaun Grech, Routledge, 2016).

My goal here is to demonstrate why and how a toolbox of methods, either old tricks or new innovations, could make the empirical investigation on intersectionality more productive and rigorous. Being obliged to explain why I have produced this book at this moment, I feel the following question would very likely emerge in the mind of the reader: why do you care about a topic of which you do not seem to have much personal experience? Given the mandate of being reflexive for anyone researching on intersectionality, I will reflect, and make as explicit as I can, on how my identities and way of thinking have influenced my writing in the final chapter. Here, let me focus on my motivation for writing this book.

We shall discuss the meaning (or meanings) of intersectionality in the first chapter. At this moment, please indulge me with a quick but hopefully acceptable definition: generally speaking, intersectionality refers to the combined effect of two or more factors on an outcome of interest. For the pioneering Black female intellectuals, the two factors were gender and race, and the outcome of their interest was being discriminated against or oppressed. My country of origin is the People's Republic of China, but I have lived in some other countries (the US, Canada, Singapore and the UK) during the past 30 years. As a member of a visible minority ethnic group (some racial or ethnic minority groups are not visible), I was bullied or attacked by some White as well as Black people on a number of occasions. As I had nothing personal to do with them, it must have been my physical form of being Chinese (or at least Asian), male and having a good education (spectacles plus walking around a good university) that gave me away as a worthy target. Because the consequences of those incidents were not very serious, the attacks never enhanced my awareness of my intersectional identities; in fact, I thought they were 'normal' or 'expected' in my life, which explained why I was not one of the academics who initiated the idea of intersectionality.

Still, I believe that as a social scientist I should study phenomena that are important for society as a whole and search for truthful knowledge and insights. I do not have to be bitterly attacked, discriminated against, or oppressed because of my multiple disadvantaged identities so as to be motivated to study intersectionality. I want to write this book not directly because of my personal experiences but because I think it is an important issue for all human beings, about which I am confident that I can do some good research and have some insights to share, which is also the reason I would like to develop a generic – as opposed to particularistic – approach to studying intersectionality. This attitude or approach may sound naïve or even unacceptable to many ideologically committed researchers. Some 'critical qualitative researchers' are frustrated to see that 'many people still believe that research, even qualitative research, should be objective' (Esposito & Evans-Winters, 2022, p. 34). We certainly cannot be completely objective in the sense of escaping from who we are and what we have experienced, but that does not mean we should stop striving to be objective. Sociology has a poor reputation for being a 'low-consensus', aka 'soft', discipline. As far as I understand, one of the reasons is that some sociologists have given up the attempt to develop sociology into a science with objective or 'ideology-free' knowledge. As C. Wright Mills advised in his *The Sociological Imagination*, sociologists can and should draw on their personal experiences, but then they must go beyond these experiences. If all researchers motivate themselves with their own personal experiences and feelings but move on to create knowledge beyond their own 'interest groups', there is a bigger chance for us to reach at least some consensuses on how we can address an important issue such as intersectionality in the most collective and effective way.

Besides my motivation for writing this book, I should also explain its USP (unique selling point). Academic work is assessed regularly in terms of its originality as well as its impact on real life – those who are familiar with the UK's Research Excellence Framework (REF, previously Research Assessment Exercise (RAE)) will know what I mean. Academics in universities are regularly encouraged to integrate their research into their teaching, but their work in teaching will not count towards their research. This book has been designated as a 'textbook', which means that it will not qualify for being submitted to the next round of REF. Fortunately, I am confident that I will survive the next REF without including this book as one of my submissions. On the other hand, I do hope that after reading the book, the reader will find some fresh or even insightful elements. While all the concepts and most methods have long existed, perhaps the most novel bit of this book is the generic approach that I have arrived at when reading and thinking about intersectionality, introduced in the first chapter and then discussed in the last chapter. It is a very simple idea: that is, intersectionality is the process of how two or more (usually categorical) factors collectively bring about an interested outcome. An important implication of this simple idea, which might count as another novel feature of this book, is that many research methods that prominent advocates of intersectionality have not used, at least not systematically or seriously, are actually useful and effective for studying this phenomenon. The reader may also find some of my interpretations, explanations and discussions useful for understanding either intersectionality *per se* or the methods for analysing it.

Many have argued that intersectionality is a knowledge project that is radically distinctive from other knowledge projects. If so, intersectionality should have its own research designs and methods that correspond to its core principles and are very different from existing methods at the same time. So far, this does not seem to be the case – no 'intersectionality-specific' methods or research designs have been invented, and existing empirical studies of intersectionality have no alternatives to employing existing research designs and methods. For researchers of intersectionality, the task is to determine which of the existing methods is more suitable for facilitating the examination of intersectional experiences rather than to create new methods in compliance with the principles of intersectionality. While waiting for such new methods to be created, the best we could do is use existing designs and methods innovatively but remain loyal to the spirits of intersectionality.

Intersectionality is a contested subject and a big umbrella under which different views and opinions live and compete side by side. It is my hope that researchers, students, activists, practitioners and policy makers will find something useful in this book. I would not be very surprised, however, if some find my approach hardly in line with their take on intersectionality; at the minimum, I hope that what I have said in this book will not offend anybody.

Keming Yang
Durham, UK

ACKNOWLEDGEMENTS

I am very grateful for the encouraging and thoughtful feedbacks that my colleagues offered after listening to my presentation of this new project, particularly those from David Byrne, Tiago Moreira, Brian Castellani, Jonathan Wistow and Matthew David. I would like also to thank Jai Seaman and her successor, Charlotte Bush, the editors at Sage, for their interest and support, and their assistant, Rhiannon Holt, for her help and patience during the production stage of this book. Charlotte Bush and Philippa Willitts combed through the entire manuscript to ensure that the language is updated and inclusive, for which I am extremely grateful. I also want to thank the production editor, Imogen Roome, and the copyeditor, Neil Dowden, for their meticulous work in preparing the typescript of this book. Finally, I want to thank the anonymous reviewer for their time and helpful comments.

1

INTRODUCING INTERSECTIONALITY

1.1 Overview and objectives

While this book is about research methods for studying intersectionality empirically, it is essential to ensure that we understand its meaning and importance before delving into the technicalities. Such understanding will help you appreciate and evaluate each of the methods to be covered, which is especially important if you are not familiar with the literature on this topic. Thus, this chapter aims:

- to trace where the idea of intersectionality comes from with a case study;
- to explain the meaning of intersectionality and its advantages over a 'single-dimensional' way of thinking;
- to introduce a 'generic' approach to studying intersectionality as a backdrop for the subsequent chapters;
- to offer an overview of the rest of the book.

Words such as 'intersectionality', 'intersectional' or 'intersectional justice' have been regularly used in academic as well as public discourses. However, that is not necessarily a blessing for the study of a concept. For example, 'social capital' is arguably one of the most popular sociological terms, but there has been an endless train of debates, disagreements and controversies over its meanings and measurements. So far intersectionality has had a similar experience – with its increasing popularity come a large number of questions over its (true) meaning, theoretical approaches (but not actual theories of explanation) and methods for empirical research. Of these questions, perhaps the most important is: what is intersectionality? Whilst a dictionary-style definition is certainly available, leading researchers of intersectionality have repeatedly argued that such a definition is too simplistic because intersectionality is not merely one thing. Not all researchers hold clarity and consistency as the two uttermost important criteria for constructing a concept; rather, some welcome ambiguities and inconsistencies because they see them as signs of the concept's growing influence.

To better understand the meaning of intersectionality, we shall start by looking at some case studies. It is some of these cases that stimulated Kimberlé Crenshaw, a law professor and a Black feminist in the US, to produce two heavyweight articles, one in 1989 and the other in 1991, which helped the growth of intersectionality into a widely adopted concept and approach. The importance of a concept should not be merely measured by its popularity; we need to understand the logic underlying the benefits of paying serious attention to intersectionality rather than the effect of a single category or factor. It is the process of uncovering such logic that led me to consider and develop a generic approach to understanding and studying intersectionality. I will give a brief account in this chapter and further reflections in the final chapter.

1.2 'Either, or', but not 'and'

'Title VII' in the USA's *Civil Rights Act of 1964* prohibits employment discrimination based on race, colour, religion, sex and national origin. For anyone with a primary school education in the English language, there should be no confusion over the meaning of this particular legal article – it is illegal for any employer to discriminate against any of their employees because of the employee's race, skin colour, religion, sex or nationality. Given that different if not necessarily conflicting interpretations of a legal code are the norm rather than the exception, perhaps we should not be particularly surprised if disputes arise over such a seemingly straightforward sentence. Of the potential controversies, the one we are interested in here is the possible relations among the five human attributes listed. The most intuitively sensible understanding of these attributes is that it is illegal to discriminate against any employee based on *any one* of the five attributes. That is, it should be correct to rewrite the sentence as the following: Title VII prohibits employment discrimination based on race, *or* colour, *or* religion, *or* sex, *or* national origin. In other words, it is sufficient to establish a case of discrimination as long as one of the five attributes is applicable. It *does not seem to be necessary* to consider cases of discrimination where the word 'and' is used, because those kinds of cases would already be covered. For example, the group 'race *or* sex' is clearly larger or more inclusive than the group 'race *and* sex'; in fact, the latter is included in the former, which I shall illustrate with more details later in this chapter.

The above introduction to the use of 'or' versus 'and' is not a trivial issue of language, which was powerfully demonstrated through a lawsuit. The case came to an American district court in 1975 although the events could be traced back to at least 1970.[1] The defendant was the American carmaker General Motors (GM). The plaintiffs were five Black women who were former employees at GM's St Louise plant. The first was Emma DeGraffenreid, which is why the lawsuit is later referred to as *DeGraffenreid v. General Motors*, and the other four were Brenda Hines, Alberta Chapman, Brenda Hollis and Patricia Bell. Their allegation was that GM's seniority system and 'last hired–first fired' layoff policy because of an economic recession was discrimination based on race and sex, thus violating Title VII of the Civil Rights Act of 1964. They wanted to represent a class of all Black women as victims of such discrimination. The court dismissed their allegation in 1976 on the ground that their complaint might be 'a cause of action for race discrimination, sex discrimination, or alternatively either, but not a combination of both' (Crenshaw, 1989: 141). Now we see why two of the simplest words in English could make a significant difference in some people's lives.

The court then gave two related reasons for refusing to acknowledge 'Black women' as a distinct class that the law was created to protect. The first was that the goal of Title VII was not 'to create a new classification of "Black women" who would have greater standing than, for example, a Black male' (ibid.: 142). There was no way for us to ascertain whether Title VII had that goal or not, and the judge seemed to have the authority to determine the interpretation, but that is not our concern here. The question of great concern to the study of intersectionality is why the judge did not think there was a need for distinguishing 'Black women' from 'Black men'. Nowhere could I find the answer, but I think it appears to be obvious: the judge thought that Black women and Black men belonged to the same racial group; therefore, the complaint made by the five Black women should be taken as representing the class of Black people as a racial group. If so, this leads to the following more general principle: it is sufficient to complain about discrimination based on a single class *without specifying further categories within that class*. In this case, the class is race, and the further categories within race are Black women and Black men. It is clear, although it is difficult to confirm now, that the judge was aware of the large number of new classes arising from multiplying the number of categories within each class, as the court confessed in the second reason for refusing the class of 'Black women': 'The prospect of the creation of new classes of protected minorities, governed only by the mathematical principles of permutation and combination, clearly raises the prospect of opening the hackneyed Pandora's box' (ibid.). In other words, accepting the Black women's allegation would lead to too many classes that the law is expected to protect separately. Note that it is not really accurate to call them 'new' classes – the classes of race and gender were already there; rather, a more accurate description would be 'classes of combined categories' or 'cross-category classes'.

Why was the word 'and' so crucial to the five Black female plaintiffs? Why couldn't they bring their case to the court as discrimination based on either race *or* gender? What was the cause of the conflict between their reasoning and the court's? The word 'and' was indeed crucial to the fate of their complaint (and their personal lives) because it would determine whether their complaint would succeed. Without going into the original details, let's do a mental and hypothetical experiment, as it is much easier and clearer. First, suppose the plaintiffs raised their lawsuit against GM for discrimination based on race alone – then they would have failed because the lawyer representing GM would argue (perhaps with clear evidence as well) that GM did not discriminate against Black people because they hired Black people or did not lay off Black employees at a higher proportion than White ones. The Black female employees could have counter-argued that the Black employees GM hired were predominantly men. Similarly, suppose that the five Black female plaintiffs brought their complaint to the court for discrimination based on gender alone – they would have failed too because the lawyer for GM would be able to demonstrate that GM did hire women or did not lay off women at a higher rate than male employees. Why was either race or gender alone not sufficient for making their case successful? As we shall illustrate later in this book, the logic underlying such reasoning is not actually complicated, but the five women would have to wait for at least a few years for some legal scholars to formally explain what was going wrong.

1.3 The idea of intersectionality

The above case was the first of the three cases that stimulated Kimberlé Crenshaw, then a professor at the University of California Law School, to develop the notion of intersectionality in her now well-known paper 'Demarginalizing the Intersection of Race and Sex: A Black

Feminist Critique of Antidiscrimination Doctrine, Feminist Theory and Antiracist Politics', published in 1989. In this paper she made a powerful case for explaining Black women's marginalized experiences because of the intersection of their race and gender, which would be ignored by the US legal system as it would only consider either race or gender separately. She referred to such 'either/or' reasoning as 'a single-axis framework'. The fundamental flaw of this framework is that the human attributes (gender, race, age, etc.) are taken as 'mutually exclusive'; that is, when one of them is being considered, the others must be excluded. This framework assumes that it is sufficient to consider one attribute alone each time, because it further assumes that when one attribute is being considered, there will necessarily be no discrimination based on any of the other attributes. For example, when a person made a complaint about discrimination based on race, it was assumed that the person was not experiencing discrimination based on any other attribute at the same time. It should be clear by now that such reasoning will result in the exclusion of any possible intersectional situations or cases. Metaphorically, Black women are located at the intersection (or 'crosscurrents', to use another of Crenshaw's metaphors) of race and gender, and when they experience discriminatory treatments because of their race and gender at the same time, they will be excluded from the protection of the legal system that was established on the principles of the single-axis framework. The above case, and others after that, clearly demonstrated that 'intersectional discrimination' did happen.

Crenshaw then went on to point out that the single-axis framework is not only a flaw of the American legal system but also a limitation of feminist theory and antiracist politics, as they all ignore, intentionally or not, the intersectional nature of Black women's experiences. This may come as a surprising puzzle to many: if feminist theory argues for the interests of all women and antiracist politics fights for the interests of all racial minorities, then Black women should enjoy 'double protections' by both feminist theory and antiracist politics. Logically speaking, this could be true, but there is a condition for this to be true, which is the absence of differential experiences among the members of any category. In reality, however, Black women become intersectionally disadvantaged when their experiences are different from those of White women in the gender category and different from those of Black men in the race category. There would have been no lawsuits like the above case and no need to consider intersectionality seriously *if all women and all Black people were protected in the same way.* The sad truth of reality is that neither all women nor all Black people are treated the same. When most of the women under protection are White and most of the Black people under protection are men, Black women could find themselves in a 'doubly vulnerable' position; the supposed 'double protections' becomes 'double disadvantages'. Clearly, the most effective remedy is for feminist theory to incorporate race and for antiracist politics to include gender, which was what Crenshaw urged the two camps to do in her article.

Because Crenshaw repeatedly used the term 'intersectionality' or 'intersectional' in her article, other researchers later recognized her as the one who 'coined' and initiated the concept of 'intersectionality'. She also made a compelling case for intersectionality as a way of reasoning by expanding her cases from Black female employees to women who experienced gender-based violence and racial and ethnic minority women in domestic work in another paper published in 1991, in which she defines intersectionality as 'the location of women of colour both within overlapping systems of subordination and at the margins of feminism and antiracism' (1991, p. 1265). It should be fair to say that she was the first to give intersectionality a most concentrated academic treatment and has been the most influential in bringing intersectionality into the centre of public and academic discourses as an important social phenomenon as well as a way of thinking.

It would be somewhat presumptuous, however, to designate Crenshaw as the very first scholar who took the idea of intersectionality seriously. The idea of intersectionality did exist before the publication of Crenshaw's article of 1989. At least a small number of people expressed the idea of intersectionality even though they used terms other than the word 'intersectionality'. Crenshaw herself cited Elaine Shoben's (1980) paper 'Compound Discrimination: The Interaction of Race and Sex in Employment Discrimination', which was published 9 years before Crenshaw's and the idea of intersectionality could not be clearer. Patricia Hill Collins, a prominent sociologist, was particularly unhappy with the fact that Crenshaw's 'ideas remain overlooked in favour of a common practice across contemporary intersectional scholarship of mentioning Crenshaw's "coining" of the term intersectionality as the point of origin for intersectionality itself' (2015, p. 10). Although it might be impossible (perhaps unnecessary as well) to pin down a particular person or a piece of writing as 'the origin' of intersectionality, some have argued that the earliest forms of intersectionality could date back to women of colour activists in the nineteenth century (Collins & Bilge, 2020; Grzanka, 2014), including Sojourner Truth, Maria Stewart, Ida B. Wells and Anna Julia Cooper. Given that 'Black feminism' as a social movement could be traced back as early as the 1850s, it is beyond doubt that Black women in the US already took the intersection of their race and gender very explicitly and seriously before the publication of Crenshaw's articles.

In his Foreword to Anna Julia Cooper's *A voice from the south*, originally published in 1892, Henry Louis Gates, Jr. designated the 20-year period of 1890 to 1910 as 'The Black Women's Era' (1988, p. xvi). He lamented the fact that many works by Black women were ignored, making Cooper's book 'one of the original texts of the Black feminist movement' (ibid: xiii). Mary Helen Washington, in her Introduction to the new edition of Cooper's book, particularly highlighted the intersectional nature of Cooper's points, although the word 'intersectional' or 'intersectionality' never appeared. In Cooper's own words, 'The coloured woman of to-day occupies, one may say, a unique position in this country. ... She is confronted by *both a woman question and a race problem*, and is as yet *an unknown or an unacknowledged factor in both*' (1892[1988], p. 134, emphasis added). There should be no doubt that this was one if not the earliest and clearest statements on intersectionality in the concept's history.

This insight into the intersectional position of Black women in the US then became lost for decades and would have to wait until the 1980s to be recognized again. The world in the first half of the twentieth century was mostly occupied with the two world wars. After the First World War, two major human rights movements made a great impact on the lives of Americans, particularly in the 1960s and 1970s; one was the civil rights movement focusing on the equality of race, and the other was the women's rights movement on the equality of gender. Looking back at these two social movements and through the lens of intersectionality, one cannot help but wonder how these two sweeping social movements occurred almost in parallel without significant interactions between them. This is particularly puzzling given the enormous efforts many prominent Black feminists made in those decades. Some of their efforts were recorded and expressed in two collections of Black feminist writings: *The black woman* edited by Toni Cade (1970), which contains writings mostly in the 1960s, and *This bridge called my back* edited by Cherríe Moraga and Gloria Anzaldúa (1983), which collects, as the subtitle indicates, *Writings by radical women of colour*, mostly in the 1970s. In both volumes we can find some clear formulations of intersectionality as a way of describing Black women's living experiences that were distinctive to those of both White women and Black men. In the Preface to her volume, Toni Cade touched on the intersection of gender and race while pointing out that male experts tended to 'clump the men and women together' when they actually focused on 'Blacks' (1970, p. 8). Furthermore, she demonstrated the limitation of focusing on gender alone: 'how relevant are the truths, the experiences, the findings of white women to Black women? Are women after all simply women? I don't know that our priorities are the same, that our concerns and methods are the same, or even similar enough so that we can afford to depend on this new field of experts (white, female)' (ibid., p. 9).

Perhaps the notion of 'double jeopardy', used by Frances Beale (1970), is the closest to the concept of intersectionality. Unfortunately, Beale only used the term in the title of her article without explaining or discussing its meaning precisely. She described the interaction between race and gender when referring to a Black woman as a 'slave of a slave', with the second slave referring to Black man; that is, Black men 'have someone who is below them' (1970, p. 94). In other words, Black men and women should not be treated the same simply because they are of the same race; rather, the factor of gender separates them apart within the same racial group, thereby demonstrating an interaction between race and gender. Similarly, Black women and White women should not be treated as the same simply because they belonged to the same gender category. As she argued, 'The white women's movement is far from being monolithic. Any white women's movement that does not have an anti-imperialist and anti-racist ideology has absolutely nothing in common with the Black women's struggle' (ibid.: 98). She went on to demonstrate this 'double jeopardy' with some statistics of wage in a table for the four combinatory groups: White Males, Non-White Males, White Females and Non-White Females, assuming that the 'Non-White' here mostly meant Black people. As far as I am aware, this was the first time that intersectional categories were presented so explicitly and quantitatively. Later, the factor of class came in as well when she criticized the labour movement, who represented the White middle-class, for not helping Black women.

One of the most powerful voices about Black women's intersectional disadvantages comes from the statement issued by Combahee River Collective (1977), a Black feminist organization in the Boston area. Using the word 'interlocking', they made intersectionality the focus of their mission at the beginning of their statement:

> The most general statement of our politics at the present time would be that we are actively committed to struggling against racial, sexual, heterosexual, and class oppression and see as our particular task the development of integrated analysis and practice based upon the fact that the major systems of oppression are *interlocking*. (1977, p. 210, emphasis added)

As they were oppressed because of both racism and misogyny, Black women's experiences became unique in comparison with those of any racial or gender group. To go back to the 'either/or' but not 'and' paradox for a moment, they particularly emphasized 'racial-sexual oppression which is neither solely racial nor solely sexual' (ibid.: 213). Correspondingly, their political mission 'was antiracist, unlike those of white women, and antisexist, unlike those of Black and white men' (ibid.: 211) at the same time.

There is a price to pay, however, for focusing on the intersectional nature of a group of people's identities and experiences. By highlighting the uniqueness of their position at the cross-intersection of race and gender, Black women took the risk of alienating themselves from both Black men and White women at the same time. This is why Black feminism was sometimes accused of being 'divisive'. They were certainly aware of this problem and did not seem to mind their estrangement from White women but did want to keep their solidarity with Black men: 'Although we are feminists and lesbians, we feel solidarity with progressive Black men and do not advocate the fractionalization that White women who are separatists demand' (ibid.: 213). In addition, although they had 'a great deal of criticism and loathing for what men have been socialized to be in this society', they did 'not have the misguided notion that it is their maleness, *per se* – i.e., their biological maleness – that makes them what they are' (ibid.: 214). Note that such logic should be applicable to White women as well – race is also biological, and it is not their biological womanhood that makes White women what they are.

1.4 What is intersectionality?

We can learn a few important lessons from the above introduction to the historical development of intersectionality. The idea of intersectionality already existed for nearly a century and a half before it became a widely used term in academic and public discourses at the end of the 1980s and early 1990s. Initially it was Black women who paid serious attention to this social problem. They used words other than 'intersectional' or 'intersectionality', such as 'interlocking', 'combined', etc., but it was the same idea. They felt strongly that they were discriminated against due to their cross-identities of being Black and women at the same time, but neither White women nor Black men would care much about their marginalized experiences; therefore, they must protect their own interests with a unique voice and by organizing their political actions. Intersectionality as a serious social problem and a concept describing the problem became particularly important when a relevant case, *DeGraffenreid v. General Motors* came to light in legal courts and mass media.

When an important social phenomenon becomes the focus for academic research, it is extremely important to clarify its meaning. This is not simply about composing a definition that researchers who use the term should agree on in order to avoid inconsistency and confusion. More importantly, it is about what the concept refers to and when it is appropriate to use the concept. At stake are a series of important questions. To start with, does intersectionality have to be about Black women? While the phenomenon was particularly astute for Black women in the US, I believe most readers would agree that intersectionality as a general social phenomenon or problem does not have to be relevant only to this particular socio-demographic group. In their writings, the Black feminists themselves included other social groups who were unfairly treated due to their multiple identities, such as lower- or working-class people, LGBTQIA+ people, Asians and Latinos, immigrants, etc. In principle, intersectionality therefore could occur to any human group that belongs to the intersection of two or more categories of identity, although in reality some intersectional groups are certainly more advantaged than others. In this sense, intersectionality refers not merely to the cross-classification of multiple identities but also to the unfair treatment of the social group whose members carry the cross-classified identities, which reflects the intersectional nature of power relations (or systems) in a particular society.

In *The Oxford English Dictionary*, there are two definitions of intersectionality, one for Mathematics and the other for Sociology. It should be clear by now why the definition for Sociology runs as follows: 'The interconnected nature of social categorizations such as race, class, and gender, regarded as creating overlapping and interdependent systems of discrimination or disadvantage; a theoretical approach based on such a premise.' In sum, intersectionality has two meanings: one, the social phenomenon of overlapping discrimination due to multiple social categories and power systems; and two, the way of thinking about discrimination and inequality by paying serious attention to the intersection of multiple social categories and systems.

As Crenshaw has been constantly recognized as the one responsible for bringing the term intersectionality into the academic as well as the public discourses, let's see what she meant when she was using the term. In an interview 20 years after the publication of her 1989 article, she explained what she meant to do with the word 'intersectionality':

> And my own use of the term "intersectionality" was just a metaphor. I'm amazed at how it gets over- and underused; sometimes I can't even recognize it in the literature anymore. I was simply looking at the way all these systems of oppression overlap. But more importantly, how in the process of that structural convergence rhetorical politics and identity polities—based on the idea that systems of subordination do not overlap—would abandon issues and causes and people who actually were affected by overlapping systems of subordination. I've always been interested in both the structural convergence and the political marginality. That's how I came into it. (Berger & Guidroz, 2009, p. 65)

To develop and establish intersectionality as a formal concept in legal or social science studies was not Crenshaw's original intention, which is perhaps why she did not present a carefully crafted dictionary-style definition for intersectionality. To her, the term 'was just a metaphor'. A metaphor is a way of speaking or writing by referring to a potentially difficult idea with a more lively and accessible word. To Crenshaw, the difficult idea was the overlapping of multiple systems of subordination, and the more accessible word for describing this difficult idea was the adjective 'intersectional' or its corresponding noun 'intersectionality'. Compared with other similar words such as 'intersection', 'interaction', 'interlocking', the word 'intersectionality' enjoys a stronger tone of abstraction and generalization thanks to the inflection of the English language.

However, the benefit of using a metaphor comes from the more accessible word, which offers little help with lessening the difficulty of the original idea; it may actually be quite risky in the social sciences to use metaphors as they may obscure or confuse the exact meaning of the original idea. In the first chapter of her book *Intersectionality as critical social theory*, Patricia Hill Collins (2019) spent two sections discussing intersectionality as a metaphor. Much of her writing was to explain why metaphorical thinking is an inherent element of intersectionality as a theoretical approach. She also mentioned another metaphor related to the idea of intersectionality, Gloria Anzaldúa's 'borderland', which refers to cases that cross borderlines between binary categories; for example, rather than the divide between White and Black or men and women, we should consider those who are mixed race, non-binary or bisexual. The 'borderland' metaphor seems to have transcended the crossroads or traffic metaphor of intersectionality. In the end, Collins pointed out that 'As metaphors, neither intersectionality nor the idea of the borderlands provide coherence, consistency, or closure' (2019, p. 33). Metaphors are certainly useful for making an idea accessible, but for serious and rigorous research, coherence and consistency are the most important.

In the social sciences, to define the exact meaning of a concept is a very tricky business, which is one of the reasons that social sciences are perceived as 'soft' and 'low-consensus'. It is next to impossible for even a highly authoritative scholar to offer a definition of an important concept with which most – don't even think about every – other scholars would completely agree. For the case of intersectionality, Collins was certainly aware of the challenge to define its meaning. She devoted the whole of her leading article in the 2015 issue of *Annual Review of Sociology* to the thorny issue of the 'definitional dilemma of intersectionality'. If the definition is 'too narrow', it will reflect only 'the interests of any one segment [of intersectionality]'. If it is 'too broad', it will lose its (distinctive) meaning (2015, p. 2). On the one hand, Collins believed that 'a general consensus exists about intersectionality's general contours. The term intersectionality references the critical insights that race, class, gender, sexuality, ethnicity, nation, ability, and age operate not as unitary, mutually exclusive entities, but as reciprocally constructing phenomena that in turn shape complex social inequalities' (ibid.). On the other hand, note that she did not say 'this is the definition of intersectionality', as she knew some would protest had she said so. Instead, she used the word 'references' to suggest that 'this is what intersectionality is mostly about' in order to accommodate potential disagreements.

To escape from the difficulty of the definitional dilemma, Collins found the tactic of Potter Steward useful: 'I know it when I see it.' We must keep in mind, however, that Steward could say that because he was a Supreme Court Justice in the US, he would not allow the difficulty of defining pornography to drag himself down. More importantly, he had the authority to say whether a particular case was pornography or not, and that would be the end of the story. Patricia Hill Collins was the 100th President of the American Sociological Association and the first African American woman to hold this office. Publishing the lead paper with a portrait photo in *Annual Review of Sociology* is an honour and privilege only a very small number of sociologists have enjoyed. All these mean that no one else has more authority than she does to say whether a piece of writing is about intersectionality or not. Still, in today's sociology it is extremely difficult to recognize anybody as *the* leading figure, let alone someone with the authority akin to that of a Supreme Court Justice. If many individual researchers think they know what intersectionality is when they see it and their understandings are very different from each other, then confusion and consistency are inevitable. As Collins herself noted, 'Scholars and practitioners think they know intersectionality when they see it. More importantly, they conceptualize intersectionality in dramatically different ways when they use it' (ibid.: 3). In the end, it should be clear that the 'I know it when I see it' tactic does not work in social science research. We need a definition that is acceptable within the academic community at large.

One definition from the United Nations (2000) presents *intersectionality* as a concept to capture:

> the structural and dynamic consequences of the interaction between two or more forms of discrimination or systems of subordination. It specifically addresses the manner in which racism, patriarchy, economic disadvantages and other discriminatory systems contribute to create layers of inequality that structure the relative positions of women and men, races and other groups.

It is only in a very recent publication that Collins and her co-author Sirma Bilge offered the following general definition of intersectionality (Collins and Bilge, 2020, p. 14):

> Intersectionality investigates how intersecting power relations influence social relations across diverse societies as well as individual experiences in everyday life. As an analytic tool, intersectionality views categories of race, class, gender, sexuality, class, nation, ability, ethnicity, and age – among others – as interrelated and mutually shaping one another. Intersectionality is a way of understanding and explaining complexity in the world, in people, and in human experiences.

There is an important point regarding the nature of intersectionality that we need to make clear when reading this definition. They define intersectionality as 'an analytic tool' or 'a way of understanding and explaining'. In other publications by either Collins or other researchers, intersectionality is also defined as a way of thinking, a critical theory, a framework, a critical perspective, etc. The differences between these terms are minor and of little concern.

A much more important difference is between intersectionality as an analytical or theoretical tool and an ideological guidance for taking actions. In the second chapter of their monograph, Collins and Bilge discussed intersectionality as both critical theory and praxis. In other words, intersectionality has moved beyond the domain of thinking and into the domain of acting; in their words, 'Intersectionality is not simply a method for doing research, but is also a tool for empowering people' (2020, p. 43). On its face value, the statement sounds nothing special – many theories or methods could be, and have been, used for either suppressing or empowering people, such as Marxism, feminism, eugenics, etc., just to name a few. However, this may not be what they and some intersectionality researchers mean. My reading of the literature suggests that they expect all researchers who study intersectionality to take actions in order to empower oppressed people or at least get involved in social movements or political campaigns; otherwise, according to them, the researchers are not taking intersectionality seriously or genuinely. Put differently, they see intersectionality as not only an analytical tool but a political one as well. But as Carbado observed (2013, p. 811): 'Scholars across the globe regularly invoke and draw upon intersectionality, as do human rights activists, community organizers, political figures and lawyers. Any theory that traverses such trans-demographic terrains is bound to generate controversy and contestation.' Whether this is the case, and if so whether it is acceptable to all, might remain an issue to be settled, an issue that I have no plan to engage with in this book. What I would like to do in this book is introduce and demonstrate how some of the existing research methods could be, and have been, employed to study intersectionality empirically.

1.5 A generic approach

Now we should have a sufficiently clear idea of what intersectionality is and is about. Because of the intersection of their multiple identities, some people are in an especially disadvantaged position. Intersectionality refers to such a situation, the way of thinking and reasoning about this situation, and the actions motivated to end the situation.

In this book, I aim to achieve two interrelated tasks. First, I would like to point out that the above understanding of intersectionality can be extended or generalized into a more generic type of situation. From the previous sections, we have learnt that the original idea of intersectionality came from some Black feminists in the US as they were among the ones who experienced the most painful effects of being disenfranchised in comparison with both White women and Black men. As we shall see in the subsequent chapters, other social groups in a similar situation were inspired by this idea, thereby bringing in factors additional to race and sex, such as sexuality, age, nationality, religion, social class, etc. In a sense, the expansion from race and sex to other factors is already a process of generalization. As Collins points out (2019, p. 28): 'Significantly, Crenshaw's metaphor was not confined to explaining racism, sexism, and similar systems of power. The metaphor of intersectionality emerged in the context of solving social problems brought on by multiple and seemingly separate systems of power.' On the other hand, and less obviously, the generalization could be applied to the target phenomenon as well – the original target was the discrimination experienced by Black women, which we now can expand to other forms of inequality, such as discrimination, injustice, humiliation, bullying, poverty, illness or any other undesirable experience. It should be made clear that the choice of the target phenomenon is not a methodological issue – it is not even an academic issue; rather, it should and will be determined by the researcher or the practitioner's substantive interest. Intersectionality is clearly in the remit of inequality and injustice which could be manifested in a variety of ways and forms.

Second, I would like to persuade and enable researchers to employ as many existing research methods as possible so that we all can study intersectionality in a theoretically clearer and empirically more rigorous manner. When the idea of intersectionality stayed within the community of Black feminists alone, the arguments for its importance were mostly constructed and disseminated via conference speeches, pamphlets, magazine articles, and a few published books, in which systematic examination with empirical evidence was rare. Since the 1970s, some legal scholars such as Crenshaw made a powerful case for intersectionality as a way to demonstrate the vulnerability of certain social groups in the existing legal and political systems. However, intersectionality would not have become as popular as it is today (more in the next section) if it has been relevant only to those involved in those legal cases. The importance and salience of an idea, a notion or a theory depends on the scope of its applicability. Even for Black women alone, accurate and systematic evidence and analysis are required for demonstrating their unique disadvantage; otherwise, we would not be able to answer a series of important questions. For example, how prevalent is intersectional discrimination experienced among Black women in comparison with other intersectional groups? Such comparison is important because it is insufficient simply to present the experiences of Black women alone. It is only through comparisons that their intersectional vulnerability can be clearly demonstrated. Further, how do their experiences depend on the industry they work in, the country they live in, and the time they live in? This question is important because their intersectionality vulnerability may depend on the context of their experiences. Obviously, we could raise even more questions when we follow the generic approach. All these questions are not merely about applying existing research methods because they have serious implications for the kinds of arguments in the end. I shall discuss this further in the next chapter and develop this generic approach by way of summarizing and reviewing the methods covered in the other chapters of the book.

Collins points out a dilemma of turning intersectionality into a generic approach: on the one hand, being generic would help intersectionality avoid the problem of being too particularistic, an issue that begets the 'race/gender/class' studies: 'intersectionality's quest for universality ... meant that it need not attend to its own particular history' (2019, p. 40); that is, intersectionality does not have to commit itself to the categories in the cases that stimulated the idea, most importantly race and sex. On the other hand, such 'generic intersectionality' may bring a different problem: 'a parallelism among these categories, one that implies that each system of power is fundamentally the same' (ibid.). In my view, this is not necessarily a problem – the word 'generic' does not necessarily mean that the factors are parallel to each other or equally important; in fact, one important analysis we can do is evaluate the relative importance of each system of power and its impact on intersectional groups. Following the generic approach, intersectionality as an analytical tool takes social categories, systems and their interactions as a general target of analysis without any priori focus on any particular categories, systems or types of interaction. It is the intention of this book to introduce the ways in which these possible forms of intersectionality could be analysed and evaluate the relevance of each method to the principles and purposes of intersectionality.

1.6 Is intersectionality important? If so, to whom?

I would not have proposed writing this book to my publisher had I not believed that intersectionality is a worthy and important subject. However, I cannot be certain that the answer to the question of its importance is always an unconditional yes, partly because it depends on who is answering the question; therefore, the two questions in this section title are tightly connected.

Within academia, the importance of a topic is usually measured by the following indicators: the amount of money invested in its research, the number of journal articles and books published, the number of courses taught, the number of sessions and presenters in association conferences, and the number of research institutes and staff members. Measured against these, it is safe to say that since the powerful case made by Crenshaw for the significance of intersectionality in both academic research and public discourses, intersectionality has been firmly established as a subject of research and study. For example, in her keynote article of 2015, Collins listed the following journals that devoted a special issue on intersectionality: *Journal of Sex Roles* (2008), *Race, Ethnicity and Education* (2009), *Journal of Broadcasting and Electronic Media* (2010), *Gender & Society* (2012), *Signs* (2013), *Du Bois Review* (2013). I could add the following more recent ones: *Societies* (2018), *Gender and Language* (2018), *International Journal of Entrepreneurial Behaviour and Research* (2019), *Sociological*

Spectrum (2020), *Critical Discourse Studies* (2021). There are a few journals now that devote themselves completely to the issue of intersectionality, such as *Journal of Intersectionality*. In her comprehensive review of the intellectual history of intersectionality, Ange-Marie Hancock (2016) covered no fewer than 10 disciplinary areas where intersectionality has become a prominent focus of research.

The establishment of research or policy centres or institutes is another sign of the institutionalization of intersectionality. For example, Crenshaw set up the Centre for Intersectionality and Social Policy Studies at Columbia Law School. The Centre for Intersectional Justice, based in Berlin, was founded in 2017. Simon Fraser University in Vancouver, Canada, has set up an Institute for Intersectionality Research and Policy. Utah State University has a Centre for Intersectional Gender Studies and Research. With the help of these centres and institutes, intersectionality has gone beyond the walls of universities into the domains of public policy. For example, the European Council has made intersectionality and multiple discrimination a focus of its policies for tackling inequality and discrimination.

Nevertheless, we would be deluding ourselves if we believed that the importance of intersectionality is universally accepted. Without attempting to be comprehensive, here I only present a few observations. First, although the core concern of intersectionality is with the inequality and discrimination experienced by some intersectional groups, it remains unclear exactly how many researchers on inequality and discrimination take intersectionality seriously. The journals that have published special issues on intersectionality do not appear to be the most influential in their respective disciplines. One does not come to see a paper with intersectionality as its focus in any of the 'top-tier' journals. As another example, in the fourth edition of *Social Stratification* (2019) edited by David Grusky, perhaps the most comprehensive reader on social inequality, only two out of the more than 130 articles are about intersectionality. The dominating majority of the selected papers are all about one factor alone: either race, or gender, or class. The second and most recent edition of Lisa Keister and Darby Southgate's (2022) *Inequality: A Contemporary Approach to Race, Class, and Gender* describes and explains inequality along each dimension separately, with intersectionality not being mentioned at all. It seems that many prominent researchers are still thinking about inequality and discrimination in a way not very different from that of the court judge in the case of *DeGraffenreid v. General Motors*. In the meantime, a search on Google Trend for intersectionality indicates that intersectionality has hardly become a global issue, as some have argued, with the appreciation of its importance being confined within a few countries, including the US, Canada, South Africa, Australia, New Zealand and in northern Europe. The significance of intersectionality has certainly increased since the 1980s but may not have reached a point at which researchers are routinely employing it as a way to study inequality and injustice.

1.7 Overview of subsequent chapters

Following this introductory chapter, it is absolutely necessary to be clear about the theoretical and methodological approaches to studying intersectionality before moving on to each specific method. The creation of intersectionality as a concept originated from a strong theoretical argument and agenda; that is, to highlight the importance of bringing in the additional and interactive effect of race to that of sex in demonstrating a neglected aspect of inequality and power relations in the American society. Therefore, it is imperative to present and discuss why and how intersectionality has been theorized, and how those theories influence the design and the choice of methods used in empirical research. Essentially, the second chapter serves as a bridge connecting the theoretical arguments to the empirical investigations of intersectionality. It is important to point out from the outset that it is not my intention to get involved in any theoretical debates in this book, especially those with an explicit ideological agenda; rather, the introduction and discussion of theoretical ideas in the second chapter only aim to demonstrate the following points: that intersectionality is not a completely methodological issue, that it is therefore important to consider the theoretical standpoint before or alongside choosing a particular research design or method, and that the chosen design or method must be able to connect the theories and the empirical investigations in a sensible way. The third section of this chapter is the most important as it will introduce different overall approaches to studying intersectionality, including the qualitative, the quantitative and the mixed-methods designs which we shall return to in Chapter 9.

Chapter 3 discusses qualitative methods for studying intersectionality. Intersectionality was initially researched with qualitative designs and methods, and since then the qualitative approach has been very popular in a number of disciplinary areas. Some researchers have explained the popularity of qualitative methods not merely as an outcome of choice but an inherent advantage over quantitative designs and methods. It has been argued that qualitative methods are particularly suitable for studying intersectionality due to their abilities to explore the complexities of the intersectional effects of multiple factors. Whilst qualitative methods could indeed reveal more details and the contingent nature of intersectionality in some special settings, researchers chose to use qualitative methods usually because the number of cases under study is very small. Illustrating with published studies, this chapter will discuss and demonstrate the conditions under which qualitative methods are especially beneficial to research on intersectionality before moving on to point out the limitations of these methods.

Chapter 4 introduces the first quantitative method for analysing intersectionality. The human attributes constantly mentioned in studies of intersectionality include sex, gender, race, sexuality, nationality, etc. From the perspective of intersectionality, it is important to note that studies in the past tend to ignore categories beyond the binary classification of sex or gender. Some attributes may have a small number of values, e.g. male and female for sex, in comparison with others such as gender or sexual identity, which have many. In addition, the fact that intersex people do exist, just as biracial people and non-binary people and bisexual people do, means that even these seemingly divisible attributes are not always so easy to categorise. The number of categories of each attribute is smaller than the number of values of a metrical variable (e.g. age in years or annual income in dollars or pounds); these attributes are usually analysed as categorical variables in statistics, and the data about these attributes could be readily presented in a table. Today, an enormously large amount of quantitative data has been accumulated and made freely available to researchers, most of which contain valuable information that could be used for analysing intersectionality. Each of these datasets covers a large number of cases, and there are many ways in which they could be used in combination for comparing different groups. Although the quantitative approach is a latecomer to the study of intersectionality, it has many well-established resources and tools at the disposal of researchers should they intend to learn how to use them. This chapter starts to introduce statistical methods for analysing intersectionality by exploring the potential intersectional patterns in contingency tables. From the statistical perspective, most of the commonly studied intersectional factors are categorical variables, such as sex, race, ethnicity and class. Data of these variables could be readily presented in a contingency table and analysed with existing statistical methods accordingly.

Chapter 5 examines perhaps the most widely used statistical method for analysing quantitative data, i.e. the regression models. A limitation of the analysis of contingency tables is the lack of distinction between the response variable and the explanatory variables (or predictors). When such distinction is important, perhaps the most common way so far of analysing the intersectional effects of multiple explanatory variables on a response variable is to include one or more interaction terms in a generalized linear regression model. However, several issues with these interaction terms have prevented them from becoming the default choice for studying intersectionality: the number of variables in an interaction term is usually no more than three; the possible configurations are not revealed, let alone studied; the relationship between the individual effects and the interactive effects is not always clear; and it may be difficult to interpret the meanings of the coefficients. In the end, although these models are flexible and the coefficients could be estimated with powerful software programmes, their capacities are quite limited for analysing intersectionality.

After studying both qualitative and quantitative methods, in Chapter 6 we look at a method that was created to go beyond the quantitative vs qualitative divide. Thanks to the work of Charles Ragin and his associates, Qualitative Comparative Analysis (QCA), sometimes referred to as set-theoretic methods, has become an alternative to completely qualitative or quantitative methods. In their monograph *Intersectional inequality* (2016), Ragin and Fiss discussed and demonstrated how this approach and method could offer some unique benefits to analysing intersectionality, such as systematic examination of all intersectional possibilities as potential and diverse pathways leading to the studied outcome. This chapter will introduce and examine the key pros and cons of QCA in light of studying intersectionality, and eventually make the point that it is not an ideal method either; for example, calibrating the conditions (essentially the factors interacting with each other) will lose a lot of information, the number of conditions cannot be very large, and there are a number of issues in linking the configurations to the outcome.

Chapter 7 introduces a relatively recent innovation in analysing intersectionality; that is, to apply the idea and logic of multilevel modelling. A major challenge to the study of intersectionality is how to formally incorporate a large number of factors and their intersectionality in connection with the targeted outcome. All the methods introduced in the previous chapters have not been very successful in coping with this issue. A paper by Evans et al. (2018) published in the journal *Social Science & Medicine* offers a solution by making use of multilevel statistical models. The idea is to treat intersectional configurations as higher-level units so that their effects could be clearly separated apart from the individual effect of each factor and modelled as such. After introducing the basic ideas and principles of multilevel models and how they are used for analysing intersectionality, this chapter will argue that they are perhaps the most effective method so far, but still not free from shortcomings, such as the lack of examination of sensible configurations prior to including them in the model and the highly uneven distribution of cases across the higher-level units.

Chapter 8 examines another set of statistical tools that we can employ for studying intersectionality, including mediation and moderation, which map out the more specific ways multiple factors affect a certain outcome. Almost all of the methods introduced in the previous chapters take intersectionality as combinatory configurations. Whilst they may be able to exhaust and examine all of the possible cross-combinations, they do not distinguish the factors' roles or functions in a logical or temporal sequence. When affecting a certain target, however, these factors do interact with each other in different sequences, either logically or temporally or both. For example, some factors already exist when another comes in, or one factor may serve as an intermediary mechanism between another factor and the response, or one factor strengthens or weakens the effect of other factors on the response. Mediation and moderation are statistical methods for representing and analysing these types of intersectionality, which have become increasingly important and popular in recent years, although they could be actually seen as simpler cases of more complicated models such as path analysis and structural equation models.

After learning the above methods, Chapter 9 discusses the situation in which we may want to use different research designs and methods in the same project. While 'mixed methods' as a research design or strategy has been increasingly popular, it is not common yet to employ it in research on intersectionality. After introducing each particular method individually in the previous chapters, it is time for this chapter to introduce and evaluate possible ways of employing them together in a single research project. Research designs that use mixed methods have been a major development in the past decades, which could be a valuable source of knowledge and insights for studying intersectionality. However, there is no consensus among researchers as to how diverse methods, not simply in terms of qualitative vs quantitative, should be mixed or integrated. In the context of studying intersectionality, the question is particularly pertinent – researchers must provide a clear rationale for employing two or more methods to analyse the interactions among a set of factors. Without attempting to create a 'standard' procedure for mixing methods, this chapter highlights the importance of a clear and sensible logic of mixing methods with some examples of published studies.

The final chapter will be devoted to reflecting on a selected number of issues in the empirical study of intersectionality. It should be clear by now that currently no single method could offer comprehensive as well as effective analysis of intersectionality without suffering from some limitations. This chapter starts by reviewing and comparing these methods and presents their relative benefits and advantages by discussing a few important but difficult issues: how the researcher should choose the factors before studying their intersectional effects; whether there is a limit to the number of factors to be included in a single analysis; what the researcher can and should do to learn about their intersectionality before conducting any formal analysis; how the intersectional effects could be analysed in relation to the target outcome; and what might be the best way of integrating different types of data and methods in a single project. Answers to these questions and the related reflections will help establish a generic approach to studying intersectionality. Without aiming to offer a rigid step-by-step procedure, the rationale behind the generic approach and its key elements will provide researchers with a flexible but useful framework for planning, designing and conducting their analysis of intersectionality.

1.8 Suggested readings and questions for discussion

For an undergraduate course, it would be useful to start learning about intersectionality by reading the first two chapters of Collins and Bilge's recently published monograph, *Intersectionality* (2nd edition, 2020), in which they introduce and discuss what intersectionality is about. For a postgraduate course, besides the two chapters for the undergraduates, it should be very useful to read and digest Patricia Hill Collins's review paper of 2015 in *Annual Review of Sociology* and Hancock's (2016) history of intersectionality. As a student, you may not find the notion of intersectionality intuitively very accessible, but it is important to ensure that you understand and appreciate its advantage over thinking of one factor or dimension alone. Perhaps it would be helpful to identify a particular form of social injustice, such as lack of access to good education, and then consider the following questions: What kind of people are mostly likely to suffer from this unfortunate experience? Describe these people with one factor initially, and then ask yourself: do they actually share the same experience? Then bring in another factor (or attribute) and examine how people are different in terms of the new factor although they all share the initial attribute. It would be even better if you could illustrate your description and analysis with at least one real-life example.

Note

1. Details of this case come from the following sources: the case study in Crenshaw (1989), Powell (1996), and casemine: www.casemine.com/judgement/us/59149490add7b049345bf04d (accessed 21 July 2021).

2

INTERSECTIONALITY
Linking Theories to Research Designs

2.1 Overview and objectives

In the social sciences, an important principle one must keep firmly in mind is that no matter how sophisticated research methods are, they alone can never determine the quality of a study, and one must always keep the methods used in line with the nature of the research questions, the context of the phenomenon under study, and the theoretical approach. The ultimate challenge to a social science research project is that these components – research questions, context of the studied phenomenon, theoretical approaches, data and related analyses – must come together to constitute a coherent whole. This is why the process of doing social science research is rarely, if ever, linear and progressive; it would indeed be naïve to assume that a student or researcher could accomplish a high-quality research project by simply following 'a recipe', a step-by-step linear progressive procedure. It is very likely that one will have to go back and forth between the steps in order to keep the components logically coherent and consistent with each other.

The goal of this chapter is to help students and junior researchers to consider how to *put different bits of a research project into a coherent whole*. For several reasons, this is particularly important for studying intersectionality. First, whilst intersectionality has been well established as a theoretical approach, what kind of theory it is and what exactly it says are questions that have not been clearly answered. Therefore, the first objective of this chapter is *to examine intersectionality as a social theory and its contents*. Many fundamental issues related to intersectionality remain unsettled; for example, although we learnt something about the origin and the meaning of intersectionality in the previous chapter, what intersectionality is remains a contested topic. We must consider whether intersectionality is a social theory and, if so, what kind of social theory it is. Patricia Hill Collins has characterized intersectionality as a critical social theory, but what does it mean for a social theory to be 'critical'? More generally, regardless of the kind of theory intersectionality might be, what does it actually say as a theory? This question is tightly related to the previous one because what the theory says largely depends on what kind of theory it is.

Second, even when its content as a social theory is sufficiently clear, it remains highly uncertain and even controversial as to how we should collect and analyse evidence in empirical investigations in order to evaluate a theory of intersectionality. It has been a long while since social sciences transformed themselves from discursive narratives to empirical investigations, although some may have gone too far in that direction. Thus, the second objective of this chapter is *to take an initial look at how research design could serve as a link between intersectional theory and empirical research*. The answers to these questions and the accompanied evaluations will have important implications for how we do intersectional analysis. There might be no such thing as 'the right way' of doing research on intersectionality, but some may tell you that your way of researching intersectionality is 'wrong' because you have not followed a certain theoretical principle of intersectionality. Therefore, we should spend some time (and space) carefully considering what kind of research should be perceived as 'appropriate' in light of the general principles and ideas of intersectionality. The discussion in this chapter is more theoretical and therefore abstract than that in other chapters, and we shall introduce more specific research designs when we introduce 'mixed-methods research' in Chapter 9.

2.2 Is intersectionality a theory? If so, what kind of theory is it?

Sociology and a few other social sciences have been beset with a lower status or reputation relative to the natural sciences and certain branches of economics, psychology or geography. There are certainly multiple reasons, but perhaps the following is one of the most important: sociologists and many other social scientists rarely agree on some of the fundamental issues of their discipline, such as theoretical premises, the core questions, methodology and the criteria of academic excellence. They keep arguing against each other about the meaning of a key concept such as social class, social status, social capital, power, conflict, inequality, the way in which research should be conducted or the criteria for evaluating the quality of research products, leaving students and readers confused and wondering which 'school' they should choose to stay with. Certainly, social scientists would even disagree and argue with each other over what these controversies mean – some characterize them as 'decomposition' (Horowitz, 1995) or 'fragmentations' (House, 2019), whilst others believe that they are healthy signs of a growing and vibrant discipline. For the case of social theory, Hans Joas and Wolfgang Knöbl (2009) devoted the entire first chapter of their voluminous *Social theory* to the question 'What is theory?', but had to acknowledge that:

> [s]ince sociology was established in the nineteenth century, its academic practitioners have never succeeded in reaching a truly stable consensus with regard to its object and mission. They have never really agreed even about core concepts. It should therefore come as no surprise that the 'correct' understanding of theory has also been fiercely debated.

No matter how one interprets them, one should not be surprised to learn that many disagreements and controversies exist for the study of intersectionality as well. There are multiple and potentially incompatible answers to the following questions: What is intersectionality? Is it a theory, or is it just an idea? Is it a philosophy in the sense of a particular way of thinking about something, or a political ideology aiming to mobilize social movements? Some researchers have surveyed and classified studies of intersectionality. Surprisingly, most of these studies have identified intersectionality as anything *but* a theory. For example, Rodriguez et al. (2016) have found many studies that referred to intersectionality as a metaphor (Acker, 2011), a concept (Knapp, 2005), a research paradigm (Dhamoon, 2011), an analytical sensibility (i.e. a way of thinking about identity and power; Crenshaw, 2015), an ideograph (Alexander-Floyd, 2012) and a knowledge project (Collins, 2015). Most recently, Collins (2020) has added further identifications of intersectionality to the list: a perspective (Browne & Misra, 2003; Steinbugler et al., 2006), a type of analysis (Nash, 2008; Yuval-Davis, 2006), or as a nodal point for feminist theorizing (Lykke, 2011), a methodological approach (Steinbugler et al., 2006; Yuval-Davis, 2006), or a measurable variable and a type of data (Bowleg, 2008).

It is important, however, to ascertain whether intersectionality is a theory or not, because the answer will help us know what we can expect when speaking of intersectionality, and the answer will facilitate the communication among researchers when their discussions come to the topic of intersectionality. If intersectionality is a theory, we would expect it to explain certain phenomena (more in the next section), and we can then evaluate whether the explanation makes sense or not. This question and its answers have serious implications for how we understand and approach intersectionality in our study and research.

Perhaps it will help if we go back to the very basic question 'What is a theory?' in order to understand why so many researchers do not recognize intersectionality as a theory. According to the *Oxford English Dictionary* (*OED*) the word 'theory' has three meanings:

1. a formal set of ideas that is intended to explain why something happens or exists;
2. the principles on which a particular subject is based;
3. an opinion or idea that someone believes is true but that is not proved;

The first is the relatively narrow meaning of theory as it emphasizes formality and the intention, if not the ability, of explaining something. The narrowness, however, is the hallmark of a scientific theory as it shows the power of explaining why something happens in a certain way. The second meaning is broader but still related to the first meaning as the principles are usually required as premises for establishing the specific theories. Principles could also serve as a more general formulation of a series of specific theories. The third meaning emphasizes the distinction between the verified and the unverified theories – an unverified explanation is a theory or a proposed explanation, whilst a verified or proved theory becomes knowledge, fact or common sense that can be used to explain other phenomena. Fundamentally, for a statement or a set of statements to be qualified as a theory, it must intend to or be able to explain something; in other words, a distinctive feature of a theory is its explanatory function. This understanding of theory seems to be shared by most prominent social scientists; for example, in his essay 'On Sociological Theories of the Middle Range', Robert King Merton defines 'sociological theory' as 'logically interconnected sets of propositions from which empirical uniformities can be derived' (1967, p. 39), and at the beginning of *Constructing social theories*, Arthur Stinchcombe emphasizes that 'Theory ought to create the *capacity to invent explanations*' (1968, p. 3, emphasis original).

So, to answer the question whether intersectionality is a theory, we need to answer the following two questions: Does intersectionality explain (or intend to explain) anything? If so, what does it (aim to) explain? Yet again, I struggle to find an explicit answer, especially an answer to the first question. At the end of a lengthy search and reflection, I have come to believe that the ambiguity or uncertainty comes from the fact that many sociologists and researchers simply do not subscribe to the *OED*'s definition of theory; to them, a theory could do many things, such as argue that something is true, point out something is wrong (i.e. to criticize), draw people's attention to the importance of an issue, expand on a general idea, etc. To them, to explain something is perhaps not even an important function of the theory they have in mind. Given these diverse understandings or uses of the word 'theory', no wonder it is so difficult to be certain about whether intersectionality is a theory or not.

Ironically, if we do stick to the definition offered by the *OED*, then it should be easy for us to answer the second question; that is, intersectionality aims to explain the discriminations, disenfranchisements and disadvantages (the explanandum, or the target of explanation) experienced by some social groups such as Black women with the intersectional effects of multiple factors and power systems (the explanans, or the explanatory part). With this more specific understanding of theory in mind, I shall try to derive some specific theories and present them in the next section. For now, it is important to know whether this kind of theory or theorizing activity is something that intersectionality researchers would like to do. After reading as many publications as I could, my answer to this question is mostly negative – researchers of intersectionality have not invested their time and effort in turning intersectionality into a theory with explicit and strong explanatory power; most of them do not even show an interest in presenting intersectionality as an explanation.

In the rest of this section, we shall focus on the work of Patricia Hill Collins again because she is the one – certainly not the only one but the most prominent one – who has been serious about taking intersectionality as a social theory. It is important to note at the outset, however, that Collins emphatically claims that she does not intend to take intersectionality as 'just another social theory'; rather, to her at least, intersectionality is a special kind of critical social theory. Clearly, the key word here is 'critical', so let's try to understand what makes a social theory 'critical' and what makes intersectionality stand out from any other critical social theory.

I will resort to the *OED* again as I expect it to provide the clearest definition of the meaning of a word in the language of English. According to the *OED*, 'critical' has five meanings. Only the first is what it means in 'critical social theory' – that is, 'saying what you think is bad about somebody/something'; the other meanings, such as something is serious or dangerous – e.g. someone is in critical condition – or judgement of critics of art – e.g. a move is critically claimed – are clearly not relevant to critical social theory. Therefore, a critical social theory says that something bad (or problematic, undesirable, harmful, etc.) has happened in a society. Given the large number of components of any society and the complicated relations among them, it should come as no surprise that a society has many 'bad things' and is criticized as such, from specific problems such as crimes, poverty, divorce, conflicts, etc., to more fundamental problems such as the decay of morality, the clash of opposing values, and the incompatibility of economic and political systems. Moreover, there are different ways of interpreting and analysing any one of these problems, which means that the task of criticizing a society or a social phenomenon can be conducted in many different ways.

While all critical social theories share the common mission of upsetting the status quo, they come in a great diversity in terms of focus, approach and philosophy. Clearly, I can only offer this introductory note here, and the reader could consult book-length introductions listed at the end of the chapter.

What we can and will do here is answer a few important questions surrounding intersectionality as a special version of critical social theory that has been explained and promoted by Patricia Hill Collins. The first relates to the function or the purpose of this theory: *What does intersectionality aim to accomplish as a social theory?* If we stick to the explanatory function of theory defined earlier, then we expect intersectionality to explain something. However, with the word 'critical' added to 'social theory', the main function of intersectionality is not to explain anymore but to challenge some existing beliefs, practices and institutions by pointing out the harms they do to certain groups of people. It is not clear how researchers of intersectionality plan to resolve the tension between the two functions (explaining and criticizing), and it is difficult to imagine it can be done easily in practice. Researchers would have to either choose one of the two to focus on or offer a feasible way of achieving both at the same time. To explain, or to criticize, that seems to be a question that many social scientists have not considered seriously but has driven a wedge between them. In his inaugural lecture at the launch of the European Academy of Sociology on 26 October 2001, the prominent French sociologist Raymond Boudon identified two basic but opposing types of sociology or sociological research: one aims to discover truth and offer explanations, and the other expresses opinions and critical comments. In his view, the former (what he called 'the cognitive or scientific program of sociology') is by definition more scientific but may not be useful for certain political or ideological purposes. In contrast, the latter (what he called, using Joseph Schumpeter's term, 'the cameral, critical, or expressive program of sociology') does not aim to identify truths; rather, their mission is to influence political decisions and processes, so they may be useful for an ideology or social movements and therefore become more well-known and supported. Clearly, Boudon and the fellows of the European Sociological Academy (ESA) are strongly in favour of the explanatory version over the critical or expressive version of social theory. Boudon did not mention any possibility for social scientists to accomplish the two functions together, thereby implying that the two functions are not compatible; therefore, sociologists would have to choose one of the two as their way of doing sociology.

Not every leading social theorist has joined the ESA. Hans Joas and Wolfgang Knöbl, for example, think that 'empirical theory' (i.e. 'explanatory statements at a high level of generality') is a bit too narrow-minded. Although they did not explicitly support the 'expressive or critical' version of social theory, they keep social theory as a broad-based enterprise that includes both empirical generalizations and 'comprehensive interpretive systems which link basic philosophical, metaphysical, political and moral attitudes to the world' (2009, p. 18). In their view, social theorists should not keep their mouths shut simply because they cannot explain certain important social phenomena; as long as the issues are important (or argued to be so), any reflective, discursive, philosophical or moral discussions would deserve the title 'theory'. In this sense, social theories do not have to explain but argue, reveal, illustrate, discuss and criticize. As a result, many social theoretical works are a mixture of all these activities – some parts are observations derived from personal experiences, other parts are rigorous analysis of available data, and still other parts are illustrated with anecdotal cases and supported with influential authors' writings.

Turing to intersectionality, unsurprisingly, there is no consensus on whether the core mission of intersectionality as a social theory is to explain or to do other things. A small number of researchers have called for increasing the explanatory power of intersectionality. In her article, for example, Jennifer Nash claims that 'it is time for intersectionality to begin to sort out the paradoxes upon which its theory rests in the service of strengthening its explanatory power' (2008, p. 14). A much louder and more influential voice is to assign some other missions to intersectionality. In her review of intersectionality, Patricia Hill Collins takes intersectionality as not only a critical social theory but also as 'an analytical strategy' and 'a knowledge project' that 'houses a dynamic assemblage of interpretive communities, each of which has its own understanding of intersectionality and advances corresponding knowledge projects' (2015, p. 3). Later, in the new edition of her monograph *Intersectionality as Critical Social Theory* (2019), she also emphasizes that intersectionality is 'a form of praxis' (p. 2), 'a lens for examining how critical analysis and social action might inform one another' (p. 3), and 'a political project' (p. 5). To Collins and some other scholars who commit themselves to intersectionality, to be clear about the content of their theories is a relatively minor objective; most importantly, they want to mobilize all resources available to them to change the world – more specifically, to rectify existing forms of unfairness and injustice.

Each researcher has the right and freedom to determine the meaning and the most important function of social theory. Taking explanation as the top function or not for intersectionality, researchers should keep these multiple meanings and functions of intersectionality in mind to avoid any unnecessary disputes and confrontations. It is in everybody's interest to keep in mind that for many researchers to enhance the explanatory power of intersectionality as a social theory is only a part, perhaps not even the most urgent or important part, of a much more ambitious mission. For now, however, let's concentrate on intersectionality as a *critical* social theory by understanding some of its defining and interrelated features.

First of all, for all critical social theories, the starting and ending points are that something 'wrong' or 'bad' exists in society. These undesirable, harmful, pernicious things motivate critical social theorists to reveal to other members of society how bad and wrong these things are. For the convenience of discussion, we refer to these 'bad things' as social problems. Clearly, the identification and condemnation of these problems could be traced far back in human history – some members of any society must have observed many problems such as crimes, poverty, conflicts, unfair treatments, illnesses, etc. Inevitably, these observers of social problems were obliged not only to show what went wrong but also to explain the reasons behind them. In doing so, they were offering explanatory theories of social inequality, unfairness or injustice. This process of observing and explaining social inequality applies to intersectionality as well: some Black women observed and experienced how unfairly they had been treated, they wanted to voice their discontent and wanted other members of (American) society to agree with them, and some of them such as Kimberlé Crenshaw offered a powerful explanation for their experiences. Obviously, such explanation or theory is far from the end of their struggle, a point we shall come back to soon. In short, to specify an explanatory theory is only a step of the whole process and something more important is at stake.

Second, a critical social theory is automatically a *normative* social theory as well, or there must be a normative theory underpinning the critical social theory, because by identifying something is wrong, bad, harmful, unjust or unfair is to make a moral judgement. By pointing out something is wrong, a critical social theory must also suggest or imply what the right should be, which is a normative theory. Put differently, simply describing or even explaining what has gone wrong in society, no matter how well this is done from a scientific perspective, is not enough; the theorist is obliged to issue a moral evaluation and verdict of the social problem. Karl Marx, the most prominent exemplar of critical social theory, not only described and explained how capitalists were able to exploit their employees by extracting the surplus value but also claimed that this was wrong and must be replaced with a more morally righteous political system. Perhaps not all studies of social phenomena would necessarily entail moral judgements, but it is difficult and even absurd to imagine that a social scientist keeps their mouth shut after demonstrating the existence of a serious social problem. Social scientists may do these two things separately in two different occasions, or they may delegate the moral judgement to others, but it can be assumed that they would not shun the moral evaluation when being requested to do so as a natural outcome of their work. For people taking intersectionality seriously, they prefer that the explanatory and normative aspects of their theories be tightly connected; to them, anybody who has simply described or explained social injustice experienced by some intersectional groups but has not openly condemned the injustice nor participated in the political struggle to change it has not sincerely or genuinely followed the principles of intersectionality.

A third important feature of intersectionality as a critical social theory is its *wide scope* of critique. As illustrated in the previous chapter, the origin of intersectionality was the unfair treatment that some Black women received in the US in the nineteenth century. Even after it became a more salient issue in public discourse in the early 1990s, it remained an issue to some particular social groups. Since then, however, some researchers have developed intersectionality into a much bigger and more general issue, a way of thinking and a guiding principle of social movements. The victims have gone beyond the initial focus on Black women, now including anyone who has been treated unfairly in any way and anybody who would like to offer support to them. Moreover, the culpable includes not only those who openly suppressed the members of a minority group of any kind, such as slave owners and White supremacists, but also academics and scholars who may have unconsciously and implicitly supported the status quo. For example, Collins has particularly criticized social theorists such as Simon de Beauvoir and Judith Butler for failing to appreciate the unfortunate living experiences of the disadvantaged simply because the advantageous social location of the two social theorists prevented them from understanding those located at the disadvantaged social locations. This does not mean that the critique of intersectionality on the existing social reality is personal; in fact, Collins has launched the attack on the more fundamental system of epidemiology. To her, what has gone wrong is not merely the contents of existing social theories, which often have been an accomplice at worst, or an inadvertent supporter at best, of the existing unfair systems, but also the way in which social theories have been produced. The ambition of intersectionality, according to her, is to create a new way of theorizing social inequality, and the mission could only be accomplished by those in disadvantaged positions.

The last but not least defining feature of intersectionality as a critical social theory, at least according to Collins, is that it is a theory *for the disenfranchised and by the disenfranchised*. Although this might be the most controversial among all the features of intersectionality, it should not come as a surprise because it is a logical outcome derived from the second feature above – if intersectionality is a normative theory, i.e. a moral judgement of a certain social situation, and if it is safe to assume that the unprivileged and the privileged make different moral judgements because of their different social locations, then it is safe to say that the two social groups will have their own respective social theories. This is not actually a new idea – again, Karl Marx, whose theory is a key source of inspiration for intersectionality, made it very clear more than a century ago that a certain social class's ideology corresponded to its economic status. China's Communist Party put this idea into practice soon after taking power in 1949, abolishing many academic disciplines, including sociology, that the Party deemed to be 'capitalist'. Drawing on Max Horkheimer's distinction between 'traditional' and 'critical' social theory, Collins applies the idea of class-based or privilege-based social theory to intersectionality (2021, p. 130):

> Social theory constitutes a site of intellectual and political contestation. Theory is neither objective nor outside of politics; rather, social theories participate in intersecting power relations by contributing explanations for and justification of the social inequalities that underpin social hierarchies.

Intersectionality as a critical social theory is therefore inherently political as it must defend, preferably consciously, the interests of certain social groups suppressed by multiple social institutions at the same time. For intersectionality, the most important classification of social groups is the disenfranchised (unprivileged, deprived, disadvantaged, etc.) vs the enfranchised (privileged, benefited, advantaged, etc.). Naturally, the latter would defend and enhance their rights and interests by mobilizing all resources at their disposal and at the cost of the disenfranchised, including inventing social theories that justify the status quo, because the status quo is the interest of the enfranchised. Privileged researchers, academics and scholars may not personally or intentionally defend, justify or promote the interests of their social groups, but their privileged position would prevent them from genuinely understanding the experiences of the unprivileged. 'Western social theories have long been placed in service to various systems of domination' (Collins, 2019, p. 4). It is seen as the responsibility of the unprivileged intellectuals to fight against the existing social structure, especially on the front of epidemiology; that is, to launch 'resistant knowledge projects' (ibid., pp. 96, 116–118). These projects are only a part of a much larger and wider political project that devotes itself to transform the existing unfair social arrangements and ideologies. In Collins's words, 'Without political resistance there would be no intersectionality' (ibid., p. 289), or to quote Marx, 'The philosophers have only *interpreted* the world, in various ways. The point, however, is to *change* it' (1978[1888], emphasis added).

2.3 What does the theory of intersectionality say?

By now, a long and ingrained division between two camps among sociologists should be very clear to us, regarding not merely the nature and function of social theory but more fundamentally the entire business of social science research. On the one hand, 'the explanatory camp' aims to discover or create social theories that are capable of explaining a large number of social phenomena by drawing on a set of widely applicable mechanisms. Starting from Robert K. Merton's 'theory of the middle range', sociologists such as Raymond Boudon, Jon

Elster, Peter Hedström and other members of the 'analytical sociology' (Demeulenaere, 2011; Hedström, 2005; Hedström & Bearman, 2009; Hedström & Swedberg, 1998; Manzo, 2014) value the explanatory power of social theory, while seeing little relevance of social theorists' social backgrounds to their theories and normative questions such as whether the existing social order is fair, or what kind of social arrangement is more desirable. On the other hand, and in great contrast, members of 'the critical camp' devote themselves to the mission of revealing how a theorist's personal background may direct the construction of their theory, what's wrong with the existing social order, and promoting what should be done to change it. Social theory cannot be innocent because it is impossible for social theorists to be free of the influence of their social positions, no matter how hard they might want to do so. As such, social theories not created and employed for resisting and changing the inequalities faced by a certain group of people have been constructed and accepted by sacrificing this group's interests. Simply criticizing the existing injustice is not sufficient; social theorists must join the larger project of changing the existing social order in practice to demonstrate the value of their work. Starting from Karl Marx, followed by the Frankfurt School, feminist theory, anti-race or critical race theory, de-colonization and intersectionality theories represent the latest development of this camp.

In principle, few would deny that both are valuable for the society as a whole; moreover, they actually need each other in order to achieve their own goal – 'the explanatory camp' cannot avoid important questions such as which social phenomena they choose to explain, whether their explanations are contaminated by their prejudices, and what the criteria are for judging the value of their explanations, while 'the critical camp' must demonstrate evidence convincing all (not only to themselves) that what they want to criticize is not a strawman or an exception, and explain the unfair or unjust social phenomena before any suggestion for changing them can be presented. In practice, unfortunately, little effort of reconciling the two has been made.

Exactly what does intersectionality say as a critical social theory? That much of the effort in developing intersectionality as a critical social theory is invested in its critical power makes it particularly valuable to identify and specify its contents. Demonstrations and illustrations of how certain groups of people have been unfairly and unjustly treated, powerful as they may be, are works of description, not explanation, and therefore not a theory in the explanatory sense. Again, it is perplexing that Patricia Hill Collins repeatedly avoided specifying the contents of intersectionality as a critical social theory. In her major publications on this topic (2015, 2019, 2021, and Collins & Bilge 2020), she devoted herself to explaining and illustrating some 'navigational tools for thinking about intersectionality' (2015, p. 3) rather than telling us exactly what her theory says. In her keynote article commissioned by the *Annual Review of Sociology*, she asked the core question about intersectionality: 'The *and* seems to matter, but how?' (2015, p. 2, emphasis original) but did not offer a straightforward answer. A few years later, she made it very clear that 'I am less concerned with the content of intersectional knowledge than with ways of thinking that people use in creating such knowledge' (2019, p. 23). It is doubtlessly important to ensure that people think about intersectionality in the ways she thinks correct, but why does that have to prevent her from clearly spelling out the content of the theory?

There seem to be two reasons for the lack of specification of the content of intersectionality as a social theory. The first is straightforward: Collins does not think 'that intersectionality is already a social theory'; rather, it 'is a social theory in the making' (2019, p. 51). It is therefore unreasonable to expect any specific or well-formulated theories when they are under construction. Personally, I do not find this argument sufficiently convincing – few social theories are set in stone and not 'in the making'. True, some theories must be more developed than others, but nothing should prevent the social theorist from presenting a very underdeveloped theory. We may add or modify the theory when we have clearer ideas or more convincing evidence, which is expected in the process of theorizing and scientific progress. So, what does intersectionality as a critical social theory 'in the making' say?

Second, three things seem to have made it very difficult to specify exactly what the theory of intersectionality says: (1) people of different social and academic backgrounds interpret intersectionality differently; (2) the target of explanation (overlapping or interlocking of multiple dynamics or systems of inequality) is not clearly defined; (3) intersectionality is trying to accomplish several objectives at the same time (describe what form of injustice has occurred, give voice to the suppressed, offer solutions, mobilize support, etc.). These, however, are not insurmountable obstacles to specifying the content of intersectionality. People of different backgrounds can produce their own theories, which could be evaluated, compared and integrated whenever it is sensible to do so. Defining the specific target of explanation should be a matter of time and effort. Finally, intersectionality could accomplish each objective in sequence, in tandem, or in an interactive manner.

After all, a few 'navigational tools' will be certainly helpful for 'thinking about' intersectionality, but it should be sooner rather than later that these tools could help us construct the exact statements of intersectional social theories; otherwise, it would be difficult to appreciate the value of these 'navigational tools'. A disclaimer is in order: although I have tried my best to make the following statement as aligned with the spirit of intersectionality as I could, not all intersectionality scholars may find it acceptable. It is only a preliminary formulation of one of the possible explanatory theories, which certainly will be modified or even rejected and replaced by other formulations. That said, I think an explanatory version of intersectional social theory can be formulated as follows:

> The interactions among two or more social attributes such as race, ethnicity, gender, sexuality, class, nationality, etc. are associated with the observed social inequalities because existing social structures and processes interact with one another in distributing the valuable resources across these cross-classified groups unevenly.

This is a social theory in the explanatory sense because it has an explanan ('interactions of multiple attributes') and an explanandum ('social inequalities'). I hope other researchers would agree that these two concepts are sufficiently clear on the one hand but capable of covering a number of specific cases on the other hand. In other words, there are certainly many different ways of representing the contents of these concepts and their causal relations in a particular empirical research project, but the meaning of the relationship between the two remains sufficiently clear. The word 'interaction' emphasizes the interactive, as opposed to the isolated, effect of any two or more of the entities mentioned, which is in line with the meaning of many similar key words used in the discourses of intersectionality such as 'interlocking', 'relationality', etc. This theory is inspired by cases such as the one presented at the beginning of the previous chapter; more specifically, the interaction between race and gender explains why some Black women were unfairly made redundant by General Motors and later why their case was initially rejected by the court. Once it is clearly formulated as a general theory, it can be used to explain other similar cases of social inequality, such as why immigrant women from developing countries take low-paid domestic jobs.

It is necessary to add a few notes here either to clarify or to avoid confusion and dispute. The first note relates to the nature and meaning of what are called 'entities' here, including but not limited to race, ethnicity, gender, sexuality, nationality, religion, age, etc. In daily and natural language, these are simply labels referring to the attributes of human beings. They are also referred to as 'social categories', because people can be classified as members of each category. Mathematically, each is a set of elements with a particular character; statistically, they care categorical variables in a dataset. For intersectionality, however, they pick up an additional meaning, 'systems of power' (Collins, 2019, p. 44), which means that some members of a particular category enjoy more power over the other members due to some formal or informal social norms and procedures that were established throughout history; for example, within the gender category, men have more power over women, which is usually referred to as 'patriarchy'. When each category is used to refer to such uneven power distributions, it becomes an 'ism', a social structure and an ideology for supporting such uneven power distribution; for example, racism refers to the social structure and ideology that White people have more power than racial groups of colour. More importantly, researchers of intersectionality emphasize that these power systems do not work alone separately; instead, they depend upon and mutually construct and reinforce each other. We would gain better understanding, therefore, if we paid serious and close attention to the power relations between social groups of cross-classified categories; for example, the contrast between White men and Black women would be more useful than the contrast between White and Black or male and female. A primary principle of intersectionality is to focus on these interdependent relations when studying the distribution of power or privilege across two or more systems.

By identifying race, gender and other terms as power systems rather than social categories alone, intersectionality as a critical social theory implicitly assumes that the following are necessarily true (see, for example, the first assumption listed in Collins, 2019, p. 45; Else-Quest & Hyde, 2016). First, within a social category, such as gender, members of one sub-category, such as men, necessarily have more power than members of the other category (or categories), such as women, and they will take advantage of their power to enhance their own interests by sacrificing the interests of the other sub-category. There does not seem to be much interest in explaining why this is necessarily true or verifying the extent (where and when) to which is true. It is taken simply as a fact or a truth of human nature although it is not very difficult to find exceptions; for example, many White people supported the rights of Black people in the civil rights movement in the US, and according to a report by the Pew Research Center (29 September 2022), the support for #MeToo varies among the Americans much more with political orientation than gender. Whenever feasible, researchers should check whether such assumptions are valid for a particular study.

Another assumption is more important to this book because it shows the value of the methods to be introduced and explained in the rest of the book. The theory of intersectionality assumes that all these power systems always depend on, interact with and mutually construct each other, and their interactions are much more significant than each category or system alone. Put in statistical jargon, the effect of the interaction terms must outweigh the effect of each individual system alone. More importantly, intersectionality as a critical social theory does not treat this statement as a theory to be verified with empirical evidence; rather, it holds the statement as necessarily true, a guiding principle, a starting point from which other observations and evaluations will be made. An important premise of this book is to keep the heavier weight of the interactions over the individual entities as a hypothesis that needs to be tested and verified with empirical data and analysis. If the evidence supports it, the credibility of the theory will be strengthened; otherwise, we may need to adjust the theory and its context of applicability.

A further important question following the above point is that suppose we can take the interdependence and intersection of these power systems for granted, exactly how do they depend on and interact with each other? Again, researchers of intersectionality have not shown much interest in answering this question with specific evidence; some of them have refused to specify the relations among the power systems. To start with, how many entities or power systems should one include in a particular study? Theoretically, this means that researchers need to decide which ones are theoretically relevant or important for their study. It is understandable that this may become an empirical question, but it would help if this could be confirmed; otherwise, a theoretical rationale for choosing the power systems would be essential. Additionally, for empirical investigations, there is a question how many of them a study could realistically analyse at the same time; while the list of power systems is not particularly long, as interaction requires the examination of multiplications of the number of sub-categories, the number of possible combinations will increase quickly, an issue we shall see in some of the later chapters. Furthermore, there is a question over the sequence in which these power systems work together, either temporally or logically. More specifically, some of the power systems are based on attributes with which people are born, such as sex, age, race and ethnicity, but others are acquired throughout the life course and can be fluid or changed, such as marital status, employment, religion, nationality and class, with disability coming under either of these. As far as gender and sexual orientation are concerned, there seems to be no consensus on whether people are born with a particular category of each attribute, or whether they develop through contexts and experiences. Of these power systems, the opposition between the powerful or privileged and the powerless or the unprivileged may be much more intensive, such as racism and classism, than others, such as ageism. In principle, it should help in refining a social theory when more specific versions of the theory are constructed for a variety of situations.

2.4 Research designs for intersectional research

Today, few social scientists would be content with a few principles for theorizing, or even some specific theories of, a particular social phenomenon. A coherent and consistent integration of theory with empirical investigation is a general expectation of social science research. A social scientist must be armed with both theoretical ideas and tools for collecting, analysing and presenting empirical evidence. Research design is about the rationale that logically links the research questions, objectives and theories to the specific methods to be used in empirical investigations. And the way in which such integration is to be achieved is the craft of research design. I use the word 'craft' on purpose as I think that research design is something in between science and art. On the one hand, no social science could promise its students a highly structured and widely agreed procedure that is so well established that it is routinely followed. On the other hand, social science research is not as intuitive and even mystical, like composing a painting or a piece of music; there are certain relatively stable principles that are applicable to most situations of research. As a craft, research design involves guided reasoning and intuitive but logical decision-making, and one becomes better at it through years of experience. It is unfortunate that many students and even professional researchers do not pay serious attention to research design; too often, they simply use the method that they feel most competent and therefore comfortable with, without thinking much about whether that method is the most logical and effective for that particular research question or phenomenon. To use a metaphor, research design can be thought of as a bridge between research target, research questions and theories on the one hand, and data collection and analysis on the other. The key question to research design, therefore, is whether the two sides could be connected in a logical and feasible way. Unfortunately, despite the efforts a few have made to develop 'a unified approach' (Gerring, 2011), social scientists have not stopped arguing with each over what this logic should be.

Research design is even more underdeveloped and unsettled for a subject such as intersectionality. With very few and recent exceptions (Misra et al., 2021), most researchers advocating and promoting intersectionality have not identified any existing research designs and strategies that they believe are useful for their purposes. In fact, as they criticize existing theories, they are highly critical of existing methods, particularly quantitative methods (Bowleg, 2008). It is this book's premise that, although we must be sensitive to the fundamental principles that are special to intersectionality, to study intersectionality does not necessarily require giving up on existing methods. In fact, it would be a great loss for intersectionality as a knowledge project to dismiss all existing research design and methods off hand. Research designs and methods, like all other tools and technologies, are neutral in the sense that they can be used for all kinds of purposes and by people with opposing positions and interests. It is people's objectives and interests that are not neutral.

In light of the objectives and theoretical principles presented in the previous chapter and sections, researchers must consider a few questions seriously and carefully in preparing and designing their research project. We shall go into the details of each specific research design and the related methods in the respective subsequent chapters (except for the last). Here, we focus on a few important elements of research design that students and researchers who intend to study intersectionality should consider.

To start with, a first set of related questions relate to the social categories (or attributes, or identities) to be included in a particular research project or study. First of all, which ones are to be included? And why? A question perhaps especially important for intersectionality is who will decide which categories are important and therefore should be studied. In intersectionality research, there is a strong distaste for the superiority of the researcher as someone coming from a privileged position who patronizes their research subjects and only lets the research outcomes benefit themselves. It is therefore highly desirable, if not entirely essential, for the participants – noting the word 'subjects' might not be used! – to advise the researcher which social categories should be studied, although the researcher may still make their contribution. Researchers of intersectionality are not yet clear about who – the researcher or the participants – are in a 'better' position of determining what to be studied and how, but at least the researcher is expected to take the participants' views very seriously.

A relatively more technical question follows. Obviously, any study of intersectionality would require at least two categories or entities. The question is: is there a maximum? So far, most studies of intersectionality include only two or three categories, such as gender, race and perhaps sexuality. Few seem to have given much thought about how many categories a researcher can handle – what would they do if it were important to study five or more categories at the same time? How would the interactions between these categories be analysed? We shall come back to this issue in some of the following chapters.

Most importantly, how do these categories or attributes interact with each other? What will happen to the people when their social location moves from a single category to a cross-classified one? What evidence do we have for demonstrating the interactive nature of the relationship between these categories? What does the interaction mean in this particular context? If it is not additive, what kind of interaction is it? What is the meaning of each of these intersectional categories and entities, especially from the perspective of its members? Has the group been identified as a disadvantaged group? Although speaking particularly to psychologists, Elizabeth Cole (2009, p. 176) has addressed some of these questions well, advising that researchers should

> understand all their participants in terms of the multiple social categories of identity, difference, and disadvantage they represent and to attend to groups that are often overlooked in psychology. This question does not imply that any given study ought to include individuals representing every permutation of race, gender, class, or other social identity; not only is this practically impossible, it is properly the cooperative work of a field. Rather, attention to who is included within any category of interest, with particular attention to groups that have often been excluded, is meant to encourage psychologists to view all samples in terms of their particularity and to attend to diversity within samples.

From the perspective of research design, what matters is to include participants who may be disadvantaged in a certain context but have been neglected due to their unique location in the cross-classification of social categories and interlocking power systems. Researchers need to think carefully beforehand which categories are to be included in order to cover this type of participants. Obviously, it is not necessarily an academic sin if a research project has failed to include any important category; if a particular category turns out to be unexpectedly important during the research process, then it can be added to either this study or the next one, which is the process of scientific discovery. To avoid this from happening, researchers could conduct a pilot study to learn whether some potential participants would think that any particular one should be included.

In choosing and determining the social categories to be included, researchers also need to consider whether they have a sufficient number of cases or participants to explore and demonstrate the variety of life experiences, especially in terms of discrimination and inequality, across the combined categories and entities. And would it be problematic to use the same research tools for collecting data from members of all cross-classification categories? This is especially important for discovering any social groups that have been neglected so far in public discourses or academic publications. This is not the same issue as sampling, although it would be helpful if the selected participants of a certain cross-classification would be deemed as representative of their group. Show the limitations of the single-dimension way of thinking, or at least show that things are more complicated than that. Research instruments, either quantitative or qualitative, are usually assumed to be equally effective and applicable to participants, which is a very strong assumption, particularly in the eyes of intersectionality. Researchers should aim to strike a good balance between covering idiosyncratic and shared situations – each participant may be unique as a human being, but it is the social scientist's job to discover something beyond individuals.

Third, what kind of disadvantage, inequality, discrimination or deprivation does the study aim to focus on? This is important because it relates to the mechanisms through which the subsequent connections are produced. For intersectionality, the most important mechanism would be power distribution and institutional arrangements (or systems of discrimination) that put, purposefully or inadvertently, the cross-classified social groups in a ranking order, thereby one or more groups end up at the bottom. It is a great challenge to identify and reveal these mechanisms with convincing evidence because they are often concealed or disguised with a legitimate façade, especially in a liberal and democratic context.

Finally, what is the logic that connects the intersectional position of a certain social group to the undesirable outcome? It is not that hard to observe such a connection when data about group attributes and the outcome are available. It is nonetheless a great challenge to argue that the connection is a cause of the outcome, because the conditions for arriving at a causal argument are much more difficult to satisfy. Many researchers rely on the members of the group to identify the causal relationship and then find out what interlocking categories may be responsible. This strategy assumes that the group members necessarily know what is actually happening to their life simply because they live in that position, which may not be the case. It is advisable that researchers of intersectionality make use of the latest development in causal analysis to enhance their capacity to construct causal arguments.

2.5 Suggested readings and questions for discussion

For theories of intersectionality, Patricia Collins's *Intersectionality as critical social theory* (2019) is clearly the most important text, and her more recent article (2021) gave an update on her thinking. Be warned, however, that if you wish to find clearly stated content of the theory, you might be disappointed, as that is what she has avoided giving; instead, you may find some concepts such as relationality or complexity helpful for you to develop a theory. For Collins and many other advocates of intersectionality, *how* one thinks is much more important than *what* one thinks. Clearly, both questions are important; unfortunately, the answers remain unclear or at least subjective. It is therefore important to discuss the following questions with your peers:

- How is intersectionality 'as a way of thinking' different from other ways of thinking? What are these ways of thinking? Is one way of thinking necessarily 'better' than another?

- What does a social theory of intersectionality say? Formulate your version of the theory and compare it with those of your peers. How different are they? If they are very different, why? What do these differences tell us about the theory in general?
- What would the 'best' evidence for intersectionality discrimination or inequity look like? How would you go about collecting such evidence in practice?

For a general introduction to research design in the social sciences, *Research design: Qualitative, quantitative, and mixed methods approaches* (Sage, 2018) by John W. Creswell and Vicki Clarke gives a very comprehensive yet accessible exposition, which will be discussed in Chapter 9. I would strongly recommend, however, John Gerring's *Social science methodology: A unified framework* (Cambridge University Press, 2011), as it offers a streamlined, generic and logical overall strategy for designing any research project. For designing a study especially for intersectionality, the papers by Cole (2009) and Misra et al. (2021) are very helpful.

3
QUALITATIVE DESIGNS AND METHODS

3.1 Overview and objectives

After introducing the basic ideas and motivations of intersectionality in the first chapter and the key theoretical principles in the second chapter, we now move on to the specific research methods that are potentially useful for studying intersectionality empirically. I say 'potentially' for two reasons. First, no method is necessarily useful – whether a method proves to be useful for a particular study depends on other factors, such as the study's objectives and resources. Second, researchers of intersectionality have not agreed on how intersectionality 'should' be studied empirically; for many social scientists, conducting empirical investigations in different ways is a liberty, even a necessity, not a weakness or constraint.

Keeping the above two points in mind, we start with qualitative research designs and methods because some researchers of intersectionality have argued that such methods are better suited for studying intersectionality than quantitative ones. This is a misconception; therefore, the main objective of this chapter is *to demonstrate to the readers why this is so*. To achieve this, it would be very helpful to *tackle a prerequisite question: what makes research methods and designs qualitative in the first place?* After discussing these questions in methodological terms, we will examine a few published studies in order *to understand more specifically the relative advantages as well as disadvantages in applying purely qualitative research methods for studying intersectionality*. The divide between qualitative and quantitative research has troubled social scientists for many decades, which has been detrimental to the progress of social science research. It is, however, encouraging that confrontations between the two sides have declined dramatically over the years. As demonstrated later in Chapter 9 when mixed-methods research designs are introduced, we should aim to go beyond such an unhelpful divide and use all kinds of methods logically and innovatively, regardless of whether the issue under study is intersectional or not.

3.2 What makes an academic study qualitative?

Innocence could be a great advantage. Suppose you were new to social science research and your brain had not been washed with any particular theoretical or methodological perspective, so you could think intuitively on your own without any presumption or prejudice. Then you would come to the conclusion that the distinction between qualitative and quantitative research in the social sciences is a really minor issue and contingent on a number of factors. It is minor in comparison with other more fundamental issues such as what the research questions are, what previous and existing studies have said about it, what sources of evidence are available, etc. The question whether your research should be quantitative or qualitative, or neither, or both, comes only after you have some clear answers to these questions. In other words, the distinction between qualitative and quantitative research is contingent on a series of factors, including the way you formulate your research (different research questions could be raised for the same phenomenon), the theories and methods you have learnt, what other researchers have done (you may want to do something different, even new), what kind of evidence is at your disposal (what if only quantitative information is available even if you are only comfortable with qualitative data, or vice versa), etc. If so, it will be very difficult to predict whether a study should be qualitative or quantitative beforehand. In fact, it is rare to find a classic of social science study – consider Karl Marx's *Das Capital*, Max Weber's *The Protestant Ethics and the Spirit of Capitalism* or Emile Durkheim's *Suicide* – to be conceived and conducted as entirely either qualitative or quantitative. To them, whether the study is qualitative or quantitative is a trivial question – one must analyse all available data with any methods logically useful; what is not trivial is how the researcher tackles the research question.

However, the reality is quite different: many researchers have already determined whether a study they plan to conduct should be qualitative or quantitative beforehand; some even keep doing entirely qualitative (or quantitative) research throughout their long careers. Clearly, they have already made up their mind about whether their research should be qualitative or quantitative long before considering their research questions, existing research, the nature of evidence and other factors. The distinction between qualitative and quantitative research is not merely about research per se; researchers identify themselves as either qualitative or quantitative in order to establish their academic identity and membership of an academic community. This is a much more serious issue because the original contingency of research methods has become a matter of identity – if researchers identify themselves as qualitative researchers, they will not touch any quantitative data or methods anymore; everything they do must be qualitative even when they know quantitative data and methods are useful for answering their questions. The same can be said for quantitative researchers as well. Locking themselves up in either the qualitative or quantitative camp for the rest of their careers is an unfortunate trap that young researchers could fall into.

This is not to deny that young researchers' choices over whether to be qualitative or quantitative are a consequence of a mixture of factors. One factor is which 'genre' of research they feel comfortable with and competent in, which in turn is a consequence of the training they received. Another factor is the influence of their seniors, especially their academic advisors and mentors. In this sense, academic commitment to a particular way of doing research is much akin to becoming a member of a religion – being young, one has no control over the environment and is unconsciously subject to the influences imposed on them by those more powerful around them. This is particularly true when powerful academics divide themselves into multiple camps that cannot get along.

Now, suppose young researchers could think and make a choice completely on their own, what merits in qualitative research will they find so attractive? As pointed out above, this is an empirical question whose answer is contingent on a series of factors, but for the sake of understanding researchers' choices, it is informative for us to identify any 'universal' or long-term benefits of qualitative research.

To start with, what do we mean by 'qualitative'? In social science research, a few things could be qualitative: the data, the methods, the approach or the empirical investigation as a whole, which is why some researchers emphasize that qualitative research is not one thing but multiple things (St. Pierre and Roulston, 2006, p. 678). What data are qualitative? Perhaps the most widely held answer is: anything other than numbers, including words, images, etc. More often than not, people think of all kinds of texts (notes of observations, interview transcripts, newspaper articles, editorials, government policies and legislations, emails, blogs, novels, biographies, etc.) as qualitative, but it is important to note that any form of texts listed here may not be produced exclusively with words alone and could include numbers or other numeric information. Other types of qualitative data include images either still or mobile, such as photos, pictures, drawings, symbols, movies, TV programmes, video recordings, etc. Research methods that have been created for collecting and analysing these kinds of data are normally referred to as 'qualitative research methods'. Methods for collecting qualitative data usually include semi-structured or unstructured interviews, ethnography and participant observations, focus groups, textual or pictorial materials, recording conversations, filming, etc. And methods for analysing these data include, for example, thematic analysis, discourse analysis, narrative analysis, frame analysis, conversation analysis, etc. It is not hard to find textbooks that explain how to use these methods, and I shall suggest a few at the end of this chapter.

A more important question is: are qualitative data (words, texts, images, etc.) necessarily or inherently more useful than quantitative data (measures, scales, numbers and statistics)? Relatedly, are methods for collecting and analysing qualitative data (interviewing, coding, thematic analysis, etc.) necessarily and inherently more powerful and effective than quantitative methods (statistical and mathematical models, computing methods, etc.)? These questions are important because the answers to them may influence how researchers carry out their studies. It is obviously impractical for me to collect responses from a good sample of researchers to these questions. However, I would expect most of them to agree that there are no definite answers as they depend on a number of situations, such as the research questions and the nature of the research target, which brings us back to the previously emphasized contingent nature of our choices.

It would not be surprising if a small number of researchers would not accept such an eclectic or pragmatic approach to choosing data and methods. They would argue that qualitative research does enjoy a certain number of inherent (universal) advantages over quantitative methods, which will lead young researchers to choose qualitative research over quantitative research. Let's examine these claimed advantages, and the interested reader could read more about these issues in the suggested readings at the end of the chapter. Note that, although I list and discuss them separately, these points are logically connected to each other so that they may mean the same thing or can logically derive one from another.

A first believed advantage of qualitative research is that collecting and analysing qualitative data will help the researcher retain the original meanings of the key concepts in a study. Correspondingly, a common critique of quantitative research is that by quantifying the key concepts, their original meanings will get lost or seriously compromised. No social scientist would dispute the importance of meanings and their interpretations in studying social phenomena. The contested issue is how meanings should be studied. Some qualitative researchers argue or imply that we could only know and understand the meanings by soliciting expressions of these meanings in natural language from the respondents; conversely, any attempt to use quantitative instruments to measure or represent the meanings would unavoidably distort them. There is a very strong desire among qualitative researchers to keep their data 'natural' or 'uncontaminated'. It is, however, untrue that quantitative researchers do not care about meanings – in fact, they take the potential loss or misrepresentation of a concept's meaning so seriously that they want to quantify such loss with a model; for example, factor analysis is such a method for representing and measuring the potential discrepancy between the original concept and the observable measures. Relatedly, quantitative researchers also attempt to ensure that their respondents mean the same concept by asking them about this concept in different ways so that we can know how consistent people's understandings of the concept are.

It is worth spending some time and space on a relatively more special issue in relation to the above discussion. Many students and junior researchers have learnt from either their senior academics or some textbooks that quantitative research follows the philosophy of positivism which naively believes that there exists a social reality for them to measure accurately. As a result, positivism has gained some notoriety among social scientists, especially those in the UK, as it has become synonymous with a rigid and simplistic perspective to understanding social reality. Many students and researchers routinely declare in their dissertations and papers that they prefer qualitative to quantitative research because the latter is guided by positivism, and they would like to follow a more 'sophisticated' or 'critical' philosophy such as interpretivism, feminism or post-modernism. All quantitative researchers are suspects of positivists, although no researchers have openly claimed that they are, making it next to impossible to identify who is a positivist.

As I was not trained as a philosopher, I am not sufficiently qualified to discuss the connection between philosophies and social science research practices. I find nothing wrong, however, with assuming the existence of a social reality for us to study; that is, social reality is real, not simply a 'social construction' of ideas all in people's minds. Qualitative researchers must keep such an assumption as valid too if they claim to study real social phenomena; otherwise, no research whatsoever is possible or worthwhile. Before organizing interviews or focus groups or collecting texts, they must believe that the materials they will collect represent a certain piece of social reality; their research would become pointless if such social reality does not exist or is so complicated that their qualitative data would not be able to represent such reality truthfully. Furthermore, they are confronted with the same challenge as quantitative researchers do; that is, they need to examine and address the potential discrepancies between the data and the reality – it would be the qualitative researchers' turn to be naïve if they believed that every word their respondents told them were true and an interview transcript truthfully represented a piece of social reality. Words and images, no matter how detailed ('rich') and vivid ('descriptive'), are not necessarily more effective or reliable in revealing the social reality than statistics.

Another claimed key advantage of qualitative research over quantitative research is that the former takes the context of the studied phenomenon seriously while the latter does not. This contrast relates to another general question that has troubled social researchers: how peculiar or general are their research results? The word 'context' emphasizes the local nature of a study and its findings; if the study pays careful and serious attention to things that are special to a particular context, then logically the results and conclusions from this study should remain valid for this context. The question is: would the results and conclusions still be valid if they were put in a different context, that is if they were generalized into other situations? Most researchers have been ambivalent and circumvent how to answer this question, because neither answer is satisfactory, leaving the researcher in a kind of conundrum: if the results and conclusions are only valid for the studied context, then the value of the study will be limited, but if the results and conclusions can be extended into other situations, their emphasis on the importance of the context is not necessary anymore. Despite the great importance attributed to the word 'context' – the American Sociological Association named its newest journal *Context* – it remains one of the least clearly defined but most widely used concepts in the social sciences; most researchers use it without defining it, assuming that the reader would understand its meaning without much difficulty. For example, if a researcher conducted some interviews with a number of women who were abused by men who they personally knew in a city, what would the context of this study be? Is it each woman's life history, their relationships with their male abusers, the neighbourhood they have lived in, the culture in terms of the male–female relationship within their ethnic group, the city's police and social work services, the national policies, or a combination of some or all of these?

More generally, what are the boundaries of a particular context? Even when the boundaries are well defined, another important yet difficult question is: how do researchers know which elements of the context are relevant to the study? What if different researchers choose to focus on different elements of the same context? To my knowledge, neither qualitative nor quantitative research has taken these questions seriously, let alone answered them properly. What qualitative studies do more than quantitative ones is the amount of information about the context, as they do usually contain more details and descriptions of selected elements of the studied context, which, however, is not necessarily an advantage, since the selection of the relevant pieces of information is usually unexplained and how well the richer details and descriptions enhance the study's value remains unknown.

On the other hand, it is not true that quantitative research does not pay serious attention to context. Quantitative researchers care more about the scale and generalizability of their studies, and they use most 'standard' or structured instruments in order to collect a large amount of comparable and scalable data. Moreover, some statistical models, such as multilevel models, are specifically designed for taking and measuring contextual effects seriously. It is fair to say that standardized measures retain far fewer peculiar features of the studied phenomenon in comparison with qualitative research, which is perhaps why qualitative researchers accuse quantitative research of ignoring contexts. Then, we will have to answer the previously posed question: how local or general do we want our study to be? Low generalizability is a price that context-specific studies have to pay. A challenge to both quantitative and qualitative studies is how to strike a good balance between contextual peculiarities and generalities.

A controversy similar to the above is that qualitative research is better positioned than quantitative research to study processes and dynamics. It is certainly true that much quantitative data, especially those collected from cross-sectional sample surveys, can only capture a 'snapshot' of the studied social reality; that is, the data contain information only about the time point when the survey was conducted. For example, many countries carry out a census (data collection on every citizen) about every 10 years, in which a specific hour of a particular date, such as midnight on the 31 December, is designated. This does not mean survey agents would knock on people's doors at midnight sharp, only that the information supplied by citizens must be valid at that hour. Although census data are clearly the most comprehensive (not really exhaustive because some citizens may not be available), they are static rather than dynamic. This does not mean, however, that all quantitative data and studies are static. In fact, many quantitative data, particularly longitudinal surveys, cohort studies, time series, etc., are highly dynamic and could be used for studying social processes and dynamics. And some powerful methods have been invented for analysing such data, such as regression models that take into account the clustering effects of longitudinal data, event history analysis, survival analysis, sequence analysis, time series models, etc. There are more quantitative tools than qualitative ones for analysing temporal trends, processes and dynamics.

Let's finish this section by addressing one more important issue – that is, the relationship between the researcher and the people that the researcher studies. Some qualitative researchers may find the word 'subjects' offending for two different but related reasons. First, the word implies an inferior position which the people under study occupy, which is certainly not true – few researchers today would seriously think they are superior to those they study. The second reason is more serious and difficult: the word 'subjects' also suggests a clear separation of the researcher from those they study. Scientists of natural phenomena are luckier as they do not have to worry about making such a distinction. Over time, the distinction has become a source of controversy for social scientists as they study those of their own kind. The argument is that it is both morally wrong and scientifically ineffective to separate the researchers from the people they study. It is morally wrong because the studied people should have the right to participate in the study and to have a say in how the study is conducted and how the results will be used. It is scientifically ineffective because the lack of involvement by the people under study will reduce the research's abilities to accomplish its goals and objectives. For some qualitative social researchers, for example those who conduct participatory action research (PAR), it is insufficient simply to *reflect* on how the social relationship between the researchers and the people they study may affect the study and the quality of the results; those people should directly participate in the study. This suggestion has been particularly welcomed by researchers of intersectionality, because they take it as a mission of intersectionality to empower the people under study and ensure that the study results will benefit them rather than merely the researchers and their institutions.

Is involving the people under study necessarily a unique advantage of qualitative research? Whilst most researchers strongly in favour of such practice appear to be mostly qualitative, it is not true that quantitative researchers cannot do the same. For example, many quantitative researchers carry out pilot studies in order to ensure that those they study understand the questions in the survey questionnaire to be used in the subsequent real study. Some quantitative researchers also try to explain their findings in a language accessible to the people they study. Perhaps the more important and difficult question is how social scientists engage those under study as much as they can without going as far as to say that the participants are no less competent and capable than the social scientists themselves; otherwise, it would be a complete waste to invest in professional training.

The key message of this section is this: whilst it is true that qualitative and quantitative studies may conduct their respective research in different ways, it is presumptuous to draw a rigid and hard line between the two. If conducted with principles and disciplines, both types of study must take great care to represent and incorporate the meanings, contexts, processes and the effect of the researcher in their findings and interpretations.

3.3 Are qualitative designs and methods better positioned for studying intersectionality than quantitative ones?

After leading Black feminists such as Kimberlé Crenshaw and Patricia Hill Collins forcefully laid out the general principles and overall spirit of intersectionality, the number of theoretical and conceptual publications has increased drastically without a corresponding development in the methods for studying intersectionality empirically. In their very recent textbook *Introduction to intersectional qualitative research*, Esposito and Evans-Winters observed that 'Of course, using intersectionality methodologically is unchartered territory …' (Preface) as 'few scholars have attempted to turn the theory into a methodological approach' (2022, p. 2). While claiming that their book 'breaks ground' by accounting 'for the "how to" of intersectional research' (ibid.), they did not seem to realize that other researchers do not think it is truly necessary to develop any specific methods for studying intersectionality. For example, after reflecting on the point of taking intersectionality as 'a way of thinking' advocated by Cho et al. (2013), Patrick Grzanka (2014) believed that they position intersectionality 'as more closely aligned with epistemology and methodology than with methods per se. Intersectionality, according to their logic, is a lens and a commitment, rather than a prescribed set of methodological procedures. This means that virtually *any* method can be considered an intersectional one, so long as the conceptualization of categories is multiplicative and dynamic, and that power is foregrounded' (p. 304, emphasis added). What matters are the principles, the general orientations and the overall spirit, not the specific methods.

If so, our question whether qualitative methods are better equipped than quantitative ones for studying intersectionality becomes irrelevant. Esposito and Evans-Winters did not explain why they wrote a book about intersectional 'qualitative' rather than 'quantitative' methods – their preference for the former over the latter is obvious but unexplained. In fact, their concern is not the qualitative vs quantitative distinction; rather, their purpose is to overthrow the existing exploitative and oppressive methods, regardless of whether they are quantitative or qualitative, and develop intersectional ones:

> Quantitative research has been vilified as limiting because it fails to provide contextual analysis in explaining norms and trends, especially across racial, gender, and economic groups. Comparatively, qualitative research has somehow been declared our saviour, since people want to hear our side of the story. But qualitative research is also limited and limiting because it continues to position the researcher as the omnipotent and omnipresent knower of other people's lives and circumstances. … Intersectional qualitative research explores ways to interrupt the inherent exploitation and voyeurism of scientific inquiry in all forms. (2022, p. 188)

The critique of quantitative research in the first sentence is not very clear: does it mean that quantitative research is inherently unable to provide contextual analysis, or that it can be done but some quantitative researchers have failed to do so? As suggested in the previous section, my view is the latter, and we shall come back to this point in the following chapters.

Esposito and Evans-Winters made it clear that not all qualitative research is suitable for intersectionality; what they want to develop is their own 'intersectional qualitative' research that resists exploitation and voyeurism. In particular, they believe that the research methods developed by Western White colonizers are certainly unsuitable for studying intersectionality, because 'the majority of our qualitative research theories, research how-to handbooks, and professors represent and are grounded in White Western middle-class culture. The descendants of the colonizers profit from their inheritance of stolen culture and consumption of Indigenous ethos' (2022, p. 15). Therefore, they must develop a new 'oppositional paradigm' as 'the marginalized and Othered have our own ways of knowing, doing, and interpreting our social and political circumstances' (2022, p. 14). It remains unknown, however, what their ways of knowing, doing and interpreting are, at least not by reading this book – all the methods of collecting and analysing data in the middle chapters of the book, including interviews, focus groups, documents, thematic analysis, discourse analysis, narrative analysis, etc., were created almost exclusively by White middle-class social scientists in the West. They have not created any method that is customized from the perspectives and experiences of the marginalized social groups. What they and other intersectionality researchers have been doing is to use the methods invented by White middle-class scholars for their purpose of resisting the White oppressions in academic research and beyond.

In his article 'Qualitative Research and Intersectionality', Adam Trahan (2011) made it perhaps most explicit that qualitative research is the right way to study intersectionality, but he made it clear in the end that he did not mean to exclude quantitative methods and called for a mixed-methods approach. However, much of his critique of quantitative research is not convincing; in fact, it is problematic. He started by saying 'The study of crime has been largely dominated by quantitative methodologies', which is at least controversial if not entirely false, but this is not our concern here. Then he argued that 'the implications of intersectionality do not lend well to rigid quantitative frameworks' without an explanation – does this mean that all quantitative frameworks are inherently too rigid for studying intersectionality, or that they would be rigid if they were not used properly? If all quantitative methods were inherently unfit for intersectionality, then it would be pointless to mix qualitative methods with quantitative ones, as he did at the end of his paper. 'It is simply not possible', he kept arguing, 'to effectively study every combination of race, class, and gender using statistical technologies' (p. 3), implying that the number of combinations would be overwhelming for quantitative methods. To illustrate, he made use of the work of Lynch (1996), explaining that 'even restricting the term to three classes, two genders, and two races (i.e., white and nonwhite) results in 36 possible class, gender, race offender-victim combinations' (ibid.). Clearly, the arithmetic is incorrect: $3 \times 2 \times 2 = 12$, not 36; even if we multiply that by another 2 (offender–victim), the result would be 24, not 36, but it is not logical to do this, because the offender–victim variable is the target, not the conditions. It is important to note that Lynch's restriction is for simplicity's sake, and does not acknowledge the gender diversity that exists in the world.

More important than the miscalculation, he did not explain why it would be impossible for quantitative methods to analyse these combinations – as shown in the following chapters, quantitative methods can certainly deal with such a number of intersectional combinations. Taking one step back, would it be possible for qualitative methods to analyse them? What is the evidence that qualitative methods are more capable than quantitative methods for studying a large number of intersectional cross-combinations? According to him, the advantage of qualitative research over quantitative research does not lie in the ability of studying a large number of combined factors, but in creating 'rich descriptive accounts of the contextual nature of people's lived experiences' (ibid.). It is important to note, first of all, that this is an advantage of qualitative research as a whole, not simply for studying intersectionality. Second, quantitative researchers never claim that their job is to produce rich descriptions of the context of people's experiences; many statisticians have made it clearer than those who detest statistics when one should not use statistics, but few qualitative researchers have clearly advised when students and young researchers should *not* use qualitative methods. Subsequently, while it is certainly important to acknowledge the advantage of qualitative research, qualitative researchers need to consider how many rich descriptive accounts they can produce and analyse and how they would detect any patterns in a large number of such accounts. It won't take long for them to realize that they will have to turn words into numbers in order to answer these questions.

Let's recap with two important points. First, the fundamental principles of intersectionality seem to demand a new set of methods to be created in order to study the experiences of the oppressed and enfranchised effectively. Unfortunately, this has not happened, and most researchers have either reluctantly or unwillingly made use of existing research methods, leaving the question whether it is truly necessary to create new methods tailor-made for intersectionality unanswered. As Grzanka suggested after reviewing some publications on methods for studying intersectionality, researchers should 'not prematurely foreclose upon thinking of intersectionality methodologically' (2014, p. 306), particularly considering that intersectionality is still a knowledge project in the making.

Second, researchers should use both qualitative and quantitative methods for studying intersectionality and stop trying to figure out how one is superior to the other. In the most recent review of the methodologies of intersectionality, Misra et al. (2021) 'hope to correct misunderstandings that intersectionality can only be qualitative, or if quantitative, can only be carried out through analyzing "interaction effects"' (p. 15). Different research methods, like tools in a toolbox, are useful in different ways, so researchers should learn to pick up the right one suitable for the job at hand.

3.4 A closer look at a selection of published studies

After discussing some of the key issues surrounding qualitative research on intersectionality, it will be helpful to learn how such studies are conducted in practice. I have identified the following four studies as examples of qualitative research of intersectionality:

- Gueta, Keren. 2017. A qualitative study of barriers and facilitators in treating drug use among Israeli mothers: An intersectional perspective. *Social Science & Medicine, 187,* 155–163.

- Medina-Perucha, Laura; Scott, Jenny; Chapman, Sarah; Barnett, Julie; Dack, Charlotte; Family, Hannah. 2019. A qualitative study on intersectional stigma and sexual health among women on opioid substitution treatment in England: Implications for research, policy and practice. *Social Science & Medicine, 222*, 315–322.
- Rosenthal, Lisa; Overstreet, Nicole M.; Khukhlovich, Adi; Brown, Brandon E.; Godfrey, Christopher-John; Albritton, Tashuna. 2020. Content of, sources of, and responses to sexual stereotypes of Black and Latinx women and men in the United States: A qualitative intersectional exploration. *Journal of Social Issues, 76*(4), 921–948.
- Young, Charlotte. 2020. Interlocking systems of oppression and privilege impact African Australian health and well-being in greater Melbourne: A qualitative intersectional analysis. *Journal of Social Issues, 76*(4), 880–898.

Here are the considerations that led me to choose these studies. First, all four studies have explicitly made intersectionality the focus of their research, and they are all qualitative, but the ways in which they conducted their respective empirical investigations are somehow different, which allows us to discern the common features as well as the variations in this type of study. Second, the studies were conducted by different kinds of researchers (single-author vs a team, same or different identities with the participants, etc.) and in different national contexts, thereby showing a variety of research situations. Third, journal articles are much shorter than book-length studies, making it easier to cover a relatively larger number of studies and to read the original study if desired. Finally, the studies are published in two highly reputable academic journals and must have gone through a rigorous process of peer-review and editing. While this does not mean that they have no shortcomings (each article has a section on the respective study's limitations), their overall quality should be high. That said, the reader is advised not to see the selected studies as 'a representative sample' of qualitative studies on intersectionality. They might be, but they were not selected in order to represent other such studies. Please bear in mind that the following discussions of these four studies focus on the methodological aspects; if you want to know more about the backgrounds, the literature review or the specific findings, please read the original study.

First of all, it might seem obvious, but it is essential that a study on intersectionality, qualitative or not, must focus on a group of people who have been disenfranchised. It is actually quite a demanding job to explain why the studied phenomenon requires an intersectional perspective. The starting point of Gueta's study (2017) is that, compared with their male counterparts, substance-abusing mothers in Israel were slow in making use of treatments available to them, so the objective of her study was to discover the barriers to their lack of use of the treatments. The intersectional approach should be useful for studying their experiences because the barriers (stigma, domestic violence, poverty, racism, lack of childcare but fear of losing parental rights, etc.) relate to each other. The social group that Medina-Perucha et al.'s study targeted was 'women receiving opioid substitution treatment (WOST) in community pharmacies in England' (2019, p. 316), who may have experienced multiple stigmas due to their gender, transactional sex, HIV status, race, social class, incarceration history, weight and sexual orientation. In their study, Lisa Rosenthal and her colleagues (2020) examined sexual stereotypes perceived by young Black and Latinx people in New York City, as these stereotypes were deemed as sources of stigmas and unjust life experiences. The target of

Young's study (2020) was the inequities in health experienced by African Australians because of interlocking discriminations based on their race, immigrant status and other attributes.

The chosen social group as the target of research has important implications for the following empirical investigation in terms of selecting the participants. Gueta (2017) recruited 25 Israeli-born and immigrant mothers known to child protection and welfare agencies with the aim of maximizing the variation of the participants' backgrounds. Practically, she designed her study to 'ensure diversity in terms of participants' age, gender, ethnicity, and geography, and permit inductive examinations' (p. 157). The participating mothers were also different in terms of stages of recovering, immigrant status, ethnicity, age, marital status and education. The first limitation she noted at the end of the paper is that the participants were 'recruited through a TC [therapeutic community] program to which most of them had been court-referred because of poor parental functioning'; therefore, her study did not cover mothers 'who are not currently in treatment and mothers whose parental rights are not at risk might reveal other salient themes' (p. 161). It is worth noting that this limitation is formulated as a lack of representing mothers of other backgrounds rather than a failure of covering different intersectional locations. Through the support of three service centres for drug-taking women and sex workers, Medina-Perucha approached 75 potential participants but was successful in recruiting only 20 participants. Rosenthal and her colleagues did not report their 'success rate' in recruiting the 75 participants for the 11 focus groups they conducted successfully (2020, p. 927); that is, they did not provide the information about how many potential participants they actually invited. Only after they analysed the data did they realize that the rate of university students was unusually high among their participants. This is an important issue for other qualitative studies as well because it raises the question of *what kinds of participants should be recruited in order to study intersectional effects more effectively*. For Young's study (2020), besides the 50 cases that already existed, she conducted 2 group interviews, with 8 and 11 people in each respective group, and 'slow interviews' with 22 people. Of the 44 interviewees, 35 were African Australians. Given the small number and the volunteering nature of the recruiting process, no attempt was made to use the group of participants as a representative sample of the interested population. Nevertheless, these studies strongly imply that the observations and conclusions derived from the data were applicable to the whole group at large, which illustrates the conundrum between contextuality and generality mentioned earlier in this chapter. None of the papers reflected on this issue as a limitation of the study. For example, how should we interpret the results from 25 Israeli mothers who took drugs? Do their experiences represent all mothers with these attributes? If yes, what is the logic of their 'representativeness'? If not, then the results are only applicable to them and should not be taken as the basis for deriving implications for policies and practices.

Second, the ways in which the researcher approaches the participants and manages their relationship affect the research results. All authors presented a reflexive section on this topic. As discussed early in this chapter, a hallmark of all qualitative studies is reflexivity; that is, the investigator is expected to reflect on the effects of their identities and attributes and their relationships with the participants on the results and conclusions. By now, the reader must have understood that this is especially important for studies of intersectionality. All authors of the four papers wrote about who they were (their 'social location' or 'author positionality'), who they were to the participants, and how their social backgrounds were similar to or different from their participants'. More importantly, they also reflected on how their identities and relations with the participants might have affected the research results, but these discussions appear to be highly speculative – it remains unclear exactly which of their attributes has affected which participants' responses to the study, as there was little evidence showing that a particular respondent answered a question raised by the investigator in a particular way due to a particular attribute of the investigator. For example, Young mentioned that her experience in Ghana, which is not one of her salient attributes, was interpreted as a sign of 'knowing' the Africans by the African Australian participants of her study. Suppose such a 'researcher (or investigator) effect' does exist, the implication then is that a study's results would have been quite different had another researcher with different identities and attributes conducted the research in the same way. If so, each study would become highly special, if not unique, which would make it very difficult to tease out any common features and findings across multiple qualitative studies.

Third, it is important to consider how the method of data collection is particularly suitable for studying intersectionality. Gueta (2017) collected data through in-depth interviews, each taking 2 to 3 hours (or 120 to 180 minutes). In the study led by Medina-Perucha (2019), the interviews lasted from 25 to 80 minutes. As mentioned above, Rosenthal's team conducted focus groups rather than interviews with each individual participant without explaining their choice. On average, each focus group had seven participants and lasted for about 90 minutes, which means that, on average, each participant had less than 15 minutes, which is much shorter than the time for each individual interview in the other two studies. If a key objective of intersectionality is to study the rich details of disadvantaged experiences, then participants should be given as much time as needed for reporting the details. Clearly, there is a great variation in the time available to them or taken by them. In a focus group, it is often the case that a small number of participants dominate the discussion whilst others do not want to or have the chance to speak. Moreover, each participant in Rosenthal's study was paid $25 plus food (pizza) and drinks, which does not seem to be consistent with the unequal contribution. As Young explained (2020, p. 885), the 'slow interview' seems to be particularly in line with the spirit of intersectionality, as the investigator used written notes as both a quality-assuring mechanism and an opportunity for the interviewee to take a more active role in the research process. Overall, it is difficult to see how the method of data collection was particularly chosen with the purposes and principles of intersectionality in mind.

Fourth, moving on to the methods of data analysis, Gueta (2017) conducted a two-step 'theoretical thematic analysis'. The first step was open-coding; that is, 'the transcribed interviews were read and re-read and initial themes were identified for each participant's experience of current and previous treatment-seeking experiences', 'guided by concepts gathered implicitly from the original words of the participants. These resulting themes were then coded into emergent descriptive categories'. The second round of coding was to read and re-read the transcribed interviews 'in a manner that was mindful of the intersection of axes of marginalization, the experience at this junction, and the potential for effective change' (p. 158). In contrast, Medina-Perucha and her colleagues analysed their interview data with Framework Analysis (FA) 'to classify and organise the data according to key themes, in order to develop a hierarchal thematic framework' (p. 317). Although they emphasized that FA was different from other methods, the procedures they followed appear to be very similar to any other qualitative data analysis – reading and coding of the transcripts, verifying the coding results by different coders and interpreting the coded results. Rosenthal's team followed a similar procedure while emphasizing they kept the key idea of intersectionality in mind when developing the code book for two students to use (2020, p. 928). Young analysed her data in a way that was almost the same as that of the other three studies. What separates Young's and Gueta's studies from the other two is that Young and Gueta coded and analysed their data on their own individually; therefore, they could not verify and modify the codes through the work of a collaborator. Again, all these methods have been used for studying many topics that are different from intersectionality, with which the authors did not have any issue.

In almost all of these studies, the results were presented and organized by the themes identified and illustrated with selected quotes from the interviews, a common practice among most qualitative studies. Obviously, given the limited space, it is impossible for the investigator to present most, let alone all, relevant words the participants said during the data collection process. The logic that the investigator followed, perhaps most often unconsciously, when selecting which quotes to be included in the paper remains obscure. For example, in Gueta's study (2017), there were 24 participants (one dropped out), but only 19 were quoted, and she did not give an explanation for why the other five did not get a chance to appear in the paper. Similarly, in Medina-Perucha et al.'s study (2019), only 10 of the 20 interviewees were quoted. Furthermore, the quotations were not equally distributed: Masha was quoted three times while others only once in Gueta's study, and the quotes were concentrated in 5 of the 20 participants in Medina-Perucha et al.'s study. The themes in the study by Medina-Perucha were organized by each of the five attributes of the studied women (being women, drug use, homelessness, transactional sex, STI/BBV status) *separately* rather than interactively, although the authors highlighted a few occasions in which evidence for interactional stigmas could be found. The study by Rosenthal et al. (2020) contains a much more condensed presentation of the results, especially worrying while considering the much larger number of participants. In Young's study (2020), only two of the nine non-African Australians and 15 of the 35 African Australians appeared in the paper. Given the demand of intersectionality for equal attention to all marginalized people, this *variation in the representation of each participant* is not a trivial issue but has not been considered in most publications of qualitative studies.

Moreover, when presenting a quote, the published study usually shows some information about the identity of the person speaking, such as 'single mother of twins aged 20'. For non-intersectional qualitative studies, such information about the speaking participants does not convey more than the speaker's limited attributes. However, it should matter significantly for studies of intersectionality, because the information is relevant to the intersectional social location of the participants, which may be essential for understanding what was said or experienced. Surprisingly, some qualitative researchers were ambivalent about this issue and continued to follow the existing 'standard practice' of reporting qualitative results. When a piece of information, such as 'an 18-year old Black man', is attached to an extraction of what the participant said, is it implied that the content of the extraction could or should be understood as a result of the person's intersectional identity? And if the answer is positive, how? In Rosenthal's focus groups, this might have been even more difficult as some participants did not provide the needed information of their identities or the relevant identity was not considered important beforehand, making it impossible to connect the data with the participant's intersectional identity or position.

3.5 Observations and reflections

Let's draw a conclusion to this chapter by making some observations and reflections on the previous and other qualitative studies on intersectionality. It is safe to say that the starting point of a study on intersectionality is a certain form of inequity or injustice experienced by at least one intersectional group. Whilst this is almost always true, the researcher would undermine their own research by taking this for granted and thus focusing on this group alone. Their research would become more powerful and convincing if *all relevant intersectional groups were included and compared*. For example, in the study on mothers who took drugs and received treatments, the researcher would have done themselves a big favour by comparing these mothers with others to demonstrate that this group of mothers have been disadvantaged in their unique way in comparison with male drug-takers or females who were not mothers.

The above logic of analysis has important implications for the design of empirical investigation. More specifically, it is useful to consider what kinds of participants should be recruited in order to study intersectional effects effectively and efficiently. A practical issue is the number of participants in the interested intersectional category vs the number of intersectional categories. Practical constraints usually do not give researchers the luxury of making both numbers as large as they wish; therefore, they must strike a balance or compromise. Currently, it is common to maximize the number of participants of the studied intersectional category, while it is highly advisable for researchers to design their study in a way to ensure that a minimum number of participants be recruited for each intersectional classification or location. For example, if race and gender are identified as the key intersectional categories, and suppose race has three categories (White, Black and Other) and gender has two categories (men and women), then theoretically there are six intersectional sub-categories. Researchers should consider recruiting an approximately equal number of participants for each sub-category in order to generate comparable data for the purpose of demonstrating intersectional inequality or injustice. Again, it is important to note that these crude classifications are used as illustrations for the sake of simplicity, which do not reflect the diversity and are not inclusive of, for example, non-binary or intersex people.

Practically, one common challenge to qualitative research is the lack of control by the researcher over the kinds of people who eventually become the participants. For example, in Karen Gueta's study (2017), social class was identified as one of the important intersectional categories; however, her participants were almost all in the lower class (except one). That is, the investigator has no control over how many participants there will be in each sub-category. There is an unavoidable but significant tension between the design requirement of recruiting a balanced selection of participants and the uncontrollable nature of the recruiting process due to volunteering. Although such lack of control is certainly understandable, there remains a large chance for the researcher to make their study more convincing and defendable in light of the overall objective of intersectionality.

The use of quantitative methods in qualitative studies is an interesting practice to observe. For example, Medina-Perucha and her team used SPSS to obtain quantitative descriptions of their participants, and Rosenthal reported Cronbach's alpha for coding consistency. More generally, in many qualitative studies, the researcher resorts to quantitative studies either to present relevant information more clearly or to justify the acceptability of their analysis. If it is unavoidable or even desirable to include certain quantitative data and analysis in the study of intersectionality, then there is no need to be orthodox about qualitative research's advantage over quantitative research, regardless of whether the topic is intersectionality or not.

Are qualitative studies better positioned for studying intersectionality? It is difficult to give a positive answer, first because the authors of the above high-quality qualitative studies admit in the Limitations section that their study might have missed some important factors or could not cover all of the complex situations. Another even greater challenge is to argue for a causal connection between the intersectional attributes and the undesirable experiences with convincing research design and analysis. To make a causal argument is the holy grail not only for the study of intersectionality but for social science research as a whole. Intersectionality as a research enterprise may have established powerful theories and arguments, but it still has a long way to go to demonstrate the causal relationship between the intersectional processes and the unjust disfranchisement.

3.6 Suggested readings and questions for discussion

It is difficult to recommend texts for introducing qualitative research methods in general – not only there are too many, but they touch on a great diversity of specific methods (in-depth interviews, focus groups, ethnography, etc.) and disciplines (sociology, psychology, business studies, education, human geography, etc.) as well. It is therefore important and helpful to consider the following questions: *Do we mean a single and coherent research approach when we speak of 'qualitative research'? What are the characteristics shared by all qualitative research methods which separate them apart from quantitative research methods?* If the reader would like to have an overview of qualitative research and related methods, a good starting reference is *The Sage handbook of qualitative research*, edited by Norman K. Denzin and Yvonna S. Lincoln (2023). Even more comprehensive than this handbook is the four-volume set *Sage qualitative research methods*, edited by Paul Atkinson and Sara Delamont (2010), which is a large collection of originally published articles. I would also recommend the similarly voluminous *The European tradition in qualitative research*, edited by Mohamed Cherkaoui, Pierre Demeulenaere and Raymond Boudon (2003), which contains a number of articles that are significantly different from the conventional perspectives on qualitative research. In addition, when having multiple items at hand, it is perhaps 'human nature' to rank them in a hierarchical order rather than see them as equal or complementary to each other. *Is it really meaningful and useful to determine among different research methods which are 'better' than the others?* If you prefer qualitative methods, then try to discuss this question with someone who uses quantitative methods, or vice versa.

Academic publications on qualitative research methods for the purpose of studying intersectionality, either books or journal articles, are scarce. A systematic and perhaps the most recent publication is *Introduction to intersectional qualitative research*, by Jennifer Esposito and Venus Evans-Winters (2022). Drawing on their own and their students' research experiences, the authors illustrated how existing qualitative research methods could be employed for studying intersectionality. While reading this text, pay careful attention to the sections about the advantages of qualitative methods and the limitations of quantitative methods – *are you convinced and why?* I would suggest that the reader read the original papers of the four studies presented earlier, search for further similar studies, and learn how to conduct qualitative research on intersectionality in practice.

4

EXPLORING PATTERNS OF INTERSECTIONALITY IN CONTINGENCY TABLES

4.1 Overview and objectives

A key objective of this entire book is to demonstrate how useful quantitative methods and mixed-methods designs (see Chapters 5 and 9) could be for analysing intersectionality. After introducing and discussing qualitative methods and designs in the previous chapter, we now move on to learn some simple quantitative methods of exploring patterns in intersectional attributes in this chapter. To avoid any misunderstanding, it is important to make it clear from the outset that it is *not* my intention to show that statistical methods and models are 'better than' or 'superior to' qualitative methods. As demonstrated in my previous book (Yang, 2010), social researchers should understand the logic of each quantitative method in order to be able to appreciate the pros and cons of these methods; put differently, they will do themselves a disservice if they simply dismiss and criticize these methods without learning the technical details. In fact, the most effective, and perhaps the harshest, criticisms of quantitative methods come from some prominent statisticians and quantitative methodologists, such as David Freedman and Otis Dudley Duncan. As some researchers have openly argued against the use of quantitative methods for studying intersectionality, it is necessary to consider and answer the question whether quantitative methods are indeed not useful for analysing intersectionality. Clearly, my objective here is to convince the reader that this is a misconception. As the discussion on this misconception may sound too abstract and negative, I will illustrate the benefits of studying intersectionality using simple statistical methods (contingency table analysis) with a few real-world examples, starting with the famous case of *Moore v. Hughes Helicopters, Inc*. If you read and try to understand these examples – particularly the tables – carefully, you will see intersectional patterns emerging, some of which you may find unexpected, while using these methods as an aid to thinking and exploring.

4.2 Are quantitative data and methods inappropriate for analysing intersectionality?

Thanks to the financial support of many research funding agents and the admirable work of many researchers, an enormous amount of quantitative data has been accumulated. Some countries have established centres with the mission of collecting the data together and making them available to other researchers at no or a very affordable cost, including the Inter-university Consortium for Political and Social Research (ICPSR) in the US, the Data Service in the UK (previously UK Data Archive), the GESIS Social Sciences Data Archive at the Leibniz Institute for Social Science (Germany) and the National Survey Research Centre at Renmin University in China. Each centre keeps at least thousands of datasets, and each dataset usually contains at least hundreds of variables from no fewer than thousands of participants. It is very likely that you will find at least some relevant data about an important social science subject in these datasets. The implication is clear: researchers working on intersectionality should make use of these 'gold mines of data'. Unfortunately, so far, they have not.

There has been a general resistance among researchers of intersectionality to analysing quantitative data with statistical or other quantitative methods. As the resistance remains persistent, it is necessary to debunk a couple of ideas that seem to be popular among some researchers but prevent them from making use of quantitative data and methods. They have deprived themselves (perhaps others as well) of the opportunity to access a large storage of useful evidence and to make a valuable contribution to the whole enterprise of intersectionality by employing a number of quantitative tools.

The first idea that stops many researchers from using quantitative data and methods is that quantitative research represents the philosophy of positivism, and because positivism is flawed, so is quantitative research. Obviously, this is too big an issue for me to address here. The dispute over positivism in social sciences has a history over several decades. At a conference of the German Sociological Association in 1961, Karl Popper presented a paper titled 'The Logic of the Social Sciences', which entailed criticisms from Theodor W. Adorno and others, accusing Popper of being positivist. These papers were collected in a volume published in 1976. Following the conference, Jürgen Habermas launched another attack on Popper's contribution in 1963, to which Hans Albert made a counter-argument. Today, many textbooks of social research methods, directly or indirectly, link quantitative methods to positivism, lending students a legitimate excuse for abandoning and attacking quantitative data and methods. Whilst philosophical arguments could illuminate certain fundamental issues underlying specific research topics or methods, it is unwise to associate a specific research method with a particular philosophy or even judge research methods in general with philosophical orientations, because it is rather unrealistic to expect philosophies to offer standards or criteria by which the value of social science research methods could be assessed. Instead, social science students and researchers should resort to their research questions, the logical rationale of their research design, the nature of their research subjects, and the kind of empirical evidence available to them for determining which research methods are suitable and therefore used.

Another criticism of quantitative research that has been frequently cited as unsuitable for studying intersectionality is that quantitative data and methods are too simplistic to capture the complexities of a piece of social reality such as intersectionality. I touched on this issue in the previous chapter, but it is imperative to elaborate here before moving on to the details of quantitative methods. Few would disagree that the social reality is complex, or at least much more complex than most of the natural phenomena – it is common sense that social phenomena are notorious for being unpredictable due to the simultaneous operations of many contingent factors and processes. That should not mean, however, that we, the people who study social phenomena, should make our own work complex as well. On the other hand, it is certainly undesirable to make our work 'simplistic'; that is, our representations and explanations fail to capture the essential features and processes in society. On the other hand, it is neither desirable nor wise to make our work unnecessarily complex, although that may make our work appear sophisticated and realistic. For all sciences, either social or natural, the most desirable is neither simplicity nor complexity, but a good balance between the two; that is, our work should be 'sufficiently complex' in representing and explaining social reality while 'sufficiently simple' at the same time in terms of accessibility and clarity.

Moving on from these abstract discussions to the specific issue of analysing intersectionality with quantitative data and methods, we need to answer the question why quantitative data and methods cannot capture the complexity of intersectionality. One charge mentioned in the previous chapter is that the number of intersections is too large for quantitative methods to analyse. Note, first of all, that this is a technical, not a philosophical, issue. It is indeed true that the number of intersections or combinations increases much faster than the number of dimensions or factors, because the number of intersectional possibilities is the product (or multiplication) of the numbers of categories of the intersectional variables. When either the number of variables or the number of categories, or both, increases, the product will increase drastically; for example, suppose the variable 'sexuality' has three categories (straight, gay/lesbian and bisexual/pansexual/queer), 'race' has three categories (White, Black and other), and class has three categories (high, middle and low), then the number of possible intersections is $3 \times 3 \times 3 = 27$, which is three times the sum of $3 + 3 + 3 = 9$. It is indeed a technical challenge to analyse 27 possibilities rather than 9. In a later part of this chapter and some other chapters we shall learn some strategies and methods for dealing with this challenge. For now, one important question is whether this relatively large number of intersections is an example of social complexity. For me, it is not, because it is much smaller and simpler than most other quantities in social life, and we can find ways to either meaningfully reduce the number of intersections or analyse them with a special technique.

Furthermore, as far as I am aware, no qualitative method can handle this challenge better than quantitative methods. As demonstrated with the four published studies in the previous chapter, qualitative researchers tend to consider only the number of intersectional variables (gender, race, etc.) but not the number of possible intersections that they need to cover when recruiting their participants; even when they do, they have no control over which intersections will be covered as it is possible that none with those intersectional attributes may volunteer to participate in their study. No qualitative study has yet systematically presented the possible intersections on which they should collect data, for which ones of these intersections data were collected, and which intersections were not covered with data and why. The results in published studies clearly show that only a small number of intersections were mentioned and analysed, with all other intersections ignored. In the sense of systematically presenting and analysing the possible intersections, which has been perceived as a sign of dealing with social complexity, qualitative methods have shown no advantage over the quantitative ones.

At the moment, the sole benefit of conducting qualitative rather than quantitative research for the purpose of analysing intersectionality lies in the rich description of the experiences of the people who have been disadvantaged in their life. If intersectionality can only be appropriately studied with rich, verbal descriptions of people's experiences, then indeed each and every researcher who wants to analyse intersectionality should employ qualitative methods. But this is a big 'if', as it remains unexplained and unjustified as to why any quantitative analysis of intersectionality is necessarily ineffective or even flawed. Rich descriptions of people's experiences in words do not logically exclude numbers, statistics or mathematical models that could describe and explain intersectionality; they approach the same social reality in different ways and therefore make complementary contributions. Simply labelling one as being philosophically advantageous over the other can only lead the entire research enterprise into a poverty of knowledge.

The next section will examine the case of *Moore v. Hughes Helicopters, Inc.*, as the plaintiff used some statistics in making her case to show why even simple statistical methods for analysing tabulated data could be useful for understanding intersectionality. From the statistical perspective, most of the commonly studied intersectional variables are categorical, such as gender, race, ethnicity and class, which means that data of these variables could be readily presented in a contingency table and analysed with existing statistical methods accordingly, which is why we will learn some simple quantitative methods for analysing intersectionality by exploring the potential intersectional patterns in contingency tables.

4.3 The Case of *Moore v. Hughes Helicopters, Inc.*

In her seminal paper of 1989, Crenshaw introduced and discussed the case of *Moore v. Hughes Helicopters, Inc.* to illustrate the failure of the American legal system in protecting intersectional social groups such as Black females from being discriminated against. At the end of the 1970s, Tommie Moore, a Black female employee of Hughes Helicopters, Inc., sued her employer for discriminating against Black females as a class. The discrimination was alleged to have occurred in promoting employees into supervisory or upper-level positions from 1975 to 1979. Jobs at Hughes were classified as a hierarchy of 20 labour grades, with 1 being the lowest and 20 the highest. In addition, some positions were recognized as 'first level supervisors', which overlapped with positions of grades 15 to 20 but were not necessarily the same ones. It was a great challenge to Moore as she had to assemble some statistics of employees in the supervisory or upper-level positions by sex and race and use them as evidence for discrimination. After the trial starting in October 1980, the case was dismissed on 27 August 1981. Here, we shall try to understand whether and why these statistics could be used for demonstrating intersectional discrimination. A caveat is in order, however – the statistics do not seem to have been always correctly recorded as the sums sometimes do not match the total reported at Casemine.[1]

As in the previous case of *DeGraffenreid v. General Motors*, the court insisted that an allegation could be made on the basis of either sex or race, but not both. For this case, it means that in the eyes of the court, if no convincing evidence was given for discrimination against either female or Black employees, Moore would have failed to make her case. Drawing on the numbers presented at Casemine, I have produced the following tables:[2]

Table 4.1 Distribution of first-level supervisors at Hughes by sex, 1976–1979

	1976	1977	1978	1979
Male	49 (96.1%)	52 (94.5%)	64 (94.1%)	74 (93.7%)
Female	2 (3.9%)	3 (5.5%)	4 (5.9%)	5 (6.3%)
Total	51	55	68	79

The statistics in Table 4.1 show that over the 4 years from 1976 to 1979, whilst the number of male first-level supervisors increased from 49 to 74, the percentages decreased gradually from 96% to under 94%. At the same time, both the numbers and the percentages of the female first-level supervisors increased slightly. Therefore, historically speaking, the status of female employees was improved, albeit only to a small extent.

Now let's look at the statistics for labour grades 15–20:

Obviously, the discrepancy between the two sex groups is even bigger among the best-paid employees – although both the numbers and the percentages of female employees increased over the 4 years, the improvement is close to being negligible.

Let's move on to the statistics by race. First, *below* is the distribution of the supervisors:

The numbers in Table 4.3 show that the contrast between the two racial groups is much less striking than that between the two sex groups, and the numbers were much more stable over time than those in the previous two tables. Let's see if this remains the case for the top-paid employees.

The numbers in Table 4.4 are very similar to those in Table 4.1 – despite the decline of percentages of White employees over the years, they were very much dominating the best-paid employees. For Black employees, both the numbers and the percentages improved, but there was too long a way for them to catch up with their White counterparts.

Each of the four tables shows the 'one-dimensional' way of thinking; that is, how supervisor or best-paid jobs were distributed across either sex or racial groups. You may think that the statistics are sufficiently strong for demonstrating the disfranchised status of either female or Black employees at Hughes, but that is not our concern here. From the perspective

Table 4.2 Distribution of employees of grades 15–20 at Hughes by sex, 1976–1979

	1976	1977	1978	1979
Male	217 (100%)	260 (99.6%)	283 (98.6%)	374 (98.4%)
Female	0 (0%)	1 (0.4%)	4 (1.4%)	6 (1.6%)
Total	217	261	287	380

Table 4.3 Distribution of first-level supervisors at Hughes by race, 1976–1979

	1976	1977	1978	1979
White	43 (84.3%)	47 (85.5%)	59 (86.8%)	67 (84.8%)
Black	8 (15.7%)	8 (14.5%)	9 (13.2%)	12 (15.2%)
Total	51	55	68	79

Table 4.4 Distribution of employees of grades 15–20 at Hughes by race, 1976–1979

	1976	1977	1978	1979
White	209 (96.3%)	247 (94.6%)	264 (92.0%)	345 (90.8%)
Black	8 (3.7%)	14 (5.4%)	23 (8.0%)	35 (9.2%)
Total	217	261	287	380

of intersectionality, even if the above statistics could not serve as evidence for discrimination – though they do, as the percentages for either women or Black people are far lower than those for either men or White people, respectively – the combination of the two dimensions may present convincing evidence for such discrimination. In this particular case, for Moore's allegation against Hughes to hold, we should expect to see even smaller percentages for Black female employees who were either supervisors or paid in grades 15 to 20. So, let's see if this is the case; statistically, this means we need to combine Table 4.1 with Table 4.3, and Table 4.2 with Table 4.4.

The effect of intersectionality becomes very clear when the statistics in these two tables are compared with those in the previous ones. For first-level supervisors, the percentages for women in Table 4.1 are from 4% to 6%; the percentages for Black employees were much higher, from 13% to 15% (Table 4.3). For the intersectional category of Black female employees, the percentages are much smaller than either: 0 for the first 2 years and 1.5 to 2.5 in the following 2 years, and the absolute numbers increased but only from 0 to 2. All percentages remained highly stable over the years. The statistics for the best-paid employees follow about a similar pattern but are even worse: women constituted from 0 to 1.5 (Table 4.2) and the percentages for Black employees are higher, from about 4% to 9%. Intersectional percentages for Black female employees, however, are down to absolutely 0 for all 4 years.

No one would dispute the unevenness of the distribution of the best jobs across the sex and racial groups at Hughes. However, not everyone would agree that these statistics, no matter how striking they appear, necessarily demonstrate discrimination against Black female employees such as Tommie Moore, because for these statistics to be used as evidence for discrimination, they must be compared with some 'reference statistics' so as to be meaningful. In other words, we need some other statistics that would allow us to claim that the statistics in Table 4.6 are 'too low' for Black female employees. In this particular case, the percentage of Black female employees among all employees (not just among the supervisors or top-paid ones) was used. For example, if Black female employees constituted 3% of all employees at

Table 4.5 Distribution of first-level supervisors at Hughes by sex and race, 1976–1979

Intersection	1976	1977	1978	1979
White Male	41 (80.4%)	44 (80.0%)	56 (82.4%)	64 (81.0%)
Black Male	8 (15.7%	8 (14.5%)	8 (11.8%)	10 (12.7%)
White Female	2 (3.9%)	3 (5.5%)	3 (4.4%)	3 (3.8%)
Black Female	0 (0%)	0 (0%)	1 (1.5%)	2 (2.5%)
Total	51	55	68	79

Table 4.6 Distribution of employees of grades 15–20 at Hughes by sex and race, 1976–1979

Intersection	1976	1977	1978	1979
White Male	209 (96.3%)	246 (94.3%)	260 (90.6%)	339 (89.2%)
Black Male	8 (3.7%)	14 (5.4%)	23 (8.0%)	35 (9.2%)
White Female	0 (0%)	1 (0.4%)	4 (1.4%)	6 (1.6%)
Black Female	0 (0%)	0 (0%)	0 (0%)	0 (0%)
Total	217	260	287	380

Hughes, then it would be reasonable for Moore and others to expect approximately 3% of the first-level supervisor or the grade 15–20 employees to be Black female as well. We have just seen that this was not the case – only for first-level supervisors in 1978 and 1979 the percentages were 1.5% and 2.5%, respectively, while it is 0 for all other cells.

Yet the lawyers defending Hughes and the judges would not accept such reasoning of 'matching statistics'; to them, and from the perspective of business management, it does not make sense to expect the two sets of statistics to correspond to each other – otherwise, the company would have put some Black female employees in supervisory or top-paid roles even when they were not qualified. Whilst Hughes, or any company for that matter, was obliged to ensure no discriminatory practices against any groups based on sex, race or any other attribute, they had to consider the business case for promoting and awarding employees as well. In this particular case, Moore had to demonstrate, besides the above statistics, that Black female employees who were sufficiently qualified for the supervisory and best-paid jobs did exist in Hughes but did not get promoted, which was a much bigger challenge than assembling some statistics. In the end, the court dismissed her case because she could not identify the qualified Black female employees. This is a powerful case, showing that to the present the striking evidence for different life experiences across intersectional groups is *only a first step* in achieving justice for the unfairly treated group. One must convince others, especially those in power such as the judges, that the unfairly treated group does deserve better treatment. To assess and determine the qualification of an employee's fitness for a well-paid position is a challenge that goes far beyond providing any evidence.

4.4 The difference that an additional variable can make

After considering the statistics in the *Moore v. Hughes Helicopters, Inc.* case, it is helpful to understand it as a special case of a more general issue so that we can apply the logic of our analysis to other cases. Essentially, here is what Tommie Moore was trying to show: the distribution of the two types of privileged jobs at Hughes might not appear discriminatory if we consider only sex or race, but it would show evidence of discriminatory practice if both sex and race were considered at the same time. More generally, we can describe the situation as the following: the relationship between the interested outcome variable (in this case, being either first-level supervisor or paid at grades 15–20) and each of the two explanatory variables (in this case, sex or race), respectively, may differ from the relationship between the outcome variable and the two explanatory variables together. In other words, another explanatory variable (either sex or race) may change the relationship between the outcome variable (better job and pay) and an existing explanatory variable (either race or sex). It is important to note that this may or may not happen, depending on the data, but it is important to give it a chance to happen, as is illustrated below. In the most dramatic scenario, both the direction of the relationship between the outcome variable and an existing explanatory variable is reversed and the magnitude of the relationship has changed (either increased or decreased). This phenomenon has been dubbed as 'a paradox' (see below for more details). However, nothing is paradoxical here because things may change once we bring in more data about a different variable. It appears paradoxical as those without proper training tend to expect the relationship between two variables to remain the same even after a third variable is brought into the analysis.

Let's look at one of the few examples with real-world data. From 1972 to 1974, a survey about certain diseases was conducted, drawing on a random sample of local residents at Whickham, a town to the southwest of Newcastle-upon-Tyne.[3] Twenty years later, a follow-up study was conducted at the same town. Information about whether the 1,314 women in the study were smokers, their age and whether they survived the 20-year period was recorded. Clearly, the response variable we are interested in here is whether a female participant survived or not, and smoking and age are the two explanatory variables, and we are interested in how they related to the response variable. First, let's examine the relationship of each explanatory variable with survival separately.

Without using any more sophisticated statistics, it should be clear that something is wrong with the percentages in Table 4.7, because they appear inconsistent with our expectations. Were the results in this table all the evidence available to us, we would have no choice but to conclude that smoking actually helped women at this town to live longer! Given our knowledge about the harms that smoking can do to our health, we would expect the percentage for being dead to be higher among the smokers than the non-smokers, or, conversely, the percentage for being alive to be lower among the smokers than the non-smokers. The results, however, have shown the opposite!

Now let's bring in the third variable, age (in groups), into our analysis and see if the results would change; that is, we shall create a table like Table 4.7 for each age group, but it's sufficient to present the percentages for death alone.

The results in Table 4.8 come much closer to our expectations: smoking does not seem to affect survival for the youngest and the oldest groups, which is not surprising – the young enjoyed lower percentages of death even when they did smoke, and the older ones suffered from higher percentages of death even when they did not smoke. For the two middle-aged groups, the percentages of death among the smokers are significantly higher than those

Table 4.7 Smoking and survival among women at Whickham

	Dead	Alive	Total
Yes	139 (23.9%)	443 (76.1%)	582 (100%)
No	230 (31.4%)	502 (68.6%)	732 (100%)
Total	369	945	1314

Table 4.8 Death percentage among women at Whickham, by smoking and age

Smoker	18–34	35–54	55–64	65+
Yes	2.8%	17.2%	44.3%	85.7%
No	2.7%	9.5%	33.1%	85.5%

among the non-smokers, which makes more sense to us. In short, the relationship between smoking and death has changed after age is taken into account.

This real-world example offers a clear illustration of the benefit of using a third variable whenever it is available. Again, it is worth pointing out that the relationship between the original two variables does *not necessarily* change, but *when the data are available, it is always worth bringing it into the analysis*. Similarly, there may or may not be an intersectional effect between the two explanatory variables; if there is none, there is no harm to check; if there is, it will show the benefit of studying intersectionality.

4.5 Searching for intersectional positions in connection to discrimination

The problem of intersectional discrimination, that is discrimination based on not just one but two or more demographic attributes, started to draw attention from lawyers and the general public thanks to the appeals made by people such as the Black female employees at General Motors and Hughes Helicopters, and later a number of other cases came under the spotlight of mass media after those two cases. No matter how powerful they might be, these cases left an impression in people's minds that the issue remains somehow sporadic, that is relevant only to a small group of people in a special situation. More importantly, intersectional discrimination seems to be an issue only when the victims voiced their complaints on behalf of others in the particular intersectional position, for example being Black and female, which could mislead the public to believe that only those in this particular position suffer from discrimination. The lack of systematic examination of all intersectional positions in connection with discrimination means that intersectional discrimination may have already existed but remains unacknowledged simply because nobody in a particular position has brought it to the attention to the authorities or the general public. It should therefore be helpful to take the initiative of *systematically* examining the relationships between certain social intersections and any experience of discrimination.

This more systematic and proactive approach comes with a price or a caveat, however: without any particular case such as *Moore v. Hughes Helicopters, Inc.* drawing our attention to the relevant intersectional attributes, our search for intersections with clear evidence of potential discrimination would be inherently exploratory. To start with, we may not have a good reason for the demographic variables that we want to focus on, although we certainly can try with some candidate variables that make sense on their face value. The search would be rewarding and our search results could be extremely revealing *only if* we discover that members of a particular intersectional position have experienced significantly higher rates of discrimination than other positions. It is useful to keep in mind that the intersectional effect might not show up at the end of our search; more specifically, the percentage of those with discriminatory experience may not change after we bring in an additional attribute to the analysis.

Both the above case-study approach and the systematic approach suffer from a common technical difficulty: we become aware of the importance of the intersection of concern, such as race and gender, only after some cases were reported or some data were analysed, a time at which we may find the sample size for that particular intersection is too small. If we pay attention to a particular intersectional category only after some analysis, it would be impossible to ensure a sufficient sample size for each intersectional group without controlling the corresponding sample sizes at the beginning of the data collection process. This could be less of an issue if the total sample size is very large, yet still the sample size for a particular intersection may turn out to be too small to be statistically useful. If we are really serious about discovering the effects of certain intersectional categories and would like to collect relevant empirical evidence for them, we should design a study by purposefully collecting sufficient data from the theoretically important intersectional groups.

To illustrate these points with a real-world dataset, here I will analyse the data collected from the UK sample of the European Social Survey (ESS) in 2018, which is the most recent at the time of writing (November 2021). Starting from 2002, the ESS is a cross-sectional and cross-national survey that has earned a reputation for being one of the most rigorously designed and executed social surveys in the world. It has been conducted every 2 years in most of the countries in Europe, although the participating countries vary from one round to another. The survey questionnaire covers a core module of questions that were repeated across the rounds and other questions added to each specific round. The valid sample size for the UK sample in the round of 2018 is 2,204.

In this survey, participants were asked not only whether they were a member of a group discriminated against in the UK but also more specifically the attribute for which they were discriminated against, including race, nationality, religion, language, ethnicity, age, gender, sexuality, disability and others. However, race and sexuality were not included in the questionnaire, making it impossible for us to analyse the relationship between each of these two attributes with the participant's report on discrimination. There is a question about the participant's citizenship (whether they were a citizen of the UK), which will be taken here as the same as nationality, although the two concepts may not be always the same. Religion is measured crudely here with the question whether the participant belonged to a religion or denomination. Similarly, in the study, disability is measured broadly – and therefore, not very accurately – with the question whether the participant's daily life was hampered by illness, disability, infirmity or a mental problem. Clearly, we should consider the understandings of disability from different perspectives and the language used for describing it as well. We shall not analyse language here, although there are questions about which language was spoken at home in the survey, as it is extremely difficult to infer which language was discriminated against.

Table 4.9 Percentage of self-reported discrimination in the UK, 2018

	Overall	Citizenship	Age	Gender	Ethnicity	Disability	Religion
Percentage	15.2%	2.0%	2.2%	2.3%	1.4%	1.4%	3.8%
Valid n	2194	2204	2204	2204	2204	2204	2204

Table 4.10 Self-reported discrimination by selected attributes in the UK, 2018

	Citizenship	Gender	Ethnicity	Religion
Odds ratio with 95 CI	4.2 (2.0, 8.7)	8.5 (3.4, 21.4)	0.03 (0.01, 0.07)	0.09 (0.04, 0.18)
Valid n	2203	2204	2192	2200

First of all, let's take a look at the percentages of the participants who reported having been discriminated against in the UK, weighted by 'design weight'.

Clearly, while the overall rate of self-reported discrimination in the UK in 2018 was as high as more than 15%, the percentage for each single attribute was quite low, from 1.4% to 3.8%. These percentages are for all participants who provided a valid answer; therefore, they do not tell us exactly who felt discriminated against. Discrimination based on religion remains uncertain, as either the atheists or the believers could be discriminated against. We must move on to study the relationship between self-reported discrimination and the categories of each attribute. Instead of showing a cross-tabulation, I have presented the odds ratio for each relationship in order to compare these relations with a more concise measure.

An odds ratio is the ratio between the probability that something occurs for one group to the probability that it occurs to the other group. As not all the statistics are shown in Table 4.10, it is necessary to interpret the meaning of these odds ratios here. For citizenship, those who were not citizens of the UK were more than four times likely to report discrimination than citizens. Similarly, women are eight and half times more likely to report discrimination than men. For ethnicity and religion, the numbers come in reverse direction: those who did not belong to an ethnic minority group were only 3% as likely as the ethnic minorities to report discrimination; similarly, those who belonged to a religion were 9% as likely as those who did not belong to a religion to report discrimination. Overall, the relationship between each attribute and self-reported discrimination is statistically both strong and significant – as shown in the brackets, none of the 95% confidence intervals (the numbers in brackets) contains 1, meaning that it is highly unlikely (less than 5%) that these odds ratios are 1 (no relationship between each attribute and discrimination).

I have recoded the values of age from specific years to three groups: 30 and under, 31 to 60, 61 and above. The variable for 'being hampered in daily activities' has three values as well: a lot, to some extent and no. As they have three ordinal values, besides the percentages presented in Table 4.11, I also have used a different statistic, Kendall's tau-b, for measuring the relationship between each of them and self-reported discrimination.

Again, it is not surprising to see that those whose life was more hampered with illness or disability reported higher rates of discrimination; the Kendall's tau-b is −0.15 with the p-value smaller than 0.001. Note that the relationship between age and discrimination is somehow

Table 4.11 Self-reported discrimination by disability and age in the UK, 2018

	Hampered a lot	Hampered to some extent	Not hampered
% discriminated against	7.2%	2.6%	0.4%
	30 and under	31 to 60	61 and above
% discriminated against	2.7%	1.4%	3.2%

different: the relationship is not linear – older people (61+) reported the highest percentage of discrimination whilst the middle-aged had the lowest percentage (1.4), and the Kendall's tau-b here is not statistically significant.

Up to now, we have analysed the relationship between only one attribute with self-reported discrimination. These single-dimensional questions included in the ESS question-naire reflect the common way of thinking about discrimination. In the spirit of intersec-tionality, it is certainly insufficient to pay attention to discrimination based on one attribute alone. To obtain some sense of 'intersectional discrimination', or discrimination based on intersectional attributes, we need to switch our attention to the general question in the ESS: whether the participant was a member of a group discriminated against in the UK. Clearly, this question was not designed to solicit information about intersectional discrimination, but at least it is flexible enough for us to explore the relationships between any potential intersec-tions of attributes and discrimination.

On the other hand, such flexibility comes as a challenge as well – our exploration becomes highly arbitrary and uncertain without a predetermined direction. Perhaps the most difficult question is: which attributes should we focus on and why? It is crucial to answer these ques-tions beforehand, because even with only six attributes (age, gender, ethnicity, citizenship, religion and disability) and a relatively large sample size, it could quickly become overwhelm-ing to examine the intersection of all six attributes in connection with discrimination at the same time. Besides these technical questions, a more important and substantive question is: why should we include these attributes at the same time? Whilst an exploratory analysis may enjoy the benefit of discovering new important intersections, it suffers the lack of a clear direction. It is my hope that this analysis demonstrates to the reader the benefits and the potential pitfalls in studying intersectionality in an exploratory manner.

Let's start with gender and ethnicity. If we were to say each has two values, which would admittedly be an oversimplification, as both gender and ethnicity have other diverse values, there would be four possible intersections (or cross-classifications): male minority, male non-minority, female minority, female non-minority. We have learnt from our single-attribute analyses above that women and people of ethnic minorities are much more likely to report discrimination, so we would expect to find the intersection 'female minority' to report the highest rate of discrimination; conversely, we expect 'male non-minority' to report the low-est percentage of discrimination; the percentages of the other two intersections should be somewhere in between the two. Let's see whether our expectations turn out to be consistent with the data.

The results are not completely in line with our expectations, which shows the bene-fit of an exploratory study: the intersectional group that reported the highest percentage

Table 4.12 Self-reported discrimination by gender and ethnicity in the UK, 2018

Intersection	% discrimination (standardized residual)	Valid n
Male + non-minority	12.9% (0.1)	940
Male + minority	45.2% (1.0)	93
Female + non-minority	12.6% (−0.1)	1043
Female + minority	33.3% (−0.9)	105

of discrimination was not the female ethnic minorities (33.3%), but the male minorities (45.2%)! The percentages for the two non-minority groups are about the same, close to 13%. It may be tempting to conclude that males who also belong to ethnic minority groups in the UK were most vulnerable to discrimination, but it is wise to be a bit more cautious here.

First of all, the sample sizes for the two ethnic minority groups are much smaller than the two non-minority groups, actually only about 10% of the latter. Also, I have included 'the standardized residual' beside each percentage in order to show how likely results would differ from a random allocation of cases. For these residuals, any value above +2 or below −2 would indicate 'statistical significance' or non-random allocations; in this case, none of the standardized residuals is either above +2 or below −2, thereby suggesting a high chance that they are not different from random allocations.

Another way of evaluating these relations is to produce and examine the odds ratios for each sub-group; there is no need to present them here, but the 95% confidence intervals of all odds ratios include 1, meaning that all connections might be due to randomness. In short, we should not take these results at their face value.

This is a good example of the Simpson's Paradox, although these relationships are not statistically significant, they may change in terms of either direction or magnitude (or both) after we include a third variable. I would not bring in citizenship as I know the number of non-citizens in the sample is very small (147). Clearly, this is a statistical consideration; if you have a very good non-statistical reason for including citizenship, you should by all means include it regardless of the sample size. As an exercise of illustration, let's add religion to our previous analysis, noting that the variable 'religion' has only two values here: either belonging to a religion (or denomination) or not.

As the number of intersections has increased from four to eight, it helps to rank order the results by the percentage of reporting discrimination. Yet again, we see that the two intersectional groups that reported the highest percentages of discrimination are males of ethnic minorities, either belonging to a religion or not, followed by females of ethnic minorities, again regardless of being a member of a religion or not. The non-minority groups have the lowest percentages of reporting discrimination, more than half of those by the ethnic minorities. Nonetheless, it would be wise for us not to jump to the conclusion that these are hard evidence of discriminations against ethnic minorities in the UK – the sample sizes for the

Table 4.13 Self-reported discrimination by gender, ethnicity and religion in the UK, 2018

Intersection	% reporting discrimination (standardized residual)	Valid n
Male + Minority + No religion	62.5% (1.2)	24
Male + Minority + Religion	40.0% (0.7)	70
Female + Minority + No religion	37.9% (0.5)	29
Female + Minority + Religion	31.2% (−0.3)	77
Male + Non-minority + Religion	14.7% (1.0)	353
Female + Non-minority + Religion	14.3% (1.2)	495
Male + Non-minority + No religion	11.8% (−0.8)	587
Female + Non-minority + No religion	10.6% (−1.2)	546

minority groups are very small and the standardized residuals are between –2 and +2. Similarly, all the other statistics – Chi-square tests or odds ratios, no need to show them here – are not statistically significant. The ESS was not designed for comparing different ethnic groups in a particular country; if we were really serious about making such comparisons, we would need a survey that is particularly designed for such purpose, more specifically with a booster sample for ethnic minorities.

Such exploratory research could be useful even when we are interested in a particular intersectional group's experience. Although our analysis becomes more directed with such interest, it focuses on only one intersectional group and therefore may have missed other groups, or at least it does not cover the whole picture with all possible intersections. For example, the case of *Moore v. Hughes Helicopters, Inc.* could lead us to a general hypothesis that women of ethnic minorities have been passed over for promotion. But is it really the case that women of ethnic minorities are least likely to be promoted into a supervisory position? Let's try to test this hypothesis with the UK sample of the ESS 2018. In this survey, participants were expected to answer the following question 'In your main job, do/did you have any responsibility for supervising the work of other employees?' with either a yes or a no. We shall take the positive answer as an indication that the participant has been promoted to a supervisory or managerial role.

Of the 2,112 valid responses to this question, 36.8% gave a positive answer. Of all responses by men, 40.3% were positive, higher than the 36.7% positive answers by women. However, the Chi-square test is not statistically significant (p = 0.09), and the odds ratio is 1.16 with a 95% confidence interval (0.98, 1.39). In other words, the higher percentage of occupying a supervisory role among males in the UK might be due to the random nature of the sample. Moving on to ethnicity, the percentage of being in a supervisory role among the non-ethnic minority respondents is 39.2%, higher than that among the ethnic minority ones, which is 30.9%. More importantly, this difference is statistically significant, with the p-value for the Chi-square test being 0.03 and the odds ratio 0.70 with a 95% confidence interval (0.50, 0.97), meaning that for an ethnic minority, the chance of being in a supervisory role could be as low as half of the chance for the non-ethnic minority ones. Putting gender and ethnicity together, we can present the results in the following table.

The percentages in Table 4.14 show that female and ethnic minority respondents in the survey did have the lowest chance of being in a supervisory role, and those of ethnic minorities as a whole were less likely to be a supervisor than the ethnic majority respondents, with men of ethnic majority being the most likely to be a supervisor. These observations are also confirmed with the standardized residuals beside the percentages: the residuals for the ethnic minorities are negative, meaning we have observed fewer cases in these groups than we would have if the data were completely random; conversely, the positive standardized

Table 4.14 Supervisory role by gender and ethnicity in the UK, 2018

	% in supervisory role (with standardized residual)	Valid n
Female + ethnic minority	28.3% (−1.3)	92
Male + ethnic minority	33.7% (−1.0)	89
Female + non-ethnic minority	37.5% (0.4)	1005
Male + non-ethnic minority	41.0% (0.3)	916

residuals indicate that we have observed more cases in the two ethnic majority groups than we would have if the data were completely random. However, none of these residuals is between -2 and $+2$, therefore lending no support to the statistical significance of these findings. That is, if we take statistical significance seriously, which we should given the sample was drawn with a scientific procedure, we should conclude that the data do not present any supporting evidence for the hypothesis that female ethnic minority people in the UK were discriminated against in terms of being promoted to supervisory roles. This may have disappointed those who wish to see a statistically significant result for the intersectional effect, particularly because the association between ethnicity and being in a supervisory role was significant, as shown above – in this case, intersectionality has actually suppressed a previously significant result for a single factor. As explained earlier in this chapter, such a reverse of relational direction or magnitude was already found many years ago. Researchers of intersectionality should be prepared for such changes and accept them without being dogmatic about any intersectional effect.

4.6 Suggested readings and questions for discussion

The reader may have realized that a technical condition for exploring and analysing intersectional patterns in a contingency table is that the categories of each intersectional attribute are clearly defined, and the number of categories is small (usually fewer than five). It is important to note that these are not statistical issues but substantive questions the researcher must answer by resorting to a theoretical approach, literature reviews and knowledge of the subject. It would help if the reader could try to answer the following questions. First, which intersectional attributes (or identities) should be included in my study? To make the subsequent analysis manageable, ensure that it is absolutely essential for an attribute to be included. If you are analysing secondary data, then you may find that a particular attribute you want to include is missing from the data; in this case, it is important to discuss this explicitly as a limitation of your analysis. Then move on to the categories of each selected attribute and consider the following question: have they included all the categories you want to analyse (exhaustive)? Again, you may find one or more categories you plan to study not included in the data. On the other hand, think carefully whether it is truly necessary to keep all of the original categories; in other words, would it be acceptable to combine or merge two or more categories into a broader one? If your answer is positive, then your table will be more concise, and it is less likely that some cells will have too few cases. More generally, you should aim to strike a delicate balance between keeping the categories meaningful while making the statistics rigorous.

To learn more about the technical details, besides the paper by Appleton et al. (1996), consult the texts by Alan Agresti, in which he explained and illustrated the analysis of Simpson's paradox, including *Statistics: The art and science of learning from data* by Alan Agresti and Christine Franklin (Pearson, 2014); *Statistical methods for the social sciences* by Alan Agresti and Barbara Finlay (5th edition, Pearson, 2018); *An introduction to categorical data analysis* by Alan Agresti (3rd edition, Wiley, 2018); *Categorical Data Analysis* by Alan Agresti (3rd edition, 2012). Finally, here is a study that has been criticized for considering only one factor at a time: Schulman, K. A., Berlin, J. A., Harless, W., Kerner, J. F., Sistrunk, S., Gersh, B. J.,

Dube, R., Taleghani, C. K., Burke, J. E., Williams, S., Eisenberg, J. M., Ayers, W., Escarce, J. J. (1999). The effect of race and sex on physicians' recommendations for cardiac catheterization. *New England Journal of Medicine*, 340: 618–626. Read it and see whether you would agree with the critique and explain why.

Notes

1. For further details, see www.casemine.com/judgement/us/59149012add7b04934570586.
2. For the data of first-level supervisors in 1976, the numbers of both January and June were available. As the change during these 6 months was very small, the numbers of June were used here.
3. The initial study was reported in Tunbridge et al. (1977), and the follow-up study in Vanderpump et al. (1995). Appleton and his colleagues (1996) discussed the two studies as an example of Simpson's paradox.

5

INTERSECTIONALITY AS CONFIGURATIONS

5.1 Overview and objectives

In the previous chapter we studied intersectionality as cross-classifications; that is, the combinations of the values of two or more attributes or identities (gender, age, class, etc.). Then we connected each combination with the occurrence of the interested outcome; for example, feeling discriminated against in a particular country. Comparing the prevalence of the interested outcome across the possible combinations of identities provides us with some evidence of whether certain intersectional identities are particularly vulnerable to discrimination. As the examples in the previous chapter illustrate, this could be an exploratory or a confirmatory process, depending on whether we have a theory or hypothesis beforehand about the connection between a particular intersectional identity and the outcome.

The objective of this chapter is to introduce another method that examines the connection between intersectional identities and a particular outcome, which looks similar to the analysis of contingency tables but actually follows a different logic. It grew out of the intention to systematically compare a number of cases along multiple dimensions at the same time; for example, political scientists were interested in comparing a number of national states in order to understand why some experienced social revolutions while others did not, under the combined conditions of economic development, class structure, and the strength of civil society. Charles Ragin was the central figure leading the process of turning such a comparative exercise into a systematically developed research approach and method. Initially, it was called 'qualitative comparative analysis' (QCA), but later the term 'set-theoretic method' became more preferable. This method appears to be almost perfectly cut out for studying intersectionality, although this only became apparent a few decades after the two lines of research paralleled each other.

A central concept of QCA or set-theoretic method is configuration, which essentially is the same as cross-classifications or combinations of attribute values we saw in the previous chapter. Conceptually, Ragin and his associates emphasize that configurations represent the special features of the cases under study, which is clearly in line with what advocates of intersectionality have argued. As illustrated in *Intersectional Inequality*, Ragin and Fiss (2016) have explained why their method is particularly helpful for studying intersectionality and demonstrated how this is done by analysing real and large datasets.

It is neither feasible nor necessary for me to explain the technical details of how to use the set-theoretic method in this chapter. It has become a fully developed method with its own terminologies, principles and procedures, and a large number of texts and articles have been published explaining the details, some of which will appear as suggested further readings at the end of this chapter. What I aim to do in this chapter is to start by explaining the basic ideas of QCA, or set-theoretic method, so that the reader can understand the logic of its technical details, and then to explain and discuss why this method is particularly suitable for the purpose of studying intersectionality. While this method seems to be innovative in making use of the set theory in mathematics and therefore has attracted the attention and support of many researchers, it has not grown without critiques and controversies, which I will discuss in order to help the readers understand some of the potential issues they may be faced with if they plan to use this method.

5.2 QCA/set-theoretic method: Basic ideas

When QCA was initially developed, two ways of doing research were dominating empirical research in the social sciences. The first could be dubbed as 'qualitative research', which draws on detailed knowledge of a small number of cases and has developed new insights and theories by comparing and interpreting these cases. A typical example of such a way of doing research is Theda Skocpol's *States and Social Revolutions: A Comparative Analysis of France, Russia and China* (1979). The idea of such analysis is to derive a causal explanation – why social revolutions occurred in some states but not others – by comparing a small number of cases (only three in this case, although Skocpol mentioned others as well). Obviously, this is a very challenging job – how could one provide a convincing answer to such a big question by analysing only three cases? Researchers must be able to free themselves as much as possible from the constraints of the limited number of cases while capitalizing on the rich details of each case at the same time. Other qualitative studies may have a relatively larger number of cases, such as 20–30 interviewees, and the data about each case might be less detailed, but the underlying rationale of the analysis remains about the same. In contrast, 'quantitative research' would collect much less detailed quantitative information about each case, but the number of cases could be as large as thousands or even more. Statistical methods enable researchers to analyse such a large amount of quantitative information very efficiently, especially with the drastic increase of computing power in recent decades.

Charles Ragin made it very clear that his motivation of developing QCA was to create 'a middle path between quantitative and qualitative social research' (2008: 1). This means that QCA and set-theoretic methods can offer some different benefits to social science research that neither qualitative nor quantitative methods can, but they are not so beneficial that they should replace the existing methods (Mahoney et al., 2013). There have been only a very few occasions in which qualitative researchers would not accept the claimed new advantages of QCA over traditional qualitative research (see the relevant papers in *Rethinking Social Inquiry*, edited by Henry Brady and David Collier (2010), and the discussion papers in the first issue of the 41st volume of *Sociological Methodology* in 2014). The main confrontation is between QCA and statistical methods, especially linear regression models. In many different occasions, Ragin has tried to demonstrate why set-theoretic methods could go beyond the limitations of linear regression models, as we shall explain soon. It is important to keep in mind, however, as Ragin reassured, 'I offer this alternate approach not as a replacement for net-effects analysis but as a complementary technique' (2008, p. 190). That is, despite the advantages that set-theoretic methods may have over statistical models, researchers should not abandon statistical methods and all switch to set-theoretic method. The two sets of methods do different things, and the advantages of one over the other are relative, not absolute.

To facilitate the following explanations and discussions, it is useful to be clear about the kind of data to be analysed. Anyone with minimum training in statistical or quantitative methods should know that the data are usually presented with a 'case-by-variable matrix'. Below is a generic representation of such matrix.

For a particular dataset, the variables will have more specific names, such as gender, age, race, etc. and each case will have a numeric ID of a few digits. Each of the other cells is a value that a case takes for a particular variable, such as 1 being 'Male' of case 001 for the variable 'Gender'. Together, these cells constitute a well-organized presentation of the information about these cases, which is simultaneously amicable to mathematical and statistical analyses because it comes as a matrix.

It is indeed true that almost all statistical methods, from simple descriptive statistics such as the mean and the standard deviation to the more complicated methods such as regression models and structural equation models, focus on the relations between the variables rather than the cases, which, from the perspective of set-theoretic methods, is a major limitation. Statisticians pay attention to some cases only when the cases may distract people's attention from the 'big picture', which is why such cases are dubbed as 'influential cases' or 'outliers'. Statistical methods designed for analysing cases instead of variables do exist, such as cluster analysis and configural frequency analysis, but the number of such methods is very small.

The most widely used statistical methods for analysing relations among variables is regression models, which could be represented as follows: let's call the target of the model (either explanation or prediction) R (for response), and the variables that explain R (either explanatory variables or predictors) P1, P2, P3, etc. Which and how many predictors should go into a particular model are up to the researcher to decide. A regression model is simply a mathematical equation that connects these variables together, and below is a generic version of three predictors:

$$R = \beta_1 P1 + \beta_2 P2 + \beta_3 P3 + error$$

What this model says is that we can predict the value of the response variable R by adding up the values P1, P2 and P3. Note that we multiply each predictor with a coefficient (the β) to reflect the relative weight (or influence) of each predictor on the response variable. This model is not perfect because $\beta_1 P1 + \beta_2 P2 + \beta_3 P3$ will not be exactly equal to the value of R, which is why there is an error term (or the difference between the actual value of R and the value predicted by $(\beta_1 P1 + \beta_2 P2 + \beta_3 P3)$). A model with variables more meaningful to intersectionality may look like this:

$$Discrimination = \beta_1 Gender + \beta_2 Race + \beta_3 Sexuality + error$$

Charles Ragin and other researchers think that the statistical way of analysing such data is very problematic, and at the same time they think that the principles of the set theory are much more useful. Their reasoning is that each case embodies multiple attributes (values of several variables) at the same time, a social reality that equations like the above cannot represent. In contrast, analysing the cases as elements of a set will make the analysis better reflect the social reality.

A set is simply a collection of elements which belong to the same set as they share a same attribute. It is important to note that by defining sets like this, we are talking about 'crisp' sets – that is, the elements either belong or do not belong to a set; a case's membership to a set could be 'fuzzy' if the *degree* of its membership could be specified, which is a technically more complicated situation we shall not go into in this chapter. For example, the set of 'females' contains all elements (people) who identify themselves as females. In this sense, each variable in a dataset such as Table 5.1 will have at least two sets, because a variable has at least two different values; for example, suppose the variable 'Race' has three values (White, Black, Other), then each is a set. In other words, a case cannot belong to a variable because the variable contains two or more sets, but a case can belong to the set of a variable's specific value. Therefore, it is more accurate to say that QCA is a '*set*-centred' rather than 'case-centred' method.

Because sets are constructed based on a variable's values, set-theoretic methods analyse more detailed information and therefore are more 'nuanced' than statistical methods, which explains why some researchers think that set-theoretic methods can go beyond the limitations that statistical models suffer from. For example, statistical models tend to conclude or at least imply that a predictor has 'symmetric' effects on the response variable; more specifically, if the effect of being male on the chance of being discriminated against is negative, then the effect of being female on the chance of being discriminated against must be positive, or so it is implied, because the two gender values are analysed at the same time of a single variable.

In contrast, QCA and set-theoretic methods separate these values apart into different sets, so we should not infer any conclusion about one value set from another simply because the two sets have opposite values. Essentially, the symmetric relationship assumed in linear regression models is now studied as *potentially asymmetric*. It is worth noting that even before QCA became a popular research method, the Harvard sociologist Stanley Lieberson (1987) had already pointed out the importance of studying asymmetrical relations and the limited ability of linear regression models to analyse such relations. To give a specific example, if females are found to have been discriminated against, that does not necessarily mean males are advantaged – they may or may not, but that is something to be investigated, not assumed. And this applies to not only a predictor but to the response or outcome as well. That is, the outcome is not a variable that covers both values of being discriminated against or not, or a

Table 5.1 A generic case-by-variable matrix

	Variable 1	Variable 2	Variable 3	Variable 4	Variable 5	Variable 6	...
Case 1	Value of Variable 1 for Case 1	...	...	...	...	...	...
Case 2	...	...	...	...	...	...	...
Case 3	...	...	...	...	...	...	...
Case 4	...	...	...	...	...	...	...
...	...	...	...	...	...	...	...

series of continuous values representing the probability of being discriminated against; following the set-theoretic method, the outcome is either the set of being discriminated against or another set of not being discriminated against, and the results of analysis of one set may be different from those of analysis of the other set; therefore, two separate analyses must be conducted. Now it should become clear that if we plan to use set-theoretic methods, we will have to conduct a series of different analyses, each on a different set.

It should become clear from the above discussion that the set-theoretic methods could conduct some analyses that are different from statistical analyses because they transform the data from a case-by-variable matrix into set-memberships. This is the first critical step in the process of conducting a set-theoretic analysis, at which point the researcher must decide on which set each case belongs to, and this decision will affect the subsequent and final analyses and results. To illustrate with a simple example, suppose the variable 'gender' has only two values, male and female, each corresponding to a set, and each case will belong to either the male set or the female set. These are examples of 'crisp sets' because the membership is absolute – a case is either a member of a set or it is not. For a variable with multiple nominal values (not in a ranking order), such as race or ethnicity, then there could be multiple sets. In this case, the researcher usually focuses on one important (or reference) set, such as those who are White, and assign each case as either a member of this set or not. Yet such analysis may miss some important information about other sets; therefore, the researcher must carefully consider which sets need to be analysed.

A different kind of sets could be created if the variable is ordinal (multiple values with a ranking order, such as educational levels) or even metrical (many values on which calculations can be done, such as monthly household income). Here, a case's membership of a set becomes 'fuzzy' because the membership is not absolute anymore; rather, it has degrees. For example, for the set 'being in poverty', members of a household belong to this set if their household income is below the official poverty threshold. You could create a crisp set of poverty by assigning membership of 1 to all cases below the threshold and the others membership of 0. However, this 'calibration' of membership is crude as it ignores the differences among the members – for those in poverty, some are much poorer than other members; similarly, for those not in poverty, a few are much richer than the majority. If we want to take such differences into account, then we need to create more refined membership scores; as a result, the sets become 'fuzzy' because the membership scores can take values not just 0 or 1 but any value between them. For example, those with income only slightly under the official threshold have a membership score of 0.6 (more in than out, with 0.5 being the cutting point), and those with income just above the poverty threshold have a membership score of 0.4 (more out than in). Clearly, if you think it is important to incorporate these details in your analysis, you must carefully consider how the memberships of each set should be scored – it is imperative to present clear justification for the score that you calibrate for each level of membership. Here, disagreements may arise as researchers may not agree with each other on the calibrated scores, which hopefully will be resolved with discussions over the substantive meanings of these sets and scores. It is important to keep in mind that if the response variable is calibrated into a fuzzy set, then the 'causal conditions' (or the predictors) can be either fuzzy or crisp, but if the response variable is calibrated into a crisp set, then all causal conditions must be crisp as well.

Why do we want to transform the case-by-variable matrix into set memberships? Perhaps the most important reason is the proposition that set memberships can allow us to discover

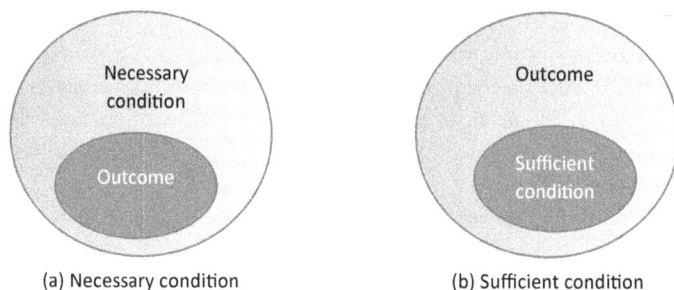

Figure 5.1 Necessary and sufficient conditions as set relationships

necessary or sufficient conditions, which is something statistical methods are not created to do. By definition, a necessary condition must be present for the outcome to occur; in other words, the absence of the condition will guarantee the absence of the outcome. By itself, however, the condition cannot bring about the outcome; that is, other conditions are required in order for the outcome to occur. In set-theoretic terms, this means that the set of the necessary condition must be bigger (or at least equal to) than the set of the outcome, as shown in Figure 5.1a. The presence of a sufficient condition will guarantee the occurrence of the outcome; however, there may be more than one sufficient condition, making each sufficient condition not necessary. In set-theoretic terms, this means that the sufficient condition must be smaller than the set of the outcome, as shown in Figure 5.1b.

To illustrate further: suppose we have a collection of employees (cases), and there are 80 female employees (the set of females) and 50 employees who claim they are being discriminated against (the set of being discriminated against). If all the 50 employees of the discriminated set are also all females, then being female is a necessary condition for being discriminated against; that is, if an employee is not female, then he must not be discriminated against. Note that there are 30 female employees who are not members of the discriminated set, which means that being female does not necessarily make an employee discriminated against; in other words, those female employees who claim they are being discriminated against are a group of a special kind of female employees – that is, they must possess a certain attribute other than being female alone. For the case of sufficient condition, we shall have 50 female employees who are all members of the discriminated set with 80 employees. We can say that as long as an employee is female, she must be discriminated against. Note that in this situation, there are 30 employees who claim they are being discriminated against but who are not female; that is, being female is a sufficient but not necessary condition for discrimination – male employees could be discriminated against as well. Clearly, things become more complicated when there are multiple conditions that could be either sufficient or necessary conditions.

It is worthwhile to point out that necessary and sufficient conditions are often referred to as 'causal' conditions, which could be misleading. As illustrated above, what we have observed are associations, not causations, between set memberships. This leads us to the following question: do these observed associations make it legitimate for us to make causal arguments? It is common sense for people with basic statistics training that association is not causation. It seems wise to apply the same caveat for set-theoretic analysis as well: *set-relations do not necessarily lead to causation*. All we observe is whether and how membership of a set relates to the membership of another set; how and why the relationship between set memberships has occurred is unfortunately something we cannot be certain about with the evidence at hand. Conceptually, it is useful to distinguish 'conditions' from 'causes'.

5.3 Analysing intersectionality with the set-theoretic method

By calling for serious attention to the disadvantages experienced by people at the intersection of two or more social categories, advocates of intersectionality have raised the importance of studying cross-classifications of categories of identities in order to understand and explain the uneven and unjust distributions of power in society. This focus on cross-classified categories is shared by set-theoretic methods introduced above, although such affinity went unnoticed until quite recently when Ragin and Fiss published their study *Intersectional Inequality* in 2016. As explained above, one important benefit of transforming data from the case-by-variable matrix to a number of sets of cases is that researchers can define necessary and sufficient conditions in terms of the cases' memberships of different sets.

This benefit will be made use of in connection with another important consequence of focusing on set memberships; that is, researchers can examine all possible simultaneous memberships of the cases in different sets. Analytically, these simultaneous set memberships are the same as cross-classifications of a number of variables' values, which are also the intersectional categories of identities. In this sense, set-theoretic methods appear to be best positioned for analysing intersectionality, ready-made with an established set of tools and procedures, because, as Ragin and Fiss pointed out, the approach of set-theoretic methods 'views cases intersectionally – in terms of the different ways they combine causally relevant conditions' (2016, p. 2). In contrast to the approach of linear regression models, which are designed for evaluating and discovering each variable's *unique individual* contribution to the explanation of the response variable's variation, the set-theoretic methods are particularly equipped for studying intersections. Instead of adding up each explanatory variable's individual variable's effect on the response variable, each 'configuration' (or simultaneous set memberships) is a separate 'causal condition' for an interested outcome although, as pointed above, the causality of such effect is more asserted than demonstrated. When analysing intersectionality with QCA in practice, we need to keep the different terminologies in mind: the cross-classifications of identity categories are now referred to as 'configurations of intersecting attributes' (ibid.: 12), which are also perceived as the 'causal conditions' for the interested outcome (the response variable in statistical models, such as advantage, power, etc.).

In a study by QCA or set-theoretic methods, such a relationship between configurations and the outcome is usually presented in a so-called 'truth table', in which each row is a configuration, the last column is the number of cases that take the value of 1 for the interested outcome and each of the other columns is one of the conditional sets. In generic terms and for the simple situation of crisp sets, let's say the outcome O has two possibilities – either it has occurred (recorded as 1) or it has not (recorded as 0) – and there are three conditional sets (S1, S2, S3), each also having two possible values (1 if a case is a member and 0 if not) – A and

Table 5.2 A generic truth table with three conditions

Configuration	S1	S2	S3	Number of cases with 1 for O
AGM	A	G	M	N1
AGN	A	G	M	N2
AHM	A	G	M	N3
AHN	A	G	M	N4
BGM	B	H	N	N4
BGN	B	H	N	N6
BHM	B	H	N	N7
BHN	B	H	N	N8

B for S1, G and H for S2, and M and N for S3. We shall have eight (2^3 = 8) possible configurations (Table 5.2).

Essentially, each configuration (or intersection, to use a term more amiable to intersectionality) is a separate set representing a particular membership of multiple sets, and we want to know how many of the cases in each configuration also belong to the set in which the outcome occurs as well, which is recorded in the last column. Recall that comparing such membership relations will allow us to infer necessary or sufficient conditions between the two sets (a configuration and the outcome). The last column could be the set that the outcome did not occur, of course; actually, researchers are encouraged, if not required, to study both situations, which is in line with the principle of asymmetric relationship (the conditions for the positive outcome are not necessarily the opposite to the conditions for the negative outcome).

Note that a causal condition does not have to be a configuration (intersection of two or more sets) – a single set can be a causal condition on its own; in that case, there will be only two columns in a truth table, the condition and the outcome. Such representation of the data, however, would not be different from a contingency table for statistical analysis. As Ragin and other researchers have repeatedly emphasized, a key benefit of using set-theoretic methods is the focus on configurations or intersections, not individual variables or sets. Such analytical focus, they have argued, reflects more truthfully the social reality; more specifically relevant to the study of intersectionality, 'In almost all known societies, inequalities coincide, compound, and reinforce' (ibid.: 6). This is a response to the following more general and important question: of the multiple potential causal factors for an interested outcome, should we pay serious attention to each factor's individual effect or the combined intersectional effect of two or more factors, or both? I think the answer should be 'both' as this is mostly an empirical question, and I believe Ragin and other advocates of QCA are of the same opinion as he was clear that the two types of methods do different things and therefore complement each other (Mahoney et al., 2013). If so, neither individual gross effects nor collective intersectional effects should take any theoretical priority and should be determined with empirical evidence. In the practice of academic research, however, those using statistical models routinely pay little attention to intersectionality, while those using set-theoretic methods tend to assume that individual factors never work alone, although a small number of researchers examine both effects.

While reading Table 5.2, the reader may have already noticed that the set-theoretic approach aims to present and examine *all possible* configurations or intersections of the set memberships included in a particular study. It is in this sense that this approach is 'more nuanced' and able to study the 'diversity' of causal conditions. On the other hand, this means that a set-theoretic analyst does not have an *a priori* intersection in mind before conducting the analysis, as most researchers of intersectionality do; therefore, it can be said that the set-theoretic approach is exclusively exploratory – little consideration is given in the literature as to whether the researcher should expect a particular configuration or intersection to be supported by the data. This is an important question for the study of intersectionality, because researchers of intersectionality, especially those who study intersectional experiences with qualitative or case-based methods, would usually be interested in the experiences of the people who are members of a particular intersectional category, such as Black queer or lesbian, racialized, self-identifying females, without intending to compare this particular intersectional group with others. While this way of thinking has a clear expectation (or hypothesis or theory), it does exclude potential intersections in the data that might turn out to be 'significant' for explaining the interested outcome. In other words, a set-theoretic study needs to explicitly consider *the tension between exploratory and confirmatory* functions of the analysis before the analysis is conducted, something that has not drawn much attention yet in existing studies using set-theoretic methods at the moment.

As configurations or intersections come from the cross-classification of set-memberships, which sets are to be included in an analysis and how the memberships of each selected set are to be calibrated are two questions of utmost importance to any set-theoretic analysis. Obviously, these are substantive rather than methodological questions that each researcher must consider carefully and make their decisions based on their study's objectives and the available data. It is worth pointing out here, however, that whilst set-theoretic methods were designed for systematically studying intersections (configurations), it may not always be the case that the set-theoretic approach dovetails the intention of intersectionality. Although both are interested in intersections, set-theoretic methods see intersections as potential causal conditions (or 'causal recipes', to use its special terminology), while to researchers of intersectionality, intersections are combined attributes of identity. Similar to the difference between exploratory and confirmatory function of analysis mentioned above, these two understandings of intersections remain currently obscured in the literature, but I think it is important to make it explicit so that researchers could pay serious attention to it. For example, in their book on intersectional inequality, Ragin and Fiss studied causal conditions for being either in poverty or not in poverty in the US, of which test scores and family income are two most important elements. They also included gender (coded as males and females) and race (coded as Black or White). However, the four intersections derived from these two attributes of identity – Black males, Black females, White males, White females – were not treated as 'causal conditions', as test scores and family incomes were; instead, the causal relationship between test scores and family incomes with poverty was analysed for each of the four identity intersectional groups separately (for details, see Tables 5.9 and 5.10 in Chapter 5 of Ragin & Fiss, 2016). Essentially, intersections of race and gender were not analysed as causal conditions for poverty; rather, they were treated in a way similar to the 'control variables' (or covariates) in linear regression models – that is, they were included in order to see whether the causal connections between the 'focal' causal conditions (test scores and family incomes) and the outcome remain the same (or 'robust', to use statistical jargon) across a number of socio-demographic groups. In contrast, sex, race and other demographic attributes of identity are usually the focus of intersectional analysis. Researchers who are serious about following the principles of intersectionality may find it problematic to treat sex and race as contextual rather than theoretically focal variables.

There is another issue that may challenge the claim that QCA or set-theoretic methods dovetail with the idea of intersectionality. As demonstrated above, in a truth table all possible configurations of set memberships are listed. An important theoretical question is: should all of these configurations be analysed? From the intersectional perspective, the answer should be negative – as the case studies in the previous chapters show, intersectional analysis is usually concerned with only one particular configuration, such as Black queer or lesbian, racialized, self-identifying women. More generally, intersectionality aims to focus on the experiences of the people who are members of the configurations that have been disenfranchised. At the least, the initial intention of intersectionality when it was formulated as a principle or approach was not to take a systematic examination of all possible intersectional categories and then find out which one was disadvantaged; instead, advocates of intersectionality already knew which intersectional groups had been suppressed and which intersectional groups had suppressed them, and the aim was to make others in the society know how unfair it was and take action to rectify the situation. The approach followed by QCA and set-theoretic methods may be more systematic, but in the eyes of intersectionality being systematic may not be an advantage, at least not at the top of the agenda, because the analysis seems to have lost its focus as no particular configuration is prioritized as the most important prior to the analysis. Put differently, the inherently exploratory nature of QCA and set-theoretic methods is not really congruent with the intention of intersectionality to focus on one or a very limited number of particular configurations.

In addition to theoretical considerations, there are a couple of practical reasons for not including all possible configurations in an analysis as well. The first is that some configurations may not make sense in real life. Obviously, whether this will happen or not depends on the conditions to be included and the meaning of each set. For example, biologically speaking, females under or above a certain age are not able to give birth to a child; therefore, the configuration of being female, of a certain age and the biological mother of children does not make sense and should be ignored or removed. For another example, a person not being a citizen of a nation is not eligible to vote in political elections, making the configuration of not being a citizen and 'voted in the last national election' meaningless and should not be included in the analysis. Configurations such as these are certainly rare, but they are not impossible. More generally, cases in real life are rarely even distributed across all logically possible configurations; conversely, the concentration of a large number of cases in a very small number of cases is the norm and nothing to be surprised about. Researchers have the obligation of examining the truth table and identifying meaningless configurations before moving on to analyse the relationship between conditional configurations and the outcome.

In this sense, a scenario much more likely to occur is that a configuration is conceptually possible but has only a very small number of cases. Those who are familiar with the analysis of contingency tables will recognize this as a problem very similar to 'sparse cells', where some cells in a usually large contingency table have very few cases; sometimes, a few configurations or cells may have no cases at all. This is actually the norm in real life because people tend to share the same set of attributes or identities in a particular society;

the diversity of socio-demographic identities is in fact quite limited in reality, which is why it is referred to as 'limited diversity'; as Ragin described, 'Naturally occurring social phenomena are profoundly limited in their diversity. In fact, it could be argued that limited diversity is one of their trademark features' (Ragin, 2008, p. 147). When examining the truth table, the researcher must determine a threshold under which a configuration will be removed. The threshold could be either absolute, such as 'fewer than five', or relative, such as 'fewer than 5% of the total number of cases'. It is only after all these are done that the truth table is ready for the next round of analysis.

Once the truth table is ready, the ultimate goal of QCA and set-theoretic methods is to find the 'causal recipes' for the interested outcome. Again, without going into the technical details which the reader can find in the suggested readings at the end of this chapter, here I will briefly explain the ideas behind the process of discovering the causal recipes and its relevance to the study of intersectionality. As explained above, the point at which set-theoretic methods fit the purpose of intersectionality is the systematic presentation and examination of all possible cross-classifications of intersectionality. Theoretically and substantively for intersectionality, and methodologically for set-theoretic methods, the intersections of categories (or set memberships) are the common target shared by the two enterprises. Nevertheless, since each has developed its own ideas separately, exactly how compatible each finds the other side remains an unexplored terrain. More specifically, as a well-established research method, QCA and other set-based methods can do a few things that may appear unexpected to advocates of intersectionality who therefore need to consider how the results produced by these methods could serve the purposes of intersectionality. Below are some of the most important ideas and analyses.

First of all, and as mentioned earlier, QCA and set-theoretic methods emphasize an asymmetrical causal relationship between the configurations and the outcome. In other words, causes for the presence of an outcome are not necessarily the opposite to the causes of the absence of the outcome. To illustrate with an example relevant to intersectionality, the fact that White men are promoted at work does not necessarily mean that Black women are deprived of the opportunity to be promoted, or vice versa. This may be true but is not necessarily true; therefore, empirical investigations are needed to confirm. For any study following the set-theoretic logic, it is mandatory to conduct two separate analyses, one for the presence of the outcome and the other for the absence of the outcome. This is an example of why Charles Ragin declared that his comparative method was 'more nuanced'. By the comparing the results, the researcher then should be able to determine whether the relationship is symmetrical or not. At the moment, most researchers of intersectionality, as users of statistical methods do, seem to take the symmetry of the relationship for granted; therefore, they may find the asymmetrical relationship theoretically unacceptable. Researchers of intersectionality need to consider this implication for their theoretical argument before adopting QCA and set-theoretic methods.

Next, another distinction needs to be made; that is, when connecting an intersectional configuration with the presence (or absence) of the outcome, the set-theoretic methods require that the analysis of necessity be conducted separately from the analysis of sufficiency. As explained previously in this chapter, a condition is necessary for the outcome if the presence of the outcome requires the presence of the condition; in other words, we observe the condition whenever we see the outcome. In contrast, a condition is sufficient if the outcome occurs whenever we see the condition. Now, the intersectional configurations in a truth table can be either a necessary or sufficient condition for the presence (or absence) of the outcome, or both, or neither. Again, researchers of intersectionality may not have thought about all these different connections between the intersectional identities and the outcome; most would have taken the *sufficiency* of intersectional identities for granted. For example, when the advocates of intersectionality demonstrated the importance of intersectional identities, they were clearly thinking that an intersectional identity such as Black and female was a sufficient condition for being deprived of the opportunities of being employed or promoted; otherwise, they would have to find other conditions in order to make a strong case for their argument. If being Black and female was only a necessary but not sufficient condition for being disadvantaged, then it means not all Black female employees were disadvantaged, so the question is: what other conditions are needed for them to suffer from a particular form of deprivation? To answer this question, Black female employees and their representatives have the obligation of identifying these other conditions. How researchers of intersectionality would find the requirement of studying these logical connections between intersectional identities and the outcome they are interested in remains a challenge.

Now we are ready to move on to perhaps the most important question in a set-theoretic analysis; that is, to discover which configurations (intersections) are necessary or sufficient conditions for the presence (or absence) of the outcome. For a particular outcome, there are four possibilities for a configuration: (1) necessary but not sufficient; (2) sufficient but not necessary; (3) neither necessary nor sufficient; (4) necessary and sufficient. Whether it is necessary or sufficient is determined by the memberships of the cases in the set of the condition and the set of the outcome. If all cases in the condition also belong to the set of the outcome, which means that the outcome set is bigger than the condition set, then the condition is sufficient. Conversely, if all cases in the outcome also belong to the set of the condition, which means that the condition set is bigger than the outcome set, then the condition is necessary. These, however, are ideal situations; the real-world data are rarely this neat. It is more likely that in a real-world dataset, only a percentage of the cases of a particular set belong to another set. Therefore, researchers need a rule of threshold so that they can determine whether the evidence is strong enough for a particular set relationship and subsequently for identifying a necessary or sufficient condition. Usually, the threshold is set at a very high level, such as 80% or even 90%. Clearly, this is not ideal as there will be a certain level of artificiality, no matter how low it is, in the results. Even a very small number of cases that violate the expected set relationship will make the researcher obliged to probe further.

By examining the computer outputs of the set relationships and applying the above rules, the researcher is in a position to identify the necessary or the sufficient conditions for the presence (or absence) of the outcome. It is normal that two or more configurations are identified as necessary or sufficient conditions, which are called 'solutions' in set-theoretic analysis. In such a situation some Boolean algebraic calculations could be used to 'minimize' the solutions in order to make the solutions as concise as possible, which is mostly a technical issue. More importantly for our concern here, these multiple solutions are taken as evidence for different causal relationships between the configurations and the outcome. For advocates of QCA and set-theoretic methods, this is a highly significant methodological benefit, because these solutions demonstrate the diversity (they call 'complexity') of causality, which is in contrast to statistical models that only show one causal relationship, or so as they conceive. It is unlikely that statistical social scientists would accept this criticism; they would argue that different statistical models could certainly estimate different causal relationships. For advocates of intersectionality, again it remains to be seen how they respond to the claimed benefits from using QCA and set-theoretic methods. They certainly will welcome the clear evidence for the set memberships connecting the interested intersection (configuration) and the interested outcome (being disadvantaged or discriminated against), but they need to be prepared for seeing set relationships that may not align with their expectations.

5.4 Critiques and controversies

QCA and set-theoretic methods aim to make the process of comparing multiple cases more rigorous by introducing a formal analytical tool developed out of set theories and Boolean algebra from mathematics and formal logic. While this is supposed to be an advantage over other methods, it may become a source of potential controversies as well. This is actually a general problem for all applications of formal methods in empirical research – there will always be a certain degree of mismatch or discrepancy between the formal procedures and the 'messy' but realistic data. Often the formal method requires that the data be transformed or analysed in a certain way which might impose a pattern on the data or generate some artificial results that the researcher has to struggle when interpreting the meaning of these results in the context of the data. It is indeed undeniable that set-theoretic methods address some of the important issues seriously and explicitly, such as asymmetric relationships and different causal conditions. This does not mean, however, that these methods are free of limitations and even flaws.

As the advantages of QCA and set-theoretic methods over statistical models have been repeatedly argued in the literature, it is useful for the reader to be aware of the criticisms of these methods in order to develop a more balanced attitude and understanding. In their review article, Gisele De Meur, Benoit Rihoux and Sakura Yamansaki (2009) discussed a list of criticisms of QCA, including dichotomization of data, the use of non-observed cases (logical remainders), case sensitivity, the difficulty in selecting conditions, the black box problem and the temporality problem. Here we focus on a few of the most important issues.

Raised by prominent social scientists such as Stanley Lieberson (1991, 1994, 2001, 2004) and John Goldthorpe (2000, 2016), a major issue with set-theoretic methods is not the focus on the cases or sets, but the determinism in defining case memberships and set relationships. This is particularly an issue with the analysis of crisp sets, where case memberships are clear-cut. In social reality, such clearly defined memberships are rare – even for supposedly simple conditions (or variables) such as gender and sexuality, it is not always straightforward to determine a case's membership of a set, let alone other more complicated examples such as political orientation or attitudes towards immigrants. To rectify this 'straightjacket', Charles Ragin (2000, 2008) introduced 'fuzzy-set' to make set memberships more flexible, which helps but only to a certain extent – case memberships now have more than two values, in fact any value between 0 or 1 (inclusive), but still they take only a few values in the range of 0 to 1. More importantly, the notion of probability, which is a foundation for statistical methods and models, is not considered in QCA and set-theoretic methods at all, even though it may make both theoretical and methodological sense to treat fuzzy set membership as the probability or degree of belonging to a set. Consequently, questions such as 'What is the probability that a case belongs to a set?' or 'How probable is a configuration a sufficient condition for this outcome?' are perceived as incompatible with QCA and set-theoretic methods. A big price to pay for analysing 'messy' realistic real-world data in a deterministic manner is that the results must be free of deviant cases and the explanation must be able to apply to all cases, which is either impossible or artificial. In contrast, statistical methods keep the original real-world values of the variables (conditions) and tolerate abnormalities such as unusual shapes of distributions or influential values.

Another price researchers have to pay when applying formal methods on real-world data is the loss of touch with the details of cases. Although QCA and set-theoretic methods are claimed to be 'case-centred' or 'case-based' as opposed to 'variable-centred' statistical methods, researchers rarely spend time and effort learning about the details of the cases they study when busying themselves with following the procedural rules and principles, either because the details are not available, or because the number of cases is prohibitively too large for detailed investigations. In 1991, the statistician David Freedman published a later very influential paper 'Statistical Models and Shoe Leather', urging social scientists to avoid using regression models blindly without learning the detailed and contextual information about the issue at hand. The advice is applicable to QCA and set-theoretic methods as well – with the analytical procedures becoming established and computing tools finely tuned, researchers now run the risk of applying these methods routinely and rigidly without knowing much about what is actually going on in the cases. This is particularly true when the number of cases is large enough to make it infeasible for the researcher to learn the details. As a research method, QCA was initially created for studying a small number of cases. Now, with the use of computer software, the number of cases (or sample size) is not an issue anymore. Unless researchers are prepared to use set-theoretical methods as something very different from the initial comparative method, they need to be aware that a lot of information is either lost or abstracted so heavily in the process of calibrating set memberships and determining set relations that they may not be able to trace from the computer outputs back to the social reality they want to understand. This is why some qualitatively oriented researchers such as David Collier (2014) suggested that QCA and set-theoretic methods should give up the algorithms and return to the 'traditional' qualitative investigations.

Finally, researchers would be wise if they refrained from deriving causal inferences from the results of QCA and set-theoretic analysis. Without getting into any disputes here, suffice it to say that to make a causal claim requires the satisfaction of some very stringent conditions. My personal view is that it is a task often beyond the realm of empirical social science research; we can construct a causal theory before conducting an empirical research project, and then produce and present as much supporting evidence as we could, but the evidence can and should never be taken as truthful representation of the actual causal process. Statisticians have been extremely cautious and therefore reluctant to make causal claims based on statistical models, and advocates of QCA and set-theoretic methods are not in a better position. Similar to any spurious associations between variables, set relationships between conditions and the outcome could be spurious as well: that the cases of one set happen to belong to another set cannot necessarily serve as convincing evidence for any causal relationship between the two sets, because we do not have information about why and how the cases end up in the two sets at the same time. It is therefore somewhat presumptuous to put a seemingly enviable label 'causal recipe' on the results. In 2014, Lucas and Szatrowski published perhaps the most systematic and unrelenting criticisms of QCA in the widely reputable journal *Sociological Methodology*. Here was their verdict: 'QCA is a wholly ineffective research method, providing a fatal distraction that, far from realizing the promise of qualitative and comparative historical research, sabotages such analyses' (p. 3) and 'methodologically, in every single test QCA failed ... researchers should reject QCA and abandon the chimerical quest for a deterministic method' (p. 70). Since the publication of this scathing review, QCA and set-theoretic methods have not disappeared and still have many followers. Researchers who are new to these methods, however, need to be informed about the potential issues involved before using them.

5.5 Suggested readings and questions for discussion

If you want to obtain an appropriate conceptual understanding of the motivation, the rationale and the logic of QCA, it is helpful to start by reading some of the books by Charles Ragin, including *The comparative method: Moving beyond qualitative and quantitative strategies* (University of California Press, 1987), *Fuzzy-set social science* (University of Chicago Press, 2000), and *Redesigning social inquiry: Fuzzy sets and beyond* (University of Chicago Press, 2008). It is of the utmost importance to understand the concepts of 'set' and 'configuration', which are the foundations of all subsequent technical details. What is a set? Try to answer this question with examples in social life. Then ask yourself: what does it exactly mean when we say someone is a member of a set? Note that your answer may depend on the set in question – the membership of the Labour Party may be quite different from the membership of the working class in the UK. The notion of 'configuration' is even more subtle, because it depends on which sets are included and how each set is defined. Taking yourself as a case, decide on a small number of sets (two or three), work out how many configurations there are, then decide which configuration you belong to.

Another important issue is the relationships between the configurations and the outcome; things could quickly become complicated and even controversial here as to what enables one to say how the configurations and the outcome are connected in a causal manner. Learning the technical details is only worthwhile after one feels confident and comfortable with these conceptual and logical issues. As mentioned above, Ragin and Fiss explained why their method is particularly suitable for the study of intersectionality in *Intersectional inequality: Race, class, test scores, and poverty* (University of Chicago Press, 2017). How enthusiastic advocates of intersectionality react to this method remains unclear, however. Consider the following questions: What makes a condition necessary or sufficient for a particular outcome? Again, use a specific example in your social life; for example, is being homosexual and Black a necessary or sufficient condition (or both, or neither) for being discriminated against in employment? Explain the logic of your answer to others and ensure they accept it.

Despite the fact that Ragin and Fiss presented and discussed many details of their analyses of intersectional inequality in their book, Ragin rarely showed others the technical processes of how to do QCA or set-theoretic analysis, a service that other researchers who are in favour of QCA have performed. Perhaps the first and the best is the text by Carsten Q. Schneider and Claudius Wagemann, *Set-theoretic methods for the social sciences: A guide to qualitative comparative analysis* (Cambridge University Press, 2012). A more recent and relatively simplified rendition is *Qualitative comparative analysis using R: A beginner's guide* by Ioana-Elena Oana, Carsten Q. Schneider, and Eva Thomann (Cambridge University Press, 2021). To keep up with the development of this method and related resources and events, please visit the following website: https://compasss.org/.

6

INTERACTION TERMS IN GENERALIZED LINEAR REGRESSION MODELS

6.1 Overview and objectives

This chapter is an extension of the previous one in that it continues to address the interactive effects of two or more predictors on an outcome. As Charles Ragin and others have argued, a fundamental limitation of generalized linear regression models (GLRMs) is their focus on the 'unique' contribution by *each* predictor to explaining the response variable's variation. Therefore, QCA and set-theoretic methods aim to shift the attention from individual effects to interactive effects between two or more predictors (or 'causal conditions'). It is incorrect, however, to say that GLRMs do not pay attention to interactive effects at all. Due to a variety of issues, such as different levels of measurement among the variables, the sample size for subgroups and the interpretation of the coefficients for interactive terms, it has been indeed a challenge for these models to include interactive terms. Nonetheless, statistical methods do exist for studying interactive effects. Charles Ragin is clearly aware of these and has made a few criticisms of these methods. Putting these together, this chapter has the following objectives:

- to clarify and explain the meaning of an interaction term in GLRM, with special attention to analysis of variance (ANOVA) and its extensions, as these models fit the situation of intersectionality very well;
- to explain why it is a challenge to include interaction terms in GLRM;
- to discuss the limitations and criticisms on interaction terms in GLRM.

We shall start this chapter by introducing the interaction terms in GLRM and Ragin's criticisms of these models. Then we shall move on to the statistical methods and models that help researchers study the interactive effects of two or more categorical explanatory variables, since such interactive effects are the most relevant to intersectionality. As the attributes of central concern to intersectionality are always categorical, such as race, gender, sexuality, etc., interactive effects of metrical (or continuous) variables are essentially irrelevant and therefore shall be skipped here.

6.2 Interaction terms in GLRM and their limitations

In the previous chapter, I introduced the following example of a generalized linear regression model (GLRM):

$$R = \beta_1 P1 + \beta_2 P2 + \beta_3 P3 + \text{error}$$

Essentially, this model says that we can arrive at an estimated value of the response variable R by *adding up* the *individual* effects of the three predictors P1, P2 and P3. Each of the three coefficients, β_1, β_2, and β_3, can be seen as a weight attached to each predictor. The product of each coefficient and the value of its corresponding predictor then represent the predictor's 'unique' contribution to the prediction of the response variable's value. The sum of these individual effects will rarely be the same as the actual value of the response variable, which is why there is an 'error' term at the end of the model. Such a model could be illustrated with a diagram (Figure 6.1).

Note the absence of line or arrow linking any two of the three predictors. In this sense, this model is in great contrast to the model of QCA or set-theoretic methods, which could be illustrated with another diagram (Figure 6.2a).

As we learnt in the previous chapter, intersections of set memberships lead to 'configurations' which are seen as potential 'causal recipes' for the outcome. We can represent the above model in a different way with the following diagram (Figure 6.2b).

In the latter example, there are three causal conditions; therefore, there are eight ($2^3 = 8$) possible configurations. Not all configurations may turn out to be a necessary or sufficient condition for the outcome, which is why there is a question mark on each arrow. It remains a question to the researcher whether these configurations are independent of each other, although the model in this diagram assumes no relationship among them. It should have become clear to the reader that the focus of analysis has shifted *from purely individual effects in linear regression models to exclusively intersectional effects in set-theoretic models*.

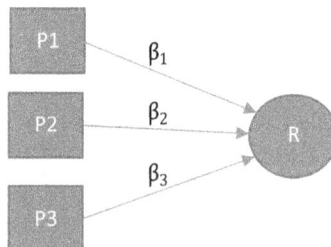

Figure 6.1   Example of linear regression model without interaction terms

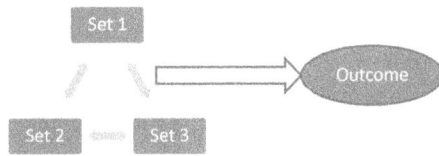

Figure 6.2a Example of set-theoretic model with three causal conditions

Statistical models that focus on interactions between variables, particularly categorical variables, do exist. For example, log-linear models aim to systematically present and discover which of all the possible ways of association between multiple categorical variables turn out to be supported by the data. Clearly, these associations are intersections of the values of the categorical variables. However, log-linear models examine associational patterns alone without aiming to explain any response variable, making them not really useful for studying intersectionality. Similarly, cluster analysis is a set of methods for discovering groups among the cases by analysing associations between multiple variables, yet it does not aim to explain any response variable with the group memberships discovered, unless a separate analysis is to be conducted subsequently. As intersectionality does aim to explain an outcome with intersectional attributes, these methods are not directly useful and therefore will not be introduced here.

To evaluate and model the effects of intersectional attributes on the experience of disadvantage, we need statistical models that can connect the interactions between categorical variables and a response variable about disadvantage. One solution is to add an interaction term to the above GLRM. However, this strategy has drawn some criticisms from advocates of both intersectionality and QCA. Previously when examining contingency tables, we discussed the criticism on the interaction term in regression models by a researcher of intersectionality. Here, let's consider and discuss the criticisms by Charles Ragin.

In the first chapter of *Intersectional Inequality*, Ragin and Fiss devoted a whole section to comparing their approach and the interaction term in regression models (2016, pp. 17–19). The first limitation of statistical interaction term they pointed out was 'saturated interaction models are not only quite demanding to compute (usually due to data limitations), but they are also very difficult to decipher and interpret' (p. 17). This is true – depending on the

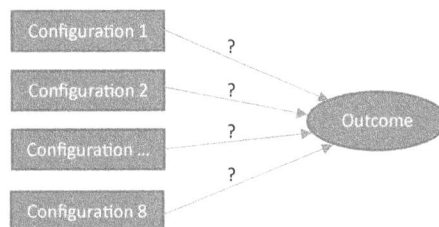

Figure 6.2b Example of set-theoretic model with configurations as causal conditions

number of variables and the number of categories that each variable has, an interaction term in a GLRM could have a relatively large number of cross-classifications of these categories. Even for a large sample size such as several hundreds or even thousands, at least one of the cross-classifications may have very few cases, a serious constraint on computing the effect of the interaction term on the response variable. However, QCA and the set-theoretic methods suffer from the same limitation; in fact, they have a special term for this limitation, 'limited diversity', which we already learnt in the previous chapter. Regardless, this is a fair warning to those who plan to include interaction terms in GLRM – researchers should examine the number of cases in all cross-classifications of each interaction term in the model outputs, and if some cross-classifications are found to have very few cases, the researcher may combine some categories together to increase the number of cases. Obviously, there is a price for doing this; that is, the number as well as the meaning of cross-classifications will change, but it should not prevent us from including an interaction term in GLRMs.

Interpretation is a more serious issue, as it may hinder the researcher from arriving at substantively meaningful observations. However, Ragin and Fiss did not explain why it would be difficult to interpret interactive terms and whether something could be done to ease the interpretation. As I see it, the challenge to interpretation comes from two sources. First, researchers must be careful of interpreting the interactive effects in comparison with the 'main effect'. It is important to note that although both intersectionality and GLRMs with intersection terms care about the interaction between two or more categorical attributes, intersectionality tends to focus on the interaction per se without caring much about the 'main effect' of each attribute, as GLRMs do. In fact, intersectionality argues against such 'main effect' because it is single-dimensional. In contrast, statistical models require the inclusion of main (individual) effects being a precondition for adding any interaction term; the interaction effect is only considered *after* the main effects are included. As Jacob Cohen et al. have defined, 'two variables are said to interact in their accounting for the variance in *Y* when *over and above* any additive combination of their separate effects, they have a *joint* effect' (2003, p. 355, emphasis original). This is important, because the interactive effects in GLRMs may not share the same meaning with set-theoretic methods methodologically or with intersectionality conceptually.

Another source of difficulty in interpreting the interactive terms in GLRMs becomes particularly acute when the number of variables in the interaction term is three or more. If there are only two variables in the interaction term, such as the model below, the interpretation is straightforward:

$$R = \beta_1 P1 + \beta_2 P2 + \beta_3 (P1*P2) + error$$

Here, the interaction term P1*P2 means that the effect of P1 on the response variable R depends on the value of P2, and vice versa. More importantly, this model *assumes* that the effect of P1 on R through P2 is *the same as* the effect of P2 on R through P1. The interactive effect, represented by β_3, is an *additional* effect *after* considering the individual effects of P1 and P2.

Things become quite complicated when the number of variables in the interaction term increases to three:

$$R = \beta_1 P1 + \beta_2 P2 + \beta_3 P3 + \beta_4 (P1*P2*P3) + error$$

Statisticians would not accept such a model, because they require that a model with a higher-order term must include all lower-order terms as well ('hierarchical models'):

$$R = \beta_1 P1 + \beta_2 P2 + \beta_3 P3 + \beta_4 (P1*P2) + \beta_5 (P1*P3) + \beta_6 (P2*P3) + \beta_7 (P1*P2*P3) + error$$

The three-way interactive effect, represented here by the coefficient β_7, is an effect *after* the effects of all other lower terms are already considered, a rule different from including a configuration of three conditions in QCA, because the latter does not necessarily consider the other lower-term effects.

More importantly, how should we interpret the meaning of the three-way interactive effect? Strictly speaking, the effect of one predictor depends on 'the interaction' of the other two predictors. Yet again, how does one predictor's effect depend on the interaction of two other predictors? One solution is to sort out the interaction of the other two predictors first, and then to interpret the effect of the first variable given each specific interaction of the other two predictors; for example, if there are four cross-classifications between P2 and P3, then the effect of P1 on R depends on each of the four cross-classifications. Such interpretation is logically sound but may remain obscured to many people.

If the number of predictors of an interaction term increases to four, to interpret its meaning will indeed become very complicated as well as cumbersome. This is a difficulty that QCA and set-theoretic methods must face as well, but if both methods face the same challenge and set-theoretic methods claim to have a better way of interpreting the interactions, why don't we borrow their interpretation? That is, we simply interpret the interactive effects as the effect of simultaneous memberships. There is an important caveat, however: we should not use only one coefficient to represent all interactive effects, as the statistical model does; instead, we must use a separate coefficient for each cross-classification. Essentially, this is the rationale of all statistical methods of 'analysis of variance', to be introduced next. It is similar to what QCA and set-theoretic methods do, except for two differences: one, these 'analysis of variance' models require a metrical response variable, whilst set-theoretic methods have a binary (crisp-set) or decimal (fuzzy-set) outcome; two, the statistical models consider the highest-order interactive effect only after taking the main and lower-order interactive effects, whilst set-theoretic methods usually do not.

The second limitation of interaction terms refers to their additive nature shown above. Ragin and Fiss phrased the question that such statistical models aim to answer as follows: 'Does the higher-order interaction produce an increment to explained variation in the outcome, beyond what is captured by the lower-order terms (and by the "main effects")?' (ibid.: 18). It becomes unclear, however, exactly what their criticism was about: initially, they said this was 'a useful practice', but then they pointed out the 'bias toward parsimony and simplicity', which refers to the simpler models without the interaction terms. The critique seems to be that for the sake of parsimony or simplicity, researchers using statistical models would be tempted to omit interaction terms; therefore, these models enjoy no advantage for studying intersectionality. Of all academic papers using statistical models, the percentage of those including interaction terms appears quite low. If this is true, then it will lend support to the claim by Ragin and Fiss. However, this is an issue with *the practice* of using statistical models, not with the models themselves. We may never know the true motivations behind the exclusion of interaction terms – researchers may claim that interaction effects were not the focus of their research. If researchers knew they should have included interaction terms in their models but omitted them purposefully to keep their models parsimonious or simple, their models could be *simplistic*, not merely simple. It is a model's ability to represent the reality, not parsimony, that should be the ultimate function of the model. Models with interaction terms are certainly more complicated than those without them, but if including interaction terms is 'a useful practice', then complexity becomes a merit, not something to avoid. All in all, there is nothing wrong with statistical models with interaction terms, and researchers should use them without attempting to omit them for the sake of parsimony.

The third limitation of interaction terms, as Ragin and Fiss explained, is the issue of multicollinearity. The two graphs below illustrate this issue.

In general, multicollinearity refers to the strong correlation between the predictors in GLRMs. The biggest circle in the two figures represents the total variation of the response variable. Suppose there are three predictors in a regression model, then Figure 6.3a shows the 'ideal' situation, in which the contribution of each predictor to the explanation for the response variable's variation has little overlap with another predictor's contribution. In addition, together, the three predictors explain a majority of the response variable's variation, leaving only a small percentage of the variation, say 20%, unexplained. The first expectation (or assumption) of no overlap between the predictors, however, is clearly unrealistic and may be even undesirable. It is unrealistic because most of the variables in real life are more or less related to each other. It may be not desirable when researchers have an interest in the interactions between the predictors. However, this could be a problem from the statistical perspective – as illustrated in Figure 6.3b, multicollinearity makes it difficult to separate one predictor's contribution from another's in explaining the response variable's variation. This is particularly undesirable if collectively the predictors only explain a small part of the variation. The multicollinearity in linear regression models with interaction terms is almost inevitable, since it comes from the interaction terms themselves. Recall in the previous model, the interaction term of three predictors is P1*P2*P3, which must be associated, at least moderately, with the three interaction terms of two predictors, P1*P2, P2*P3, P1*P3, respectively, because both variables in the two-variable interaction terms are components of the three-variable interaction term.

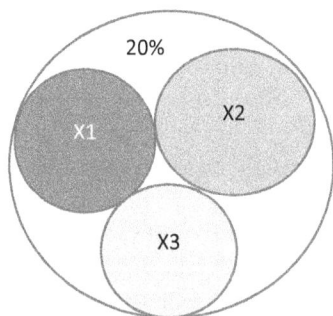

Figure 6.3a The ideal: no multicollinearity

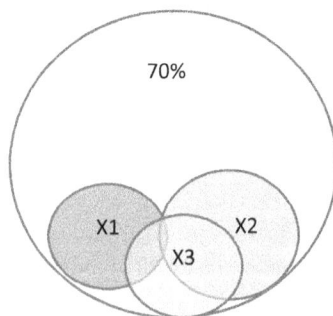

Figure 6.3b The undesirable: multicollinearity

Ragin and Fiss argued that multicollinearity would have 'a noxious and often lethal impact' on the model (2017, p. 18). Then they continue, 'Small empirical differences can spawn impressive-looking interaction effects via suppression and other data issues' (ibid.), yet they did not spell out their explanation for how this could actually happen – what suppresses what, and what are the other 'data issues'? Finally, they pointed out that 'when multicollinearity is severe, as is usually the case when higher-order interaction terms are examined, many different subsets of interaction terms will fit the evidence equally well—deciding which ones to trust becomes a rather difficult task' (ibid.). It remains unclear why this has to be a difficult task – if the subsets of the interaction terms could do an equally good job as the higher-order interaction term, then surely the researcher should choose the lower-order term; the principle of parsimony should prevail here because there is no benefit of including a higher-order term.

If multicollinearity is almost unavoidable in linear regression models with interaction terms, then it is pointless to avoid it. Instead, researchers should embrace it by shifting the focus of analysis from the study of individual effects to the study of interaction terms. In other words, whenever researchers have a theoretical or substantive reason for including interaction terms in their linear regression models, they should focus on the interaction terms. As long as they pay careful attention to the representation and interpretation of interactions, such models can still be very useful.

The last and final criticism that Ragin and Fiss charged on the intersection terms refers to the two different approaches – statistical and set-theoretic, implying that the set-theoretic approach has a clear advantage. In their own words, set-theoretic methods 'are more concerned with connections that are uniform or close to uniform than with connections that reflect differences in tendencies' (ibid.). Let's try to understand what they mean here. When following the set-theoretic approach, researchers examine the connections of multiple set memberships to the set of a particular outcome; they would have discovered strong evidence for the causal relationship if they had found that all (or almost all) cases – this is what they meant by 'uniform or close to uniform', being members of the sets of causal configurations, were also members of the outcome set. Nonetheless, this is why QCA and set-theoretic methods were seen as deterministic (or almost deterministic), which, in the eyes of some prominent social scientists (e.g. Stanley Lieberson and John Goldthorpe), is a major liability, not an advantage. In contrast, GLRMs estimate the cases' 'tendencies' by drawing on the combined values of chosen predictors. Here, the word 'tendencies' means the chance that the cases take a particular value such as the mean or the probability of having a particular attribute. In this sense, the set-theoretic approach is indeed more suitable for systematically examining the intersections between the values of the conditions (predictors), but it appears rigid in defining the conditions and the outcome as well as in connecting the intersections to the outcome. Statistical models, on the other hand, are more flexible in the sense of keeping all of the variables' *original* values but somehow more cumbersome in connecting the interactions between the predictors and the outcome in a *statistically efficient and substantively meaningful* way.

In the rest of this chapter, we shall focus on GLRMs with the interaction effects of two or more categorical predictors.

6.3 Studying intersectionality with ANOVA

The following is a typical situation in which intersectionality would demonstrate its distinctive effect: people with a particular combination of racial and gender attributes, such as Black women, are disadvantaged with a lower average income than those in other cross-classifications of race and gender. If we examine such a situation from a generic perspective, we will be able to see why some well-established methods can be of great use for studying intersectionality. Here, we have two categorical attributes, for example race and gender, and each has two or more categories. In this example, the response variable is average income; again, generically, it *must be a metrical* variable in order for us to use the methods of ANOVA; for example, time spent on physical exercises, monthly salary, body mass index (BMI), blood pressure, etc. Our discussion starts with a simple situation and then moves on to more complicated ones.

To keep the illustration simple, suppose the variable Race has only two values, White and Non-White, and similarly, Gender has two values too, Men and Women, then the data could be represented as in Table 6.1 below.

The Greek letter μ is usually used to represent a variable's mean; here, it is the mean of income, and its subscript represents the categories or values of each categorical attribute, except for μ_G, usually called 'the grand mean', i.e. the mean of the entire sample. The four marginal means (μ_M, μ_F, μ_W, μ_{NW}) represent the mean of each categorical attribute, respectively; therefore, they do not tell us any useful information about intersectionality. It is the mean for each of the four cross-classifications (μ_{MW}, μ_{MNW}, μ_{FW}, μ_{FNW}) that contains the information for intersectional effects on average income. If these four means are the same, which is commonly stated as the null hypothesis in ANOVA, then it should be clear that there is no intersectional effect of race and gender on income. With real-world data, these means are bound to be more or less different, and the question is: how should we analyse the differences between these means so that we can claim that there are intersectional effects of race and gender on income?

Statisticians and quantitative methodologists have followed two approaches to answering this question. As James Jaccard (1998) explained and illustrated, the first approach compares and takes *the difference between the mean differences* as the evidence for interactional (intersectional) effects, and the other approach removes the main effect of each categorical attribute and any lower-order interactional effects so that the 'gross' targeted interactional effect could be identified. Jaccard calls the second approach 'Interaction Effects as Treatment Effects' or 'Residualized Means', of which Robert Rosenthal and Ralph L. Rosnow are the leading advocates. Unfortunately, the two approaches do not seem compatible with each other, with Rosenthal and Rosnow criticizing the first approach for not really studying the interactional effects. Jaccard's view was that both were valid and should be used for different

Table 6.1 Race, gender and average income

	White	Non-White	Row mean
Male	μ_{MW}	μ_{MNW}	μ_M
Female	μ_{FW}	μ_{FNW}	μ_F
Column mean	μ_W	μ_{NW}	Grand mean μ_G

purposes (1998, p. 20). This shows that the term 'interaction effect' has more than one meaning. As this is not merely a statistical issue and has conceptual implications for studying intersectionality, it is worth spending some time learning about the fundamental difference between the two approaches.

The first approach has two steps: in the first step, we need to find the differences between the two categories of one categorical variable at each of the other categorical variable's categories, respectively, regarding the response variable. For the above example, for men, the difference of mean income between the White and the non-White is ($\mu_{MW} - \mu_{MNW}$), and the same difference for women is ($\mu_{FW} - \mu_{FNW}$). Obviously, we could also compare the two gender groups for each of the racial groups. In the second step, we compare the two differences by taking their difference, ($\mu_{MW} - \mu_{MNW}$) – ($\mu_{FW} - \mu_{FNW}$), which is why this approach is called 'difference between mean differences'. This second difference between the initial two differences of means represents the interaction (or intersection) effect of race and gender on average income, because it shows how the effect of race depends on gender. In the statistical literature, such a relationship is also usually referred to as moderation; that is, the effect of race on average income has been moderated by gender, although in fact the two categorical variables moderate each other. In statistics, moderation means that one variable's effect varies with the values of another variable. Therefore, we can call this approach 'interaction (or intersection) as moderation'. A common practice – not necessarily the best – is to reject the null hypothesis that the difference between mean differences is zero if the difference turns out to be statistically significant.

In a number of publications, Robert Rosenthal and Ralph L. Rosnow have argued that the above logic is misleading at best, because it does not separate different effects apart from when comparing the means or the differences between means. To interpret interaction (or intersection) effect as the moderated effect of one variable by another may be intuitively appealing and accessible, but it is not the 'pure', 'gross' or 'real' effect of interaction (or intersection). We can only find the 'real' interaction effect *after removing the effects of all lower-order terms*, including the grand mean, the effect of each predictor, and the effect of lower-order interaction terms. In their textbook, Rosenthal and Rosnow provided an equation for representing the relationships between the components of the data in a two-way ANOVA design (2008, p. 467):

Group mean = Grand mean + Row effect + Column effect + Interaction effect

As our interest is in the interaction effect, we can rewrite the above equation with the interaction effect as the subject:

Interaction effect = Group mean – Grand mean – Row effect – Column effect

In this equation,

Row effect = Row mean – Grand mean

Similarly,

Column effect = Column mean – Grand mean.

Therefore,

> Interaction effect = Group mean – Grand mean – (Row mean – Grand mean) – (Column mean – Grand mean)
> Interaction effect = Group mean – Grand mean – Row mean + Grand mean – Column mean + Grand mean
> Interaction effect = Group mean – Row mean – Column mean + Grand mean

The term 'group mean' refers to each of the cell means. Therefore, the number of group means is equal to the product of the number of categories of each explanatory variables. Consequently, there will be the same number of interaction effects, and the researcher should compare these interaction (or intersection) effects in order to gain a sense of how they affect the response variable collectively.

Now, let's apply this equation to our example above. As there are four cells in the original table, we have four different interaction effects:

- Male and White = $\mu_{MW} - \mu_M - \mu_W + \mu_G$
- Male and Non-White = $\mu_{MNW} - \mu_M - \mu_{NW} + \mu_G$
- Female and White = $\mu_{FW} - \mu_F - \mu_W + \mu_G$
- Female and Non-White = $\mu_{FNW} - \mu_F - \mu_{NW} + \mu_G$

Clearly, this understanding of interaction (or intersection) effect is more restrictive (or 'pure') than the above 'interaction as moderation' interpretation, because all of the other effects have been removed, making the interaction (or intersection) effect a 'leftover' or 'residual' effect.

Rosenthal and Rosnow (2008) urged researchers to ask themselves an important question: what exactly do we want to know? If you really want to know the interactive effect, then you must first remove the lower-order effects, including the main effects and the lower-order interaction effects. Whilst Rosenthal and Rosnow would like researchers to accept their answer, I think researchers should be allowed to make their own choice. The answer from Rosenthal and Rosnow may be different from what researchers want to know. Jaccard (1998) also thinks that both approaches are valid despite the fact that they serve different purposes. All in all, the guiding principle seems to be the following: you can adopt either of the two approaches as long as it suits the purposes of your research, but you should be aware of the difference between the two.

The second approach is consistent with the linear model of ANOVA:

$$\mu_{Cell} = \mu_{Grand} + \mu_{Row} + \mu_{Column} + \mu_{Interaction} + \mu_{Cell}$$

This is a linear model because all the effects are added up on the right-hand side of the equation. An important implication of such a linear relationship between the effects is that each is an effect *after the other effects have been taken into account*. It is therefore also important to note that μ_{Row} and μ_{Column}, which are usually referred to as the 'main' effects, should not be interpreted directly as the effect of each categorical explanatory variable. Instead, each is a 'gross' effect after the other effects have been considered, especially when there is an interaction term in the equation, because the interaction term has rendered the interpretation of each individual variable's effect meaningless. It is for this reason that statisticians warn us against interpreting the main effects if there is an interaction term. For example, in their textbook *Statistics: The Art & Science of Learning from Data*, Alan Agresti and Christine Franklin emphasized that '*It is not meaningful to test the main effects hypotheses when there is interaction*' (2014, p. 709, emphasis original), because the main effect of each explanatory variable depends on the value of the other categorical variable – there is no constant main effect!

Conceptually, the two statistical approaches to comparing and analysing means discussed so far may have serious and important implications for understanding intersectionality. The reader may be able to recall from the first two chapters of this book that the key principle of intersectionality is to pay serious attention to the *simultaneous and combined* effect of two or more socio-demographic attributes when examining disenfranchisement; thus, it is insufficient, misleading, even immoral, to focus on one categorical attribute alone. The debate between the two approaches to ANOVA introduced above has posed the following question to advocates of intersectionality: which one of the two approaches would you like to follow when discussing the meaning of intersectionality? At the moment, advocates of intersectionality seem to have followed the first approach; for example, when making a case for the intersectional effect of race and gender on either pay or opportunities to be promoted at work, Black feminists presented evidence for the differentials of income or employment between intersectional groups, such as Black women vs White men. The second and more restrictive definition of intersectional effect may lend extra support to the mission of intersectionality as it could be used as a counter-argument to the single-factor argument held by some judges in the past. More specifically, advocates of intersectionality could argue that even if we seriously consider the individual effect of each single-factor one at a time, *there still remains an intersectional effect* of the two or more factors, as the single factors may not explain the entire variation of the response variable; it is therefore desirable and important to include and examine the intersectional effect. It is worth mentioning that as stated previously, this is a principle, and whether the empirical analysis of a specific set of evidence turns out to support it depends on the evidence.

6.4 Extending the ANOVA model

Both the situation and the methods in the previous section are intentionally simple to illustrate the key idea and logic rather than the technical details. It is this section's purpose to introduce methods and models for analysing more complicated situations, yet we shall still focus on their logic and principles rather than the technical details which the reader could find readily in other texts, including those at the end of this chapter.

6.4.1 Increasing complexity with more categorical values and variables

In the example above, there were only two categorical attributes as explanatory variables, and each categorical variable has only two values. The situation becomes more complicated when either the number of values of each variable, or the number of the variables, or both, increases, which is usually the case in social reality. For example, the increasingly liberal attitudes and policies towards sexuality in recent decades have led to a large number of values for the variable 'sexuality'; even a conservative classification needs to include a range of values, including heterosexual, queer, lesbian, gay, bisexual and more. Similarly, 'race' could have a large number of values, depending on the context in question; in a liberal democracy, which racial or ethnic minority groups are to be listed in census or sample surveys has been a highly controversial question, but the number could easily reach five to ten; the omission of any minority group, no matter how small, will likely entail protest. These and other attributes, such as age groups, marital status, social class, immigrant status, etc., are relevant to intersectionality because they are often used as categories of identity, which will make the situation even more complicated due to the number of possible intersections. If we intend to include five categorical attributes with each having five values, then there will be $5^5 = 3125$ intersectional groups! Even when each attribute has only two values, there will be $2^5 = 32$ intersections.

Advocates of intersectionality have criticized the inclusion of interaction terms in linear regression models as being unable to analyse so many intersectional groups, which is only valid to a certain extent. Technically speaking, the large number of categorical attributes or their values does not pose an insurmountable obstacle to analysing their intersectional effects on a metrical response variable; for example, in their textbook, Rosenthal and Rosnow presented an illustrative example of analysing a 'five-way interaction', with five categorical explanatory variables and a metrical variable (2008, pp. 524–526), and Jaccard touched on the analysis of 'four-factor design' (1998, pp. 79–80). Statistical methods and computing power are available for clearly presenting and analysing such 'high-dimensional' intersectional effects. The procedure of such analyses usually involves an initial test of the 'omnibus' intersectional effect – whether there is a statistically significant overall interactional effect across all of the categorical cross-classifications in terms of their means of the response variable, and if the result turns out to be significant, then more analysis will follow to specify which of all the intersectional effects are the sources of the overall intersectional effect.

Thus, the large number of possible intersections should not be a source of complexity that will prevent researchers from using ANOVA or related statistical models. Instead, researchers should pay serious attention to the following two interrelated issues when they intend to use these models to study intersectionality. The first relates to the meaning of the possible intersectional groups. As demonstrated above, when either the number of categorical attributes or the number of values of these categorical variables increases, the number of intersectional groups will increase multiplicatively. The question is: is it truly necessary and informative to include all these possible intersectional groups in the analysis? Researchers must carefully think and select the categorical attributes and their values in statistical analysis. At the moment, few empirical studies of intersectionality included more than three categorical attributes and even fewer included five or more. We shall introduce a relatively new method for dealing with a large number of attributes in the next chapter. Here, I would like to emphasize the conceptual and theoretical reason for selecting the number of categorical attributes: What is the theoretical justification for including more than three categorical attributes in an analysis? Which intersectional groups are we truly interested in? And how do we expect them to be different from other intersectional groups in terms of the metrical response variable?

For some researchers, it may be truly necessary to study people at the intersection of four or more attributes, such as gay (sexuality) Asian (ethnicity) men (gender) who are middle-aged (age) and married (marital status) with children (parenthood), but a stronger case needs to be made for focusing on a strictly defined group. The more categorical attributes are included in an analysis, the more specific the studied group will be, and the smaller the sample size will likely to be, ultimately demanding a much stronger justification for targeting a strictly defined group.

The second issue addresses the meaning of intersectional groups again but from a different perspective. Supposing that we have justified the inclusion of four or five categorical attributes in our analysis and that we have the technical capacity to model these attributes, how are we going to *interpret* these intersectional effects *meaningfully*? In the several short monographs on interaction effects (see details in 'Suggested Readings'), James Jaccard has proposed to interpret interaction effects by distinguishing the explanatory variables into two types: a 'focal' variable that the researcher would focus on due to its theoretical importance, and one or more 'moderators' on which the focal variable's effect on the response variable depends. If we follow this strategy, as we did in the example discussed in the previous section, first of all we need to decide which of the two categorical attributes, gender and race, is the focal variable. Suppose gender is the focus of our theoretical concern, then the intersection effect of gender and race on average income would be interpreted as the following: the effect of gender on average income depends on race. When the number of explanatory variables increases to three or more, the highest-order interaction effect would be interpreted as the effect of the focal variable on the response variable depending on the lower-order interaction terms.

However, Jaccard's interpretation of interaction effect appears incompatible with the spirit of intersectionality. First of all, the distinction between the focal variable and the moderator means that researchers must rank the intersectional attributes in the order of theoretical importance; thus, they do not treat these attributes equally and study their simultaneous or 'combined' effects at the same time. It is one of intersectionality's key principles that these categorical attributes are equally important, both theoretically and practically. In addition, the arbitrary separation of the focal attribute from the moderating attribute ignores the fact that statistically, the two attributes mutually depend on each other, because there is only one coefficient for the interaction term in the ANOVA model. Perhaps more importantly, the single coefficient for the interaction term does not help us see and compare the intersectional groups in terms of their means of the response variable. Jaccard did discuss the methods for comparing these means, for example with confidence intervals, but doing so means that there is no need for us to consider the meaning of the coefficient of the interaction term other than its statistical significance.

Finally, Jaccard's interpretation becomes clumsier with the increase of variables in the interaction term; for example, what exactly do we mean when we say 'the effect of one attribute on the response variable depends on the interaction of the other two attributes'? The interpretation would become even more obscured if there were four or five variables in the interaction term. In contrast, it would be much clearer to interpret the interaction effect as simultaneous attributes of a particular intersectional group, such as Black (race) widowed (marital status) women (gender) above the age of 60 (age). Clearly, this interpretation requires that we examine and compare all intersectional groups. In interpreting statistics, clarity and sensibility are the most important principles.

6.4.2 Logistic regression models with an interaction term of categorical attributes

Recall that the appropriate use of ANOVA models requires the response variable to be metrical. Given that most of the variables in social science research are categorical or count (integers), the number of situations in which this requirement is satisfied is probably quite small. Fortunately, statisticians have developed a 'logistic regression model' that can go beyond such restriction. It is neither desirable nor feasible to present the technical details of this model here; instead, this section focuses on the logistic regression model with an interaction term of categorical attributes, as this is the situation most relevant to the study of intersectionality.

Before introducing the logistic regression model, it is worth pointing out that if the response variable as well as the explanatory variables are all categorical, then the data could be presented with a contingency table, the situation that was covered in Chapter 4. So why don't we analyse the data in a contingency table without constructing a logistic regression model? It is certainly useful to study the contingency table as a preliminary analysis, but the logistic regression model offers more benefits. For example, the logistic regression model could predict the probability that each case takes a particular value of the response variable, something the analysis of a contingency table will not do. Additionally, the model is much more flexible than the table in terms of including the explanatory variables; for example, a logistic regression model could include a metrical covariate, which is impossible for a contingency table.

Categorical variables can be classified into three types: binary, multi-nominal and multi-ordinal. It is important to realize the differences between them because the researcher should choose the logistic regression model that is most suitable for a particular type of categorical response variable. Here, we focus on the simple situation in which the response variable is binary.

Suppose the response variable is whether an employee has been promoted at work after working for a certain period of time, and we are also interested in the intersectional effect of two categorical attributes, gender and race. An important difference between a logistic regression model and an ordinary linear regression model is that we cannot directly put our response variable at the left-hand side of the model, because it has only two values (binary), while the right-hand side will predict many values that are very different from these values. To avoid this problem, statisticians have found it useful to take a special transformation of the binary response variable as the new response variable, which is the natural logarithm of odds. Explanation for some details is in order here.

First, given the response variable takes two possible values, 1 and 0, and let π be the probability that it takes the value of 1.

Next, the odds that the response variable takes the value of 1 will be $\dfrac{\pi}{1-\pi}$.

Now we take the natural logarithm of the odds as the response variable in the model:

$$\log_e \frac{\pi}{1-\pi} = \alpha + \beta_1 \text{Gender} + \beta_2 \text{Race} + \beta_3 \left(\text{Gender*Race} \right) + \varepsilon$$

The left-hand side is usually written as $\ln \dfrac{\pi}{1-\pi}$ and referred to as 'the logit', a transformation that helps us circumscribe the problems due to the binary nature of the original response variable, because this new response variable can take many values, either negative or positive, and it could have a relatively normal distribution as well. However, this smart transformation has a catch: it is much more difficult to interpret the meaning of this new response variable than to interpret the original response variable – the natural logarithm of odds simply has no clear intuitive meaning. One solution is to change the right-hand side into either the odds or the probability. If the reader knows the algebraic relations of logarithm and exponentials, then the following equations would come as no surprise. If we use the odds as the response variable, the model becomes:

$$\frac{\pi}{1-\pi} = e^{\alpha + \beta_1 \text{Gender} + \beta_2 \text{Race} + \beta_3 (\text{Gender}^*\text{Race}) + \varepsilon} = e^{\alpha} \times e^{\beta_1 \text{Gender}} \times e^{\beta_2 \text{Race}} \times e^{\beta_3 (\text{Gender}^*\text{Race})} \times e^{\varepsilon}$$

It is important to note that the effects of the explanatory variables, including the interaction (intersectional) effect, are now multiplied rather than summed as they are in ordinary linear regression models. That is, the interaction effect is a multiplying factor, not an effect added to the other individual effects. Once this is taken into the interpretation of the intersection or intersection effect, the rest is about the same as the interpretation discussed above.

Sometimes, it may be desirable to take one step further by taking the probability π as the response variable:

$$\pi = \frac{e^{\alpha + \beta_1 \text{Gender} + \beta_2 \text{Race} + \beta_3 (\text{Gender}^*\text{Race}) + \varepsilon}}{1 + e^{\alpha + \beta_1 \text{Gender} + \beta_2 \text{Race} + \beta_3 (\text{Gender}^*\text{Race}) + \varepsilon}}$$

The purpose of this equation is to make predictions about the probabilities that the original response variable takes the value of 1, so the interaction term is only part of the prediction function. These transformations are mathematically equivalent, but the researcher may choose one of them out of theoretical or substantive considerations.

6.4.3 Two technical expansions

Finally, two technical expansions of the simple ANOVA model are worth mentioning. Of the two, the expansion on the response variable is perhaps more important than the other on the inclusion of more explanatory variables. So far, the models we have discussed have only one response variable, which is either the original one or a transformation of the original. In some situations in social science research, there may be two or more response variables, which measure the same concept repeatedly either at different times or for different aspects; therefore, they are called 'repeated measures', such as political interest, political trust, loneliness, etc. For example, in the European Social Survey, the concept of 'social trust' is measured with following three questions:

- 'Generally speaking, would you say that most people can be trusted, or that you can't be too careful in dealing with people?'
- 'Do you think that most people would try to take advantage of you if they got the chance, or would they try to be fair?'
- 'Would you say that most of the time people try to be helpful or that they are mostly looking out for themselves?'

As they are all about social trust, they should be modelled together as response variables in the same model. In statistics, methods for analysing this kind of variables are referred to as 'multivariate statistics'. The requirements for these variables are about the same as for the single response variable in an ordinary linear regression model; that is, they are supposed to be metrical with a normal distribution. If the predictor side remains the same with two or more categorical attributes, then substantively the question we want to answer is whether people at the intersection of two more social categories have been disadvantaged in terms of several measures at the same time. A statistical benefit of analysing these response variables in a single model is the efficient use of the data. The researcher may prefer to combine the values of these variables into a single variable, which is fine as long as these variables are found to be sufficiently correlated with each other. One statistic that has been widely used for determining whether the variables are 'sufficiently' correlated is the Cronbach's alpha; a value of more than 0.8 is usually taken as sufficient support for combining the variables into a single indicator.

The other expansion of the simple ANOVA model is to add one or more explanatory variables into the model. As the interested categorical variables should already be in the model, the added variables are supposed to be metrical, such as age in years, income, BMI, etc. I would suggest that the term 'control variables' be avoided for these variables, because nothing was controlled when our data were collected from observational studies; the word 'covariate' is more appropriate. The purpose of adding such variables into an ANOVA model is to increase the 'robustness' of the model; that is, we may want to examine whether the interaction or intersection effect of the categorical attributes remains about the same when we consider an additional variable. The researcher, however, should provide a theoretical reason for doing so.

6.5 Assumptions, limitations and cautions

One statistical method or model is more preferable than another not because it is mathematically more sophisticated, but because it suits the purpose of study. As we have seen in this chapter, a mathematically more sophisticated model may become less interpretable, which makes it actually less preferable. All of the methods introduced in this chapter have assumptions that may be difficult to satisfy, which limit their use in the practice of social science research.

For ANOVA models, the response variable is assumed to be metrical and has an approximately normal distribution, a condition or assumption that is not very easy to uphold as such variables are the exception rather than the norm in data of social reality. The reason that the distribution is expected to be normal is because we compare the means across groups, and it is only sensible to use the mean as the statistic for describing the centre of the data when the distribution is at least roughly normal; otherwise, we should use the median as the statistic for the centre. Essentially, ANOVA models are methods for comparing group means, but if so, why are they called 'analysis of variance', not 'analysis of means'? To answer this question leads us to another assumption of these models – in order for our comparisons of the means to be fair, the variances of the response variable across the groups should be about the same as well; otherwise, if some groups have about the same mean but very different variances, then it is misleading simply to focus on the mean alone. A carefully conducted statistical analysis always considers both the centre and the spread of the distribution at the same time. When conducting ANOVA analysis, researchers are expected to check whether the group variances are about the same.

The fundamental logic of ANOVA analysis is to compare two types of means, the 'between-group means' and the 'within-group means', and to see which one is relatively bigger than the other. If they are about the same, then group membership does not matter – in other words, it is statistically insignificant. Note that group membership is conceptually about the same as set-membership in QCA and set-theoretic methods. In this sense, interaction terms in ANOVA models are simultaneous set memberships, representing intersectional groups of interest to the study of intersectionality. The important difference is that the interaction term in ANOVA and other regression models tend to focus on the overall interaction effect, and I think they should learn from QCA and set-theoretic methods to pay serious attention to the effect of each specific cross-classified intersectional group. It is only when we discover how each intersectional group is associated with the response variable that we have studied the interaction or intersection effect properly. Statistical methods such as Bonferroni confidence intervals are very useful for this purpose; unfortunately, they are not always used.

It is also worth pointing out that both the ANOVA and the set-theoretic methods focus on the between-group differences rather than the within group differences. Individual differences within any particular group are treated as 'errors', which are often ignored. Whilst this is a justifiable choice, researchers may want to move on to look into these within-group differences should there be a good reason for it. This is why it will not help simply to add more interaction terms in regression models – the interaction terms are only useful for comparing groups but not useful for determining who within a group will be discriminated against or disadvantaged – it is assumed that members of the same group are homogeneous. If only a proportion of people within an intersectional group are disadvantaged, then a regression model with interaction terms will not be able to inform us. As Green et al. aptly pointed out, 'While inter-categorical intersectionality is a useful tool for studying differences between populations, regression models with numerous interaction terms inherently overlook the heterogeneity of risk that remains within these identities' (2017, p. 214).

Finally, when the intersectional groups are compared, it is assumed that they are about the same size in terms of the number of cases. Again, in real-world research this is rarely the case. As we learnt from the discussion of QCA and set-theoretic methods, the lack of diversity is normal in cross-set or intersectional groups, which threatens the comparability of the group means or any other response variable. It is advisable to check the sample sizes across the intersectional groups so that at least the information is made available with caution.

6.6 Suggested readings and questions for discussion

Before learning the technical details of the methods covered in this chapter, in fact all statistical methods for the purpose of using them properly in social science research, it is important to ask and answer two questions:

1. Do the statistical models or methods fit the situation of the research target? In other words, would the results from using these methods and models serve the purposes of the research? In the context of this chapter, the more specific question is: would the analysis of interaction terms in GLRM reveal any effect of intersectional attributes on the interested outcome (a certain form of discrimination or injustice)? In what sense could we give a positive answer?

2. Are the data ready for conducting the analysis with the methods and models? A positive answer is needed because most statistical models and methods require that the data be in a certain form. More specifically for ANOVA, the response or target variable should be a metrical variable with an approximately normal distribution, which are only two of the conditions (or assumptions) for conducting ANOVA. At the same time, do the categorical explanatory variables serve the theoretical purposes?

Students would benefit from considering these questions by analysing a specific issue of intersectionality that they are familiar with.

Both ANOVA and logistic regression models are topics covered in most statistics textbooks, although special monographs about each method are available as well. In at least two papers, Rosnow and Rosenthal (1989, 1991) argued against the comparison of cell means as a way of studying interaction effects. They then expanded their argument with more details of illustration in several chapters of their textbook (Rosenthal & Rosnow, 2008). Almost at the same time or perhaps a little later, Jaccard and his colleagues published a series of short books, each focusing on the study of interaction effect in a special context or modelling situation; see Jaccard, Turrisi and Wan (1990), Jaccard and Wan (1996), Jaccard (1998) and Jaccard (2001), all in the Sage series Quantitative Applications in the Social Sciences. The most recent and technically more comprehensive treatment of interaction effects is by Robert L. Kaufman (2019). Whilst Kaufman's work has several merits, such as mathematical rigour, new ways of presenting and examining the interaction effects, and even a new Stata package for plotting the interaction effects, it appears to follow Jaccard's strategy of having a focal variable and studying its varying effect on one or more moderating variables, which, as I pointed out above, could pose difficulties to interpretation.

7

ANALYSING INTERSECTIONALITY WITH MULTILEVEL MODELS

7.1 Overview and objectives

The statistical models to be introduced in this chapter are a direct response to the issue of interaction terms discussed in the previous one. The overall idea of the methods introduced in the previous chapter is to represent and analyse intersectionality as interaction terms in generalized linear regression models, although one must be careful of choosing the appropriate models for the specific level of measurement of the variables. As we saw previously, the interest of intersectionality in social, demographic and other attributes means that these models are expected to formally represent the effects of cross-classifications of these attributes on a particular form of disadvantage or disenfranchisement. While this makes sense in principle, such models will soon run into a practical difficulty that other methods such as QCA and set-theoretic methods encountered as well: even for a relatively small number of variables and each variable having only a small number of categories, the number of possible intersectional groups, as the multiplication of the numbers of these categories, will easily reach a very large number, thereby stretching the data thin at least for some of the intersectional groups. For example, with five variables (socio-demographic attributes) and each having only two categories, there will be $2^5 = 32$ intersectional groups; if each variable has three categories, the number of intersectional groups will increase dramatically to $3^5 = 243$! To represent each of these groups as an interaction term in a regression model, we will need to include a very large number of dummy variables. As each dummy variable will have a corresponding regression coefficient, the model will struggle to estimate so many coefficients (or parameters) at the same time, very likely with little or even no data for some of them. As we shall see below, analysing intersectionality with interaction terms has other limitations as well.

To overcome these limitations, some statisticians and methodologists have come up with the idea of representing intersectional groups as units at a higher level; that is, higher than the individuals that are usually the units of data collection in most surveys of human participants. This is a perfect example of using an 'old' method to deal with a new problem – statistical methods and models for analysing data at more than one level have been established and developed during the past decades, but only quite recently have researchers started to realize their usefulness for analysing a large number of intersectional groups. If you are familiar with multilevel (or hierarchical) modelling, then all you need to do in order to use such models for analysing intersectionality is to create a new variable 'intersectional group' whose values will be the cross-classifications of the interested attributes. However, as such models are technically more sophisticated than those in an introductory statistics course, and for the sake of smoothing the introduction of more sophisticated models, I will explain what multilevel data and multilevel models are in the first section. Then we move on to the strategy of turning individual-level data into two-level data with intersectional groups as the higher-level units, and I will explain and discuss the benefits for doing so. Please note, however, that the objective of this chapter is to explain the logic of applying multilevel models for the purpose of analysing intersectionality, not to explain the technical details of multilevel modelling; these mathematical details are extensively covered in many other books, and the reader can find some suggested readings at the end of this chapter. After explaining the idea and the logic of these models, I will reflect on the conditions under which such models are to be used fruitfully for the purpose of analysing intersectionality.

7.2 Multilevel data and models

At the beginning of Chapter 5 I used a table (Table 5.1) as a generic example of the data matrix – that is, a table with cases as rows and variables as columns; therefore, the data in each cell represents the value that a particular case takes for a particular variable. Although such a dataset could be very large with up to tens of thousands of rows (cases) and hundreds of columns (variables), it is actually a rather simple form of data because all of the cases are at the same level; for example, they are all different individual persons. Obviously, in real life these individuals belong to – or are 'nested in' – some geographical areas, such as districts or counties, or some organizations, such as schools, universities or commercial companies. When we want to include the information about these areas or organizations in our data and to study whether they make any difference to our analysis at the individual level, both the data and the analysis become a bit more complicated than the analysis of data at only one level, as we covered in the previous chapters. As these areas or organizations usually contain a large number of individuals, they are units at a level higher than the individuals. The most widely used example of multilevel data is that students are the lowest-level units who belong to classes, units of a higher level, which in turn belong to schools or universities, units of an even higher level. Obviously, data with more levels are more complicated than data with fewer levels, but it is not obvious how data collected at different levels are to be analysed in the same model. Since the objective of this chapter is to explain the basic ideas and logic, it is sufficient for us to focus on data that have only two levels.

First of all, let's take a look at what multilevel data look like. When we would like to include higher-level units in our data, it is intuitively tempting to simply add a variable to indicate whether a case belongs to a particular higher-level unit or not. For example, suppose

Table 7.1a An example of 'wide' multilevel data: adding membership of higher-level unit

	Variable 1	Variable 2	Variable 3	Variable 4	University 1	University 2	...
Student 1	...	...	...	...	1	0	0
Student 2	...	...	...	...	1	...	...
Student 3	...	...	...	...	0	1	0
Student 4	...	...	...	...	0	1	0
...	...	...	...	...	...	...	...

the data were collected on the students of 20 universities, then we could add 20 variables after the other variables, one for each university; to illustrate, the following table includes only two of them.

Suppose each student studies only at one university, coded as 1 (and 0 being not studying at that university), then there should be a 1 for only one of the 20 universities in each row; for example, the first two students are members of the first university, the next two students are members of the second university, and so on. The above way of recording the data is the 'wide' format because we add memberships of the higher-level units as variables.

An alternative way of recording the same data is to keep the universities as rows – that is, cases rather than variables. If we do so, we must make it clear which student's value it is for each variable; in other words, there will be several variables for the same student.

Clearly, neither is an efficient way of storing the data: the first wastes a lot of space for keeping the 0s, and the second would be 'very wide' if there were many students (or cases) in each higher-level unit (here, university).

A more efficient format is to have only one variable for recording the membership of any higher-level unit, as shown in Table 7.2.

This is usually referred to as the 'long' form of multilevel data, which is also the preferred, sometimes even required, format for storing multilevel data before the data are analysed. We can also add variables that describe the higher-level units, such as the type of university (for example, private = 0 vs public = 1, shown in the last column in Table 7.2), to the dataset; as all units of the lower level share the same attribute of their higher-level unit, the values of that variable are all the same for all lower-level units of the same higher-level unit.

The addition of a higher-level unit to the dataset has important implications for how we represent and analyse the data. First of all, the higher-level units need to be reflected in the

Table 7.1b An example of 'wide' multilevel data: higher-level units as cases

Higher-level units	Variable 1 for Student 1	Variable 2 for Student 1	Variable 1 for Student 2	Variable 2 for Student 2	...
University 1	...	...	...	...	0
University 2	...	...	...	...	...
University 3	...	...	...	...	0
University 4	...	...	...	...	0
...	...	...	...	...	...

Table 7.2 An example of multilevel data (the long format)

Higher level	Lower level	Variable 1	Variable 2	Variable 3	Public or private?
University 1	Student 1	...	...	...	1
University 1	Student 2	...	...	...	1
University 2	Student 3	...	...	...	0
University 2	Student 4	...	...	...	0
...	...	...	...	...	...

notations of our statistical models. Supposing our response variable Y is a metrical variable which also has an approximately normal distribution, it would be sensible to use the mean of Y as an estimate of the value of Y if we do not include any predictor X in the model; in other words, the mean of Y should be our best guess of Y's value if we do not have any other information. But clearly each value of Y is not the same as its mean, so there is a difference between each observed value and the predicted mean, which is usually called 'the error term' in statistics. As a result, this simplest model could be represented with the following equation:

$$Y_i = \beta_0 + \varepsilon_i$$

Note that both Y and the error term ε (Epsilon) have a subscript i which is a convenient indicator of each individual case in the dataset; for example, if the sample size of a dataset n is 2000, then i will be any number between 1 and 2000. In contrast, the mean of Y, represented here by β_0, does not have an i because there is only one mean. We can use any other letter to represent the mean and here we put a 0 as its subscript because we shall add more βs later to the model. Essentially, this model says that the value of Y could be represented as its mean plus an error, which is the difference between an observed value and the mean. This may sound too obvious to be useful, but as with any axiom it is useful as a starting point.

The i represents only the individuals as the lowest-level units. If the data contain information about higher-level units, how should we include them in the model? The answer is to add another indicator for the higher-level units, and it is common practice to use j, as shown below:

$$Y_{ij} = \beta_{0j} + \varepsilon_{ij}$$

In this equation, the values of Y are indexed by both an individual number (i) and a higher-level unit number (j), so the meaning of i has changed – it is not a number between 1 and the sample size anymore but a number between 1 and the sample size of its higher-level unit. For example, Y_{23} means the value of Y for the second case in the third higher-level unit, and its corresponding error term is ε_{23}, which is the difference between the observed value of Y_{23} and β_{03}, the mean of the third higher-level unit. It is important to note that now β_0 has a subscript as well – the j tells us that each higher-level unit has its own mean; for example, β_{03} is the mean of the third higher-level unit. In essence, this model says that the value of the response variable could be estimated with the group mean of each higher-level unit plus a certain error term.

The first model above has only one (the lowest) level, and the second has two levels (the individual and a higher level), so if we could put them together, then we would have a multilevel model. Whilst the first model uses the total (or grand) mean β_0 and the second model uses the group mean β_{0j}, the two can actually be connected with the following equation:

$$\beta_{0j} = \beta_{00} + \mu_{0j}$$

This model says that a group mean (β_{0j}) can be represented as the sum of the total (grand) mean (β_{00}) plus an error (μ_{0j}). Here, we use β_{00} instead of β_0 simply to keep two subscripts for each term. I have purposefully used these simplest models as I hope the reader could appreciate the idea of multilevel models without getting distracted with the notations.

It is important to note two things in what we have done so far. First, before we consider the model of a higher level, we used the model $Y_i = \beta_0 + \varepsilon_i$, which uses a *fixed* number β_0 to make an estimate of Y's value. After we consider the model at a higher level, $Y_{ij} = \beta_{0j} + \varepsilon_{ij}$, we do not use one number anymore; instead, we use a different number for each higher-level unit. In other words, the key regression coefficient in the model has changed from a fixed parameter to a *varying* one. Conceptually, this is a major and significant shift that the reader should pay attention to.

Second, while making the coefficient depend on the higher-level unit, we also bring in another source of error, μ_{0j}, which represents the *random* difference between the mean of each higher-level unit and the grand mean. When we put the two models together by bringing $\beta_{0j} = \beta_{00} + \mu_{0j}$ into $Y_{ij} = \beta_{0j} + \varepsilon_{ij}$, we will have one model that includes two error terms:

$$Y_{ij} = \beta_{00} + \mu_{0j} + \varepsilon_{ij}$$

In words, this model says that the value of Y could be estimated with the total (grand) mean plus the error term at the group level and another error term at the individual level. It is fine to use either two shorter equations or one slightly longer equation to represent the idea, but it is important to note that the estimation of the response variable's value is now made with information at two levels. Because the total (grand) mean is a fixed number, the main objective of the above multilevel model is to compare the variance of the higher-level error term μ_{0j}, usually written as $\sigma^2_{\mu_{0j}}$, with the variance of the lower level error term ε_{ij}, usually written as $\sigma^2_{\mu_{ij}}$, because the result of such a comparison will indicate whether the higher-level units make any difference, in addition to the lower-level information, to the estimation of the response variable's value. A particular statistic is usually calculated to represent such a comparison; that is, the intra-class-coefficient (ICC), usually represented by the Greek letter ρ:

$$\rho = \frac{\sigma^2_{\mu_{0j}}}{\sigma^2_{\mu_{0j}} + \sigma^2_{\mu_{ij}}}$$

For those who would prefer words to Greek letters or numbers, we could write this equation in words:

$$\text{ICC} = \frac{\text{variance between higher level units}}{\text{total variance}}$$

The rationale of ICC is very similar to the equation of the F-test in ANOVA – if the variance between the higher-level units counts as a 'significant' percentage of the total variance, then we have evidence for effect of the higher-level units; in other words, the higher-level units make a significant difference in terms of explaining the response variable's variation. Then we need to answer the following question: how high does the percentage have to be in order for us to make such a claim? As with other statistical procedures and decisions, there is no consensus, only a widely adopted convention or threshold; for example, some researchers would prefer the ICC to be at least 5% while others prefer 10%. The rule of thumb is to report your ICC so that your readers are well informed about how you have made your decision. We shall come back to this issue after linking this measure to the analysis of intersectionality.

We could build more complicated models by adding predictors and their coefficients to the above simple models. For example, we can add one predictor to the model of the higher-level units so that we could better estimate the group mean of each higher-level unit, as shown below:

$$\beta_{0j} = \beta_{00} + \beta_{01}W_j + \mu_{0j}$$

In this model, W is a predictor at the higher level, and we assume that all higher levels share the same coefficient β_{01}; if there is an even higher level that affects β_{01}, then we could make it randomly varying across the units at a third level.

Or, we may want to add a predictor to the model at the lower level:

$$Y_{ij} = \beta_{0j} + \beta_{1j}X_j + \varepsilon_{ij}$$

Here we need to decide whether each of the two regression coefficients is to be predicted by a group mean and an error term or by an additional predictor as well. The researchers must specify the components of the models in terms of being fixed or random; that is, whether a particular coefficient is assumed to be fixed or to be treated as randomly varying across the higher-level units with an error term. The details of model specification depend on the objectives of each study, which are not the concern of this book, as it is sufficient for us to learn how to demonstrate the higher-level effect.

On the other hand, the meaning of 'random' vs 'fixed' effects could be confusing for students and people without much training in more advanced statistics, so it is useful to explain what these words mean here. Essentially, in linear regression models, the word 'fixed' means 'the same'; therefore, 'fixed-effects' refers to the effects that are the same for all the cases under study. As mentioned previously in this chapter, if a statistical model is assumed to be valid for all of the cases under study, then the effects of the predictors in the model are 'fixed'. In contrast, if the effects are assumed to change from one higher-level unit to another, then the effects are specified as 'varying randomly', hence 'random effects'. Because more than one level of data is required in order for any effect to vary, an effect cannot change 'randomly' if there is only one level in the data; therefore, it is only meaningful to talk about 'random effects' models for multilevel (or longitudinal) data. In this sense, longitudinal data are a special form of multilevel data, with the individuals being the higher-level units whilst the values taken at different time points on the same individual are the lower-level units; therefore, an effect could vary randomly across individuals. That said, the reverse is not necessarily true – a dataset with multiple levels does *not necessarily* require a multilevel model, because there may be little evidence for the 'clustering' effect of the higher-level units; if so, a single-level model would be sufficient. As Garson explains in his recent textbook on multilevel modelling:

> Fixed effects refer to effects in the level 1 regression model. Fixed effects may be associated with predictors at any level. Random effects refer to the effects of clustering of the outcome variable within categorical levels of a clustering variable which defines a level in a multilevel model. Random effects are used to adjust estimates for the intercept of the level 1 outcome variable or slope (b) coefficients of one or more predictor variables. The same variable may be both a fixed effect (it is a predictor in the level 1 regression model) and a random effect (its slope estimates are conditioned by random effects of the grouping variable). (2019, p. 16)

Moreover, when a model contains several higher-level coefficients, the researcher may decide which coefficient's effect is either fixed or random by drawing on theories or substantive knowledge; usually multilevel models contain both fixed and random effects, and if so these models are 'mixed-effects' models.

7.3 Turning intersectional groups into higher-level units

Conceptually, the core idea of the multilevel approach to studying intersectionality is very simple: turn the intersectional groups into the units at a higher level and then analyse the data with multilevel models. To illustrate, suppose we would like to include four attributes, sex (male, female), age (young, middle-aged, old), class (lower, middle, upper) and race (White, minority); there will be $2 \times 3 \times 3 \times 2 = 36$ intersectional groups.[1] (Again, a caveat is needed here for the simplified classification of sex which is widely accepted now to be not as simple as a binary (male or female) variable.) Then we create a new variable whose values include these 36 groups. Assuming each individual belongs to one and only one intersectional group, the data could be presented in the form of Table 3.

It should be clear immediately that this is a very efficient way of representing and subsequently analysing intersectional effects – in this particular example, rather than including and analysing 36 separate variables in a model, we only need to incorporate *one new* variable in our analysis. The larger the number of intersectional groups, the more efficient this strategy will be, if we do not have to worry about the sample size for each group. The intersectional groups are not variables anymore; rather, they become the values of only one variable. As it is much easier for a statistical model to handle a variable with many values than to estimate the coefficients of many variables, turning intersectional groups into higher-level units is a technically efficient solution to the multiplicative increase of the number of intersectional groups.

The literature on this methodological innovation suggests that although Juan Merlo, a Swedish social epidemiologist, and others already proposed to use multilevel models to include contextual as well individual factors in the area of public health at the beginning of this century (Merlo, 2003; Merlo et al., 2004, 2005, 2006), it was Clare Evans who, in her PhD thesis (2015) at Harvard University, initially came up with the idea of turning intersectional groups as higher-level units so that multilevel models could be used. Then as either the lead

Table 7.3 Intersectional group membership as a new variable

Higher level	Lower level	Variable 1	Variable 2	Variable 3	Variable 4	...
Intersectional group 1	Person 1	...	...	...	...	...
Intersectional group 1	Person 2	...	...	...	...	...
...	...	...	...	...	...	
Intersectional group 2	Person 1	...	...	...	...	...
Intersectional group 2	Person 2	...	...	...	...	...
...	...	...	...	...	...	...
Intersectional group 36	Person 1	...	...	...	...	...
Intersectional group 36	Person 2	...	...	...	...	...
Intersectional group 36	...	...	...	...	...	...

or the sole author, she published a few papers in the journal *Social Science & Medicine* (Evans, 2019; Evans et al., 2018, 2020), explaining this approach and illustrating it with an empirical study. Others have then made contributions to this development as well (Axelsson Fisk et al., 2018; Green et al., 2017; Jones et al., 2016; Merlo, 2018; Wemrell et al., 2017).

Clearly, this is a statistical solution to a statistical problem, but it has important conceptual and theoretical implications for the study of intersectionality as well. In the rest of this section, I will explain the statistical case for adopting this approach and reflect on the conceptual and theoretical implications in the next. Here, since Evans and others have developed the multilevel approach to studying intersectionality as a solution to overcoming the limitations that single-level models have suffered from, let's learn about these limitations and understand why the multilevel modelling approach makes sense.

The first and perhaps the most important limitation of the single-level (or conventional) models is the lack of 'scalability', an issue we touched on a few times earlier, albeit briefly; that is, such models find it very difficult or at least cumbersome to include many parameters for the interaction terms in a single model. When the number of interactional groups is small, as we saw in the examples in the previous chapters, it is not that hard for a single-level model to include them as intersection terms. However, when either the number of attributes that are of great interest from the intersectional perspective or the number of each attribute's categories increases even moderately, the total number of intersectional groups will increase multiplicatively. As we saw in the above example, with only four variables of attributes, each of the three having three values and one having two values, we need to include 35 dummy variables (one for each group and the last when all these dummy variables equal 0). In their study with the body mass index (BMI) as the response variable, Evans et al. (2018) included five socio-demographic attributes, but because three of them have four categories, the total number of intersectional groups quickly reaches a very large number:

1. Gender (two categories: male and female)[2]
2. Race/ethnicity (three categories: (1) White, not Hispanic or Latino, (2) Black, not Hispanic or Latino, and (3) Hispanic or Latino)
3. Education (four categories: (1) less than high school, (2) completed high school (or equivalency), (3) some college no degree, (4) college degree or more)

4. Income (four categories: low income, low-middle income, high-middle income and high income)
5. Age (four categories: (1) 18–29 years, (2) 30–44 years, (3) 45–59 years, (4) 60 years and older).

Therefore, the number of intersectional groups is:

$$2 \times 3 \times 4 \times 4 \times 4 = 384.$$

It is truly difficult to imagine a statistical model with 384 predictors or parameters as the *main* effects. After these intersectional groups are transformed into units at a higher level, the number of dichotomous dummy variables representing the *main* effects decreases to 12, because for each variable the number of dummy variables is the number of its categories minus 1. Therefore, in the study by Evans et al. (2018), the total number of dummy variables needed is:

$$(2-1)+(3-1)+(4-1)+(4-1)-(4-1) = 1+2+3+3+3 = 12.$$

Had we used interaction terms at the individual level, our model would have had to include 384 – 1 = 383 main effect terms! By putting individuals into higher-level intersectional units, there is no need to include the interaction terms anymore as *these higher-level units are intersections*, not the variables at the lowest level anymore. Therefore, the large number of groups has become much less of an issue, at least technically. I said 'much less' purposefully – while I certainly accept that it is very smart to turn the large number of intersectional groups from variables to values of one variable, which clearly has substantially increased the scalability of intersectional groups, I do not think such transformation has entirely resolved the issue. I will come to the conceptual aspect of this issue in the next section.

Here, let's discuss two further issues about this methodological innovation. The first is both a statistical as well as a conceptual issue, which relates to the difference between intersectional groups and other higher-level units in multilevel models. Starting with the statistical aspect, note that one important difference between intersectional groups and other 'natural' higher-level units such as classes or schools is that intersectional groups are *exhaustive*, while schools and classes are (or expected to be) usually a random sample drawn from a large population. This is because intersectional groups are *analytical* units created by cross-classifying the categories of a number of variables; as a result, they do not actually 'exist' in social reality. In contrast, classes, schools, companies, neighbourhoods, areas, cities or other real-world entities already existed before a study involving these units was conducted. Usually these 'natural' units have existed in large numbers, and it is both desirable and necessary to draw a random sample of these units rather than including all of them in a study. In this sense, it is meaningful, sometimes even essential, to specify the sample size not only of the lowest-level units (individual persons in most social science studies) but of the higher-level units as well; that is, researchers are expected to ensure that the higher-level units are selected as elements of a random sample and of a sufficiently large size (Hox et al., 2017).

In contrast, sampling is meaningless for intersectional groups because they come as an exhaustive list of all possible units, all of which the researcher is obliged to analyse; in other words, they are, by definition, the population. When the number of intersectional groups, or the population size, turns out to be a very large number, such as 384 in the study by Evans et al. (2018), we may wonder whether we could draw a random sample from these units. Yet is it really sensible, both conceptually and statistically speaking, to do so? Would it be meaningful to draw 'a random sample of intersectional groups'? Probably not, because the intersectional groups are not equally important in the context of a particular study. In fact, it would be actually more meaningful to focus on a 'non-random' sample of intersectional groups; that is, to select certain intersectional groups out of theoretical or substantive considerations. It is perhaps for this reason that as far as I am aware, existing studies include *all* possible intersectional groups as higher-level units without attempting to select a 'sample' from them, because the sensible rationale of making such a selection is simply unavailable.

It is worth noting two consequences of including all possible intersectional groups. One is the difficulties in making any statistical inferences and conducting statistical analysis at the higher level. Because the intersectional groups come as a population, it is not meaningful anymore to talk about inferential statistics that could be used for inferring from an estimated statistic of a random sample to the corresponding value of the population. In the meantime, while it is usually useful to include variables of the higher-level units in multilevel models, for example the type of school, it is rather difficult to consider what variables could be included that describe the intersectional groups, as any of such variables should have already been considered when selecting the variables that were used for creating the intersectional groups – if school type is an important attribute of schools as higher-level units, then the type of school should have been used for creating the intersectional groups.

In the end, whilst the multilevel approach is successful in improving the scalability of analysis, as Evans et al. admitted (2018, p. 71), this approach remains *exploratory* – it is more useful for *exploring* the *overall* clustering effect of the possible intersectional groups than for confirming any hypothesis or theory that focuses on *particular* groups or other attributes of these groups.

Another important technical benefit of turning intersectional groups into higher-level units is that multilevel models could incorporate the sample size of each intersectional group in the models, which is particularly useful when some of the group sizes are very small. Again, this is both a statistical and a substantive issue. To focus on the statistical aspect of this issue here, we already encountered this problem previously when we were studying QCA and the set-theoretic methods – recall the 'lack of diversity' in terms of the distribution of cases across intersectional set-memberships. Similarly, when we have a large number of intersectional groups, it is highly likely that there will be very few cases in some of these groups. In their study, Evans and her colleagues analysed the data collected from the second wave of the National Epidemiologic Survey on Alcohol and Related Conditions (NESARC) in 2004–2005. Even though the final sample size for analysis, 32,788, is very large, 2 of the 384 intersectional groups have no cases, less than 10% – that is, up to 38 groups – have fewer than 10 cases, and less than 20% (up to 56 groups) have fewer than 20 cases. What do we make of these numbers? Statistically, these numbers do not appear to be high, especially in light of the very large number of intersectional groups, and we shall come to the implications for our substantive analysis in the next section. Here, let's concentrate on the statistical solution to the issue.

If we still analyse intersectionality with interaction terms with single-level regression models, and if some intersectional groups have very small numbers of cases, then the estimated values of regression coefficients will be unstable and unreliable, because the smaller sizes will lead to bigger standard errors, or it would be much easier for one or two extreme case values to influence the estimation. The idea of a statistical solution is to make these small intersectional groups exercise less influence on the estimation of coefficients by attaching a weight to the estimation (Evans et al., 2018, p. 67):

$$w_j = \frac{\sigma^2_{strata}}{\sigma^2_{strata} + (\sigma^2_{e0} / n_j)}$$

The word 'strata' in this equation refers to the intersectional groups, and σ^2_{e0} is the variance of the individual level error terms. Given the weight defined as this, when the size of the intersectional group, n_j, decreases, σ^2_{e0} / n_j will increase, which will make the whole denominator, $\sigma^2_{strata} + (\sigma^2_{e0} / n_j)$, increase, and as a result, W_j will decrease. That is, the size of each intersectional group is related to the weight in a positive correlation; in other words, smaller intersectional groups will have a correspondingly smaller weight, and therefore will make a smaller contribution to the estimation of the coefficients because this weight will be used to estimate the higher-level regression coefficient:

$$\beta_{0j} = w_j\beta^*_{0j} + (1 - w_j)\beta_0$$

Here, β^*_{0j} is the estimated coefficient for an intersectional group based on the fixed-effects (or single-level) model, and β_0 is the grand mean for all levels. As W_j is attached to β^*_{0j}, a smaller weight for a small intersectional group will reduce the contribution of β^*_{0j} to the calculation of β_{0j}. In the meantime, $1 - W_j$ will become bigger when W_j is smaller, and as $1 - W_j$ is attached to β_0, β_0 will make a bigger contribution to the estimation of β_{0j}. All in all, this whole process will almost literally generate a more 'balanced' estimation of regression coefficients given a particular size of intersectional group. Intersectional groups with a very small number of cases will play a correspondingly less influential role in the modelling process.

The last benefit of the multilevel modelling approach to studying intersectionality that Evans et al. (2018) have argued for is the ease of interpreting the results. Presumably, it should be easier to interpret the meaning of the effects of higher-level units than to interpret the meaning of a large number of parameters, but this is more a conceptual than a statistical issue, so let's discuss it in the next section.

7.4 Reflections on conceptual and theoretical implications

To start, it is worth highlighting the core idea of the multilevel approach introduced in the previous section: by recoding a large number of intersectional groups into the units at a higher level, we could capitalize on the power of multilevel models and avoid a large number of interaction terms in a single-level model. The question is: does this statistical solution, which is admittedly smart and helpful, make sense conceptually and theoretically as well? We can break down this relatively general question into a few more specific ones. The first is whether it makes sense to treat intersectional groups as higher-level units. I discussed the question in the previous section in relation to the distinction between a sample and a population; now let's move on to its conceptual aspect. The creation of multilevel models was motivated by the need to incorporate clustering or nesting relationships between the cases (Goldstein, 2011; Raudenbush & Bryk, 2001). This is why the most typical multilevel data come from the study of education – pupils are clustered in classes that in turn are clustered in schools which then are clustered in geographical areas, etc. Note that here the higher-level units – classes, schools, and areas – are pre-existing social organizations. It is meaningful to treat classes, schools, areas or other aggregate units as higher-level units – they are not simply labels, because valuable resources are distributed across these social units by following certain processes and mechanisms that are responsible for the fact that people of different units have different life experiences. This 'clustering effect' means that elements of the same higher-level unit are expected (or assumed) to be more homogeneous than the elements across all units.

In contrast, intersectional groups are higher-level units artificially created by researchers; they are analytical or 'man-made', not 'natural'. For this reason, the ground is much weaker for us to expect any clustering or nesting effect to exist among intersectional groups, as we do for classes or schools, which is exactly what theorists of intersectionality have attempted to argue. In the context of multilevel modelling, intersectionality as a theoretical approach would expect a very high level of homogeneity among members of the same intersectional group, because various rules, laws and institutions work together to 'interlock' individuals into different social locations or organizations. Consequently, applying multilevel models in the study of intersectionality is not simply a statistical task – it requires a strong theoretical case prior to statistical analysis; in other words, the hierarchical relationships among intersectional groups appear to be 'unnatural' and need to be established in the first place.

For the sake of illustration, let's consider only two attributes, gender and race, with each having only two simplified categories, making each individual belong to one of the following four intersectional groups: White man, White woman, Black man and Black woman. To study the effect of intersectionality, a multilevel dataset and model would include the individuals and these four intersectional groups, but note, however, that these groups belong to units at an even higher level, namely race and gender. When the focus of analysis is the effects of intersectional groups, these single factors are ignored as they are not intersectional; these factors should be included as units at an even higher level if we follow the multilevel way of organizing our data strictly. To exclude these factors from the data and the modelling process would mean that our models have missed some important information, which perhaps explains why, as we shall see below, intersectional groups can only explain a very small percentage of the response variable's variation.

And even if a certain level of clustering is found among some intersectional groups, it remains a task for researchers to be explicit about or to discover the reasons for such clustering effect. This brings us back to one of the most important questions for the study of intersectionality: what has made people of a certain intersectional group more (or less) disadvantaged than other groups? The answer cannot be simply that they carry a few socio-demographic attributes simultaneously; the simultaneous attributes themselves do not come automatically as an explanation for intersectional disadvantage. This is perhaps why advocates of intersectionality have repeatedly argued that intersectionality is not about identities, socio-demographic labels or attributes, but about the social processes and systems that are responsible for the discrimination and disenfranchisement experienced by people with these attributes. Despite the attempt that advocates of the multilevel approach have made to justify the value of this approach for intersectionality, the creation of intersectional groups as higher-level units offers little information about the *context or causes* of intersectional inequality; the hierarchical structure of the data itself offers no explanation. Like so many other terms in the social sciences, the word 'context' has become too ambiguous and elusive to be useful and meaningful. It is all too easy to call simultaneous memberships of intersectional groups 'contexts' or 'contextual factors', but we learn nothing from them about how and why the members have been deprived of certain rights, privileges or opportunities. For the word 'context' to be a useful and meaningful concept, it must tell us something about the social processes and arrangements through which some members of society are more likely to be disadvantaged than others. Researchers may not be able to incorporate these processes and systems empirically in their research, but if they seriously intend to keep their research aligned with the spirit of intersectionality, they are expected to identify and theorize the *mechanisms and processes* that are behind the clustering effect of intersectional groups. It is only when this is done that the creation of analytical intersectional groups could become a strategy useful for intersectionality. The creation and analysis of intersectional groups as higher-level units alone is not enough; such statistical manoeuvres must come with substantive understandings and explanations.

Besides the meaning of intersectional groups as higher-level units, another question relates to the large number of these groups, which has been claimed as a major benefit of following the multilevel approach. It is indeed true that with the use of multilevel models an original limitation of including a large number of interaction terms in regression models, which qualitative researchers often drew on to demonstrate the shortcoming of quantitative methods, has now been overcome. However, with the technical difficulty resolved, a new question has arisen: Is it really necessary to study so many intersectional groups? And if so, why? As we learnt from the first few chapters of this book, when intersectionality was initially being established by Black feminists as an approach to explaining and understanding social inequalities, the focus was on the theoretical and substantive arguments; empirically, the number of intersectional groups was restricted almost to the minimum, usually only four (Black men, Black women, White men and White women). Today, our enhanced computing ability to incorporate several hundred intersectional groups is indisputably a technical progress; in the meantime, however, we cannot help asking ourselves: why do we need to study so many groups? Early advocates of intersectionality had a good reason for focusing on Black women in relation to other racial and sexual groups – a number of cases demonstrated why and how Black women were deprived of certain privileges and opportunities, something we do not possess today in the context of the large number of intersectional groups. Our improved statistical ability has not come with the corresponding focus needed on identifying the intersectional groups who have been disadvantaged and why. Besides 'the limited diversity' as an issue for empirical investigations, our analysis remains completely exploratory and descriptive despite the employment of a technically more sophisticated tool. In their important study, Evans et al. (2018) did their best in identifying which among the 384 intersectional groups were particularly vulnerable to a high BMI score, but still they were only able to present some overall patterns while struggling to learn about specific groups, let alone explain why these groups suffered from BMI scores higher than others. The large number of intersectional groups remains overwhelming, perhaps not technically anymore, but in terms of interpretation and explanation. It should be clear by now that for the empirical research on intersectionality to move forward, we need not only sophisticated analytical tools but also theoretical guidance and substantive knowledge about specific intersectional groups. By no means, I must add, does this aim to dismiss the value of the multilevel approach – there is no doubt about the value of exploring the overall effect and pattern of a large number of intersectional groups.

My last reflection expands on a point briefly made previously: while accepting the statistical benefits of using the multilevel approach to studying intersectionality, how helpful is it for us to understand and explain intersectional inequality? As Evans and her colleagues admitted in their paper (2018), the key function of their approach is to *explore* any significant effects among the large number of intersectional groups (or strata, to use their own terminology). There is little doubt that the multilevel approach has fulfilled this function successfully – not only can we know the overall 'clustering' effect of intersectional groups, but we can also compare these groups in terms of their values on the response variable. Nevertheless, when researchers want to do more than explore these effects, the multilevel approach appears to be able to offer limited help. In a series of papers, Juan Merlo (see the citations in the next section and the References at the end of this book) developed an approach referred to as Multilevel Analysis of Individual Heterogeneity and Discriminatory Accuracy (MAIHDA), but later accepted the multilevel approach developed by Evans et al. as 'more superior'. Note, however, the key function Merlo emphasized was to *predict* health outcomes at the *individual* or the lowest level, not to predict or explain differences at the higher level of intersectional groups. Indeed, for many studies, the objective is to make accurate predictions of individual life experiences given these individuals' intersectional attributes.

That said, it is worth noting a few points, however. First, sometimes the objective of research may be to compare and contrast differences across intersectional groups rather than predict individual experiences, and in such a situation there is no need for multilevel data and models. In this situation, it should be sufficient to conduct the analysis at the group level alone. Second, the relative contribution made by the intersectional groups towards the explanation of individual experiences, measured with the statistic ICC introduced above, is usually low or even very low, such as less than 10%. In their study, Evans et al. found that only about 5% of the total variance is attributable to between-strata differences (2018, p. 69). In a more recent study conducted on a Canadian sample (Ickert et al., 2021), the percentage is somewhat larger, 12%, which means that the vast majority of explanation for the response variable's variation lies in the differences among the individuals, not the intersectional groups. Finally, and in connection with a point made above, so far few studies have added variables at the intersectional group level in order to incorporate potential intersectional factors that could explain life experiences at the individual level. Therefore, multilevel analysis of intersectional effects remains a much more statistical exercise than a theoretical explanation based on attributes of intersectional groups.

7.5 Suggested readings and questions for discussion

To use the methods and models covered in this chapter, it is important for the reader, first of all, to understand the meaning of 'multilevel' in the statistical sense and connect it to the context of study on intersectionality. Note that the world 'level' in statistics does not necessarily correspond to a 'level' in life. Sometimes they correspond to each other; for example, a school is at a higher level than the level of classes. Other times, they don't; for example, a person is at a higher level than the time points at which data were collected on that person. This is why 'multilevel' or 'hierarchical' models deal with 'clustering data', that is the situation in which some data of a lower-level unit are clustered within a higher unit of analysis, and the unit could be anything, not necessarily a social organization. Therefore, discuss the meaning of 'multilevel' in the study of intersectionality with your peers, asking: what is a 'level' in a particular study? How many levels are there? How is 'higher' or 'lower' defined? How could we be certain that members of a lower-level unit all belong to a higher-level unit? While treating individual persons as members of an intersectional category is a smart statistical manoeuvre, does it really make sense in light of intersectionality's principles? You should start learning and using these methods and models after you become satisfied with your answers to these questions.

Once you understand the basic concepts and logic of multilevel modelling, you can move on to read some publications about using the multilevel approach for analysing intersectionality. Note that these publications, almost all published as articles in peer-reviewed journals, may not reveal all of the details of how the authors managed their data and constructed their multilevel models. As shown in the previous sections of this chapter, the paper by Evans et al. (2018) is perhaps the most important on this topic, so try to read it carefully and understand as much as you can. Evans then expanded the discussion about the differences between multilevel models and single-level models (what she referred to as 'conventional models') in a subsequent paper (Evans and Lépinard, 2019), reinforcing her argument for the benefits of following the multilevel approach. Some years before Evans published her papers, Juan Merlo, a Swedish social epidemiologist, developed the framework Multilevel Analysis of Individual Heterogeneity and Discriminatory Accuracy (MAIHDA) (2003), and in an invited commentary he offered his strong endorsement of the multilevel approach (2018). For another published study that has followed the multilevel approach, the reader may find the study by Ickert et al. (2021) useful.

For readers who would like to learn more about multilevel models in order to understand and use these models for the purpose of studying intersectionality, I would recommend starting with two short and accessible texts: *Introducing multilevel modelling* by Ita Kreft and Jan de Leeuw (Sage, 1998) and the second edition of Douglas Luke's *Multilevel modelling* (Sage, 2020). In my view, the former does a better job of making a case for the value of multilevel models, whilst the key benefit of reading the latter is to see the entire process of conducting multilevel analysis with an example. If the reader feels more comfortable with mathematical symbols and equations, reading either of the following texts will help to gain a more rigorous grasp of the technical details: the second edition of *Multilevel analysis: an introduction to basic and advanced multilevel modelling* by Tom A. B. Snijders and Roel J. Bosker (Sage, 2011); and the third edition of *Multilevel analysis: Techniques and applications* by Joop Hox, Mirjam Moerbeek and Rens van de Schoot (Routledge, 2017).

If the reader would like to learn how to construct and interpret multilevel models with a particular computer program, the following texts should help: for readers using SPSS, the third edition of *Multilevel and longitudinal modelling with IBM SPSS* by Ronald H. Heck, Scott L. Thomas and Lynn N. Tabata has recently been published (2022); for those who prefer Stata, the fourth edition of Sophia Rabe-Hesketh and Anders Skrondal's *Multilevel and longitudinal modeling using Stata* (two volumes, Stata Press, 2021) is a widely adopted reference; for users of R, W. Holmes Finch, Jocelyn E. Bolin and Ken Kelley have published the second edition of their *Multilevel modelling using R* (Chapman & Hall/CRC, 2019), and Andrew Gelman and Jennifer Hill's *Data analysis using regression and multilevel/hierarchical models* (Cambridge University Press, 2007) contains R scripts for their examples.

Notes

1. Again, a caveat is needed here for the simplified classification of sex which is widely accepted now to be not as simple as a binary (male or female) variable. Note that the number of intersectional groups will increase multiplicatively if the number of categories of any of these attributes increases, making the data more stretched across these groups.
2. The previous caveat applies here: the authors of this study used a binary classification of gender, which would appear inadequate in today's public discourse.

8

MEDIATION, MODERATION AND INTERSECTIONALITY

8.1 Overview and objectives

The methods introduced so far take intersectionality as combinatory configurations of the interested attributes. These attributes are referred to as 'explanatory' or 'independent' variables, predictors, or 'causal conditions'. Whilst the methods could examine all of the possible cross-combinations, they do not distinguish the attributes' roles in a logical or temporal sequence when affecting the outcome. Essentially, these methods represent intersectionality as cross-classifications or interaction terms, and the key message that the analyses generated with these methods is consistent with the notion of 'moderation'; that is, one attribute's effect on the outcome depends on the value of another attribute. In plain English, 'moderation' means 'it depends'.

When affecting a certain outcome, whether the attributes or conditions relate to each other in a logical or temporal sequence, rather than mutually and simultaneously without any sequence, is a theoretical matter that the researcher must settle before choosing a relevant method. This could be potentially important for the study of intersectionality, particularly when it is theoretically important to stress on the *simultaneity of human attributes*; put differently, researchers need to consider whether they would put the attributes into different positions in an analytical structure or prefer analysing these attributes simultaneously without any order. As we shall discuss in the rest of this chapter, this is an open-ended question, both theoretically and empirically, as the answer may make sense for some situations but not for others. For example, one attribute may precede another, or one attribute serves as an intermediary mechanism between another attribute and the outcome.

The overall aim of this chapter is to consider and discuss the structural relations among the predictors (or conditions) of an interested outcome. Methods and models for analysing such structural relations are important because the structural relations represent a special form of intersectionality. More specifically, this chapter has the following objectives:

- To introduce and study the situations in which the effect of one attribute on the outcome is theorized as going through the effect of another attribute, which is the basic idea of mediation. When the effect of an attribute on the outcome is mediated through a mediator, the effect could be classified and analysed as either direct or indirect. In this sense, the studies involving one or more mediators require and represent more specific theories of the structural relations among the interested attributes.

- To clarify the meaning of moderation and explain how a variable's moderating effect could be empirically analysed and demonstrated.
- As mediation and moderation are usually represented with graphs, they leave people with an impression that they represent a certain form of causal relations among the studied variables. It is important to explain in what sense this is the case.
- To put mediation and moderation in the context of intersectionality so that the reader will appreciate the ways in which methods for analysing these structural relations could aid the examination of intersectional injustice and inequality.

Statistics books on mediation and moderation tend to cover these two subjects together. For two reasons, here we focus on the methods for analysing mediation and how they could help us study intersectionality. The first reason is that we already covered moderation in the previous chapters, especially Chapter 7. The second reason is a consequence of the first: perhaps because moderation has been extensively studied as cross-classifications and inter-action terms, few publications analyse moderation alone for the purpose of understanding intersectionality, although moderation is in fact more general and complicated than interaction terms. There are only a small number of studies that have included both moderation and mediation in the context of intersectionality. Our discussions will remain at the conceptual level without going into the mathematical or statistical details which interested readers could find in the suggested readings.

8.2 Mediation: Direct and indirect effects in structural relations

At the minimum, three variables are needed for constructing a mediating or moderating relationship. It is helpful to make the notations clear at the outset: if our theory or hypothesis says that X predicts the mean of Y with a certainty of probability through a mediator, then X will be the predictor, Y the outcome and ME the mediator. In some sub-disciplines of statistics, such as econometrics or latent variable modelling, the terms 'endogenous variables' and 'exogenous variables' are used. The former is similar to dependent (or response) variables and the latter independent (or explanatory) variables, respectively, but they are not completely the same. Strictly speaking, an exogenous variable explains at least one endogenous variable and is not explained by any other exogenous variable. In a structural model with multiple variables, however, a particular variable could be both endogenous and exogenous at the same time; if so, the variable becomes a mediator. We use ME here in order not to confuse it with the moderator (MO).

In the simplest situation where there is no mediator, the relationship between X and Y could be represented with the following diagram:

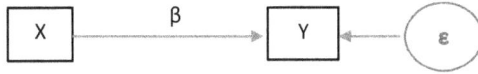

Figure 8.1 Structural relationship with no mediator

The following explanations for the letters and symbols in a figure like this could be useful to readers not familiar with them. In statistics, especially path analysis and structural equation models, it is a widely adopted convention to use squares (or rectangles) for observable (or manifest) variables and circles (or ovals) for unobservable (or latent) ones. We shall not need the Greek letter ε in the diagram if we think that X could explain the *entire* variation of Y, which is virtually impossible in reality; therefore, ε represents the 'residual' (or 'the error term') of Y's variation that is not explained by the model. As we have no available information about the error term, it is usually treated as 'latent' and therefore put in a circle. The β on the arrow from X to Y is the effect of X on Y. Now the meaning of the following equation should become clear:

$$Y = \alpha + \beta X + \varepsilon$$

The alpha (α) is included because we can still have an estimated value of Y (usually its mean) if X has no impact on Y (in other words, $\beta = 0$).

Now let's add one mediator to the above model. Note that even with only one mediator, there is more than one way to map out the possible relationships between these variables. Perhaps the simplest is the following:

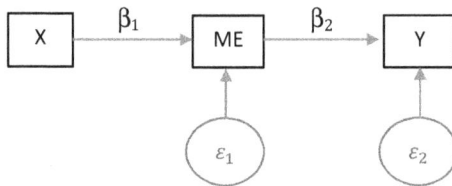

Figure 8.2 Mediation with only indirect effect

This diagram represents a theoretical model that all of the effect that X has on Y goes through the mediator; in other words, there is *no direct* effect of X on Y; otherwise, there should be an arrow pointing directly from X to Y. Besides the error term for Y (ε_2), there is also an error term (ε_1) for the mediator ME, because ME is the response variable that X explains and again, such explanation cannot be exhaustive. With one predictor X and two response variables (ME and Y), we need two equations to represent this model:

$$ME = \alpha_1 + \beta_1 X + \varepsilon_1$$
$$Y = \alpha_2 + \beta_2 ME + \varepsilon_2$$

As X is not in the second equation, you may wonder which coefficient represents the effect of X on Y, which is the main value we want to know, but none of the symbols in these two equations represents such an effect. This is so because the effect of X on Y is indirect; therefore, it needs to be derived from the other coefficients as the product, $\beta_1 * \beta_2$.

If we want to add the direct effect of X on Y to the model, we need a slightly more complicated diagram (Figure 8.3):

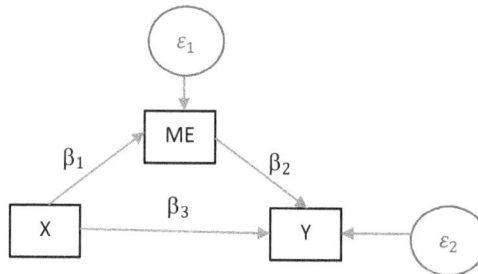

Figure 8.3 Mediation with both direct and indirect effects

This model also has two response variables (ME and Y), so we need two regression equations, with the first the same as the previous, but the second equation on Y is different:

$$ME = \alpha_1 + \beta_1 X + \varepsilon_1$$
$$Y = \alpha_2 + \beta_2 ME + \beta_3 X + \varepsilon_2$$

This is a most typical representation of the mediation model used in current research, in which X has both a direct and an indirect effect on Y. The direct effect is measured with the coefficient β_3, and the indirect effect is the product of its effect on the mediator (β_1) and the mediator's effect on Y (β_2), that is $\beta_1\beta_2$. It is worth pointing out that the direct effect in Figure 8.3 is the direct effect *after taking the indirect effect into account, and vice versa*.

How important is the mediator for explaining the variation of Y? Answering this question requires careful consideration of a few subtle issues. First of all, it might make intuitive sense to compare the direct and the indirect effects in order to see which one exercises a bigger impact on Y, but such comparison would not make sense if the coefficients were not comparable if they had different units; in that case, we would need to standardize the coefficients in order to make the coefficients comparable. For example, if X is age in years while ME is income in pounds, then it does not make sense to compare years with the product of year and pounds. A common way of standardizing a regression coefficient is to multiply it with the division of the standard deviation of X and the standard deviation of Y.

Another important condition for comparing the direct and indirect effects of X on Y is that all regression coefficients must be statistically significant, because if any of the coefficients are not statistically significant, then it means the probability that it is zero would be intolerably high, so at least one arrow should be removed. As a result, either the direct or the indirect effect would disappear, making the comparison of the two effects meaningless.

Given the standardization and statistical significance of all coefficients, we can consider the relative importance of the direct (β_3) and the indirect effects ($\beta_1\beta_2$). We are certainly more interested in the indirect effect as it represents the impact of the mediator. We should pay attention to their signs as well, which may be particularly important for the indirect effect, because its sign might change due to the signs of β_1 and β_2 – for example, if β_1 is positive but β_2 is negative, then the indirect effect of X on Y ($\beta_1\beta_2$) will be negative; therefore, the mediator has changed the direction of X's effect on Y. If β_1 is negative and β_2 is also negative, then the sign of the indirect effect ($\beta_1\beta_2$) will also be positive; that is, the mediator will have changed the sign of X's effect on Y, this time from negative to positive. In the other two scenarios, the signs of X's direct and indirect effects on Y will remain the same.

Once these issues are considered, we could compare the magnitudes of the direct and indirect effects with either their difference or their ratio. If we want to have a sense of their relative importance of the overall impact of X on Y, we could calculate the proportion (or percentage) of the indirect (mediating) effect of the 'the total effect' (the sum of the direct and the indirect effects). Like many other statistical values, we could assign a particular value as a threshold, but it is more informative to report the exact value of such proportion (or percentage).

A good practice in statistical analysis is carefully checking the assumptions that underlie a model or method. As mediation models are analysed with a series of interconnected regression models, it is also imperative to examine whether the assumptions for these models hold given the data at hand. David MacKinnon (2008, see sections 3.9 and 3.12 in particular) classified these assumptions for mediation models into two groups: one for the linear regression models, which are the same for all linear regression models, and the other for the set of assumptions that are specific for mediation models. MacKinnon listed the following four assumptions for linear regression equations, although there are other assumptions in the literature:

1. The first and perhaps most important assumption is that the equations are the correct mathematical representations of the actual relations between the variables. The word 'linear' means that the effects of the independent variables (the Xs) could be added up to predict the average value of the dependent variable Y, with the coefficients as the weight of each independent variable. One implication is that no interaction terms exist in the model, because interaction terms represent a multiplicative (non-linear) relationship. This assumption can be relaxed to let the model include non-linear relations and interaction terms.
2. No important independent variable is missing in the proposed model, which is a more theoretical than a statistical issue and therefore cannot be checked with statistics.
3. All variables are accurate measures of the corresponding concept. This is a very important issue because the results and conclusions of analysis may be different if the data contain large errors. Even for a variable whose meaning is very straightforward, such as age and employment, the data might not accurately represent the reality – people may round up their age, and people may not agree on whether a housewife or househusband is a form of employment.
4. The residuals of the response variable are random. This is derived from another assumption: the linear regression equations could predict the majority of the response variable's variation significantly well; if so, the residuals should be not only small but

also lack any clear pattern, because the pattern should have already been captured by the independent variables. A simple plot of the residuals or a scatterplot of the residuals with the response variable would show whether this assumption is violated or not.

MacKinnon then listed eight 'inferential assumptions for the single mediation model'. Four of them are similar to the above assumptions 2, 3 and 4. The first of these four is the same as the second assumption above: no external important predictors (external influences) are missing in the model. The other two assumptions are about the normality of the variables' distributions. The first one assumes that each of the three variables in the single mediator model – X, ME and Y – has a normal distribution. This makes sense for ME and Y, because they are the response (exogenous) variables in the linear regression equation; as the equations aim to predict their mean, and the mean is only meaningful for a normal distribution, ME and Y are supposed to have at least an approximately normal distribution. There is no need to require or assume X as an independent variable to have a normal distribution. The expected normality is applicable to the distributions of the regression coefficients, $\hat{a}$ and $\hat{b}$, $\hat{a}\hat{b}$, because inferential tests will be conducted on them, which are valid only for normal or approximately normal distributions. This is particularly important for the coefficient, $\hat{a}\hat{b}$, not only because it measures the mediating (indirect) effect of X on Y but also because it is a product rather than a sum of two coefficients.

The fourth assumption is a specific version of assumption 3 above, which requires that the timing of measurement of the variables appropriately matches the true timing of the relation between changes in each respective variable. While this may make perfect sense conceptually, it could be very difficult to satisfy in the practice of data collection. Even for longitudinal data, researchers must collect the data for many variables at the same time point; unless for a strictly controlled process of data collection for the purpose of demonstrating the temporal relations between the variables, it is practically very difficult to satisfy this assumption.

8.3 Moderation as interaction or condition

The meaning of moderation is not as clear as that of mediation. By definition, a moderator moderates the effect of one variable on the response variable. In his book, MacKinnon defines a moderator as 'a variable that changes the sign or strength of the effect of an independent variable on a dependent variable. It is typically (but not always) an interaction such that the effect of an independent variable on a dependent variable depends on the level of the moderator variable' (2008, p. 11). The question is: how does a moderator change the sign or strength of the effect of an independent variable? The answer seems to be, by interacting with the independent variable. If so, then moderation is the same as the interaction term introduced in the previous chapter. However, as we shall see, moderation has been used in a broader sense than the interaction term. Such ambiguity is reflected in the graphic representation of moderation:

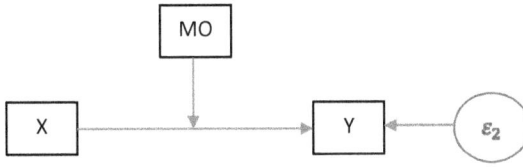

Figure 8.4 A most commonly used diagram of moderation

Whilst this diagram clearly shows that the moderator influences the effect of X on Y, it is difficult to know which equation it corresponds to, because the arrow of the moderator points to another arrow rather than a variable. As a result, we cannot put a regression coefficient to the arrow from MO. Moreover, there is another way to depict a moderated relationship:

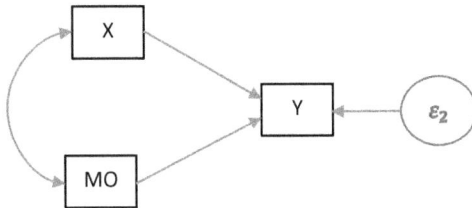

Figure 8.5 Illustration of moderation as interaction

For two reasons Figure 8.5 is more desirable than Figure 8.4 for depicting the role of a moderator. First, every arrow (or double arrow) is pointing from one variable to another, thereby eliminating the confusion over the arrow from a variable to an arrow. Second, the double arrow between X and MO clearly represents the interaction term which is the most common understanding of moderation. More importantly, in Figure 8.5 the independent variable and the moderator moderate each other, so their positions are interchangeable. In this sense, we could break down the moderation relationship into two mediating relations, one starting from X through MO and the other starting from MO through X, which offers another illustration for why mediation is clearer than moderation.

Furthermore, rather than representing moderation as a term of interaction in linear regression models, it is now common to treat a moderator as a condition under which the interested relationship is examined. In practice, this means that the interested relationship is studied at each level of the moderator, and if the relationship changes significantly across the levels, then there is clear evidence for the moderator's effect on the relationship. For example, suppose the moderator MO has three levels, then the moderating effect of MO could be represented as shown in Figure 8.6.

Clearly, this way of analysing a moderator's effect takes the moderator out of the targeted relationship. It also assumes that the moderator is a categorical variable, and these categories are comparable sub-groups. Finally, our comparison of the βs should be statistically rigorous; for instance, their distributions are approximately normal, and the sample sizes of the sub-groups are sufficiently large. When the moderator is a metrical variable or the distribution and the sample sizes are not satisfactory, we will have to find another way of studying the

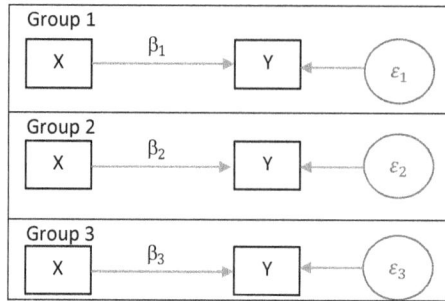

Figure 8.6 Moderation as conditioning with three sub-groups

moderating effect, such as creating an interaction term or transforming the metrical variable's values into a small number of categories.

8.4 Mediation, moderation and causation

Mediation and moderation are now routinely represented with a diagram in which variables are connected with arrows. What do those arrows mean? It should be obvious that an arrow indicates a 'causal' relationship between the two variables. However, the relationships in a diagram are represented by linear regression equations that, on their own, neither constitute nor describe any causal relationship. The causal relationships are our beliefs, theories or hypotheses, which are external to the equations. The statistical analyses on the regression coefficients and other statistics may give us more accurate information about the relationships between the variables, but they offer no evidence for the causal relationships themselves. Indeed, one of the 'inferential assumptions' for mediation MacKinnon listed is the following: '*Causal Inference.* [all coefficients] reflect true causal relations of the correct functional form (Holland, 1988s; Rubin, 2004). ... In many situations, the results of a mediation analyses are descriptive rather than implying causal relations' (2008, p. 67). If we take the causation seriously, we need to realize that the intuitive sense of casual relations among the variables represented by the arrows falls short of the scientific requirement for establishing causal relationships. It is important for the reader to appreciate the conditions required for interpreting mediation and moderation as causal relations.

MacKinnon also made the distinction between 'theoretical mediator' and 'empirical mediator'. The former is a 'true' or 'genuine' cause of the outcome, whilst the latter is only an indicator or proxy of the former. In an empirical study, our findings are derived completely from the empirical mediator. If the empirical mediator fails to represent the true mediator, then our findings will be at least inaccurate or at worst biased. Unfortunately, we normally do not have access to information about the true mediator; therefore, it is crucial for researchers to assess the validity and reliability of the empirical mediator. While statistical methods do exist for assessments, researchers must make use of all available sources of evidence, much of which are not statistical, to establish any causal relations.

The other two assumptions for mediation that MacKinnon specified simply reflect the essential nature of mediation; that is, the sequential order represents *both the temporal and the logical* relations among the variables. Temporally, this means that X occurs first, followed by ME, and then Y occurs last. 'In this regard', MacKinnon pointed out, 'assessment of mediation with cross-sectional data is problematic as generally no information regarding temporal precedence is available, but must be based on theory or some other means' (2008, p. 64). It is true that cross-sectional data, which are collected at one point of time, are less capable of representing the temporal sequence of attributes and events than longitudinal data that are collected on the same sample at a few different time points. This should not mean, however, that cross-sectional data cannot give us information about the temporal sequence of events; some attributes or events inherently precede others; for example, birth came certainly before migration, parents' ages must be older than their children's, and so on. This is why MacKinnon added these situations 'in which the meaning of the variables measured in a cross-sectional study do imply some temporal precedence that may shed light on mediation such as when X is measured before M (Smith, 1982)' (ibid.). Finally, the interested mediator may be in a chain of mediation that includes mediators at both micro and macro levels, and if so we must have data that measure these mediators at the right time.

Of these assumptions, the one about causation is simultaneously the most important and the most difficult. Let's focus on two challenges. The first is the presence of a confounder that may invalidate the proposed mediating model, which is a variable that affects both the independent variable X and the response variable Y:

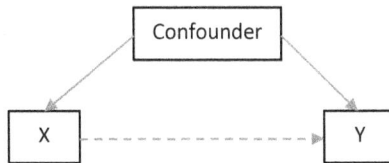

Figure 8.7 Confounder

This diagram looks very similar to the one depicted in the single-mediator model in Figure 8.3 (the error is omitted to simplify the diagram), but pay attention to the important difference between the two: in the mediator model, an arrow points from X to the mediator; in the confounder model, an arrow points from the confounder to X. The confounder confounds the relationship between X and Y, because the observed relationship between X and Y is not a genuine consequence of X's causal effect on Y; instead, the confounder is the true cause responsible for the observed relationship, making the observed causal relationship 'confounded' and therefore misleading, shown with a broken arrow. The single-mediator model (Figure 8.3) would be seriously compromised if there was a confounder for each important causal relationship (errors and coefficients omitted), as illustrated below (Figure 8.8).

As Wang and Sobel pointed out, 'unless it can be assumed that there are no confounders for the M–Y relationship, the partial association between M and Y should not be given a causal interpretation' (2013, p. 216). In fact, to make the observed relationship between two variables weaker, insignificant or even disappear is only one possibility. Sometimes, a

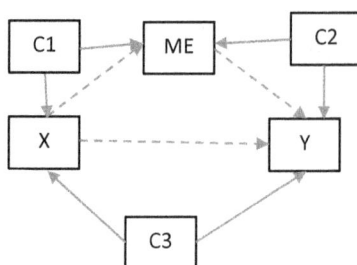

Figure 8.8 Mediation with confounding factors

confounder could make a weak or even non-existent relationship stronger or reappear once the confounder is included in the analysis, which is why the confounder has other names, such as 'suppressor' or 'distorter'. Essentially, any variable that could seriously change an observed relationship once this variable is brought into the analysis is a confounder.

How do we know which variable is a mediator or a confounder? More specifically, how do we determine the direction of the arrow connecting X to the variable in between X and Y? The regression equations cannot help us, because they are the same. In the single-mediator model, as the arrow points from X to ME, the equation is

$$ME = \alpha_1 + \beta_1 X + \varepsilon_1.$$

However, if we believe the ME is a confounder, then we could rearrange this equation by taking X as the subject:

$$X = \frac{ME - \alpha_1 - \varepsilon_1}{\beta_1}.$$

As the same equation could be used for either mediator or confounder, we cannot rely on linear regression equations for determining whether a variable is a mediator or a confounder. It is our theory, not an arrow or any equation, that is causal, so we must make use of our knowledge rather than statistics to identify the role of each variable in the model and ensure that all possible confounders have been considered in our model. Then the interested causal relationship could be analysed by 'controlling' the confounder's effect. In observational studies, we cannot literally control the confounder; what we can do is conduct the analysis on the cases taking the same (or at least very similar) value for a confounder. What has troubled social scientists for many years is the challenge that because the identification of a variable as a predictor or a confounder becomes inevitably arbitrary, it is difficult to determine whose theory or decision is correct. Things may become less contested if the findings from a large number of studies on the same set of variables all point to the same structural relationship, but such studies are very rare.

Currently, the 'best' solution for demonstrating a proposed causal relationship is to conduct randomized controlled trials (RCTs). The basic idea is that since we shall never be confident of having included all possible confounders in our analysis, the safest way to avoid the inference of any missing confounder is to randomly allocate the subjects (or participants) of a study in different states of the proposed cause. Random allocation to causal states leaves no opportunity for any potential confounding variable to interfere with the proposed causal relationship. Whilst this sounds logical in principle, the conditions for conducting an RCT in practice could be too demanding to be practically satisfied, including ethical concerns and noncompliance. Without random assignment, non-experimental (observational) studies, such as small-scale interviews or large-scale sample surveys, which are the most common ways of collecting data in the social sciences, are always vulnerable to the critique of missing a confounder.

Fortunately, there have been some encouraging endeavours to improve the rigour of causal analysis in observational studies, of which the counterfactual (or potential outcomes) approach and Acyclic Directed Graphs (ADGs) are particularly encouraging. More specific methods and techniques include stratification, difference-in-difference (DID), instrumental variables (IVs) and propensity score matching (PSM). Although some of these methods are related to mediation and moderation – for example, Tyler VanderWeele (2015)'s analysis on mediation and moderation from the counterfactual approach – their main concerns are with causation rather than mediation and moderation. The reader can find the references to some key texts at the end of this chapter. Our central concern here is with the ways in which mediation and moderation could be applied for analysing intersectional relations, which we now turn to in the next section.

8.5 Intersectionality as mediated and moderated relations

The methods of mediation and moderation were created before intersectionality became an influential approach; thus, they were not designed for analysing intersectionality. How could we ensure that the use of these methods would be in line with the fundamental principles of intersectionality? This is a far more important question than the technical details of a particular method. From the perspective of intersectionality, the response variable in a model of mediation or moderation is most likely a form of disadvantage, such as unemployment, poor health, a specific experience of discrimination, etc. Methods of mediation and moderation become useful when they make the researcher carefully consider the role of intersectionality in the overall structural relationship of the chosen attributes: is an intersectional attribute a predictor (independent variable), a mediator or a moderator? Intersectional attributes could certainly take any of these roles in a model, but even a simple model with three or four variables will have multiple possible scenarios, so it is important to think about our conceptual and theoretical models before producing and interpreting statistics. Given that some of the most intersectional attributes are socio-demographic attributes, it is theoretically unlikely that they would take a mediator role in a structural model, because no other variables could precede them, either temporally or logically; instead, they are more likely to be predictors or moderators in a model of intersectional inequality or injustice.

Without resorting to interaction terms in linear regression models, as introduced and explained in the previous chapter, a common practice is to model a mediating structural model for each value of an intersectional attribute, essentially treating intersectional attribute values as contexts or sub-groups in which the coefficients of the same model have different values. If the intersectionality of multiple attributes is the most important independent variable in the model, the first major form of application of mediation methods to the analysis of intersectionality, then we should aim to study its direct and indirect effects on the outcome variable by producing and examining their statistical significance, relative magnitude and other statistics. Before conducting these statistical analyses, the researcher must carefully consider the theoretical case of taking intersectional attributes as the key predictors. One important question, for example, is whether all intersectional categories should be treated as the values of a single intersectional variable, or the intersectional attributes should be treated as separate variables that have a certain temporal or logical sequence among themselves. As advocates of intersectionality tend to stress on the simultaneity of intersectional attributes, the first option appears to be more desirable. On the other hand, in some situations, it may make sense to separate the interested intersectional attributes apart as there might be an inherent sequence among them; for example, while the biological sex describes somebody from birth, their gender identity develops throughout life and may differ from the sex they were assigned. Other attributes, such as education and socio-economic class (SES), certainly come later. It is therefore sensible to treat these intersectional attributes separately. The researcher must draw on their theoretical reasoning and knowledge of the substantive issue to determine the role each variable should take in the proposed model.

The rest of this section illustrates each of these analytical strategies with a published study. The first example involves both mediation and moderation, but intersectional attributes were treated only as moderating groups so that the overall mediation model was statistically estimated for each group. In her study, Rica Vina Cruz (2022) modelled the mediating effect of 'sex guilt' between satisfaction with a marital or love relationship and satisfaction with sex life among Filipino heterosexual adults. As shown below, her theoretical model can be represented with a triangle-shaped diagram introduced earlier:

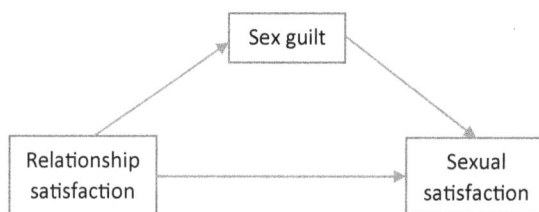

Figure 8.9 Cruz's model of sex guilt as a mediator between relationship and sex satisfaction
Used with permission.

Source: Cruz, R. V. (2022). The role of sex guilt as a mediating variable in the association of relationship and sexual satisfaction: An intersectional approach. *Sexuality & Culture*, *26*, 616–639. Springer Nature.

Empirically, data were collected from a snowball sample of heterosexual adults, either married or unmarried, who were recruited through social media and other channels and then completed an online questionnaire. Relationship satisfaction was measured with the Global Measure of Relationship Satisfaction (GMREL) subscale of the Lawrance and Byers' (1995) Interpersonal Exchange Model of Sexual Satisfaction Scale (IEMSS), a five-item questionnaire on an individual's satisfaction with their overall relationship with their current partner. Each item is a seven-point Likert scale, with 1 being very unsatisfying to 7 very satisfying. Similarly, sexual satisfaction was measured by the Global Measure of Sexual Satisfaction (GMSEX) subscale of IEMSS, also a five-item questionnaire with each item a seven-point Likert scale. Sex guilt was measured with an adapted shortened version of the Revised Mosher Sex-Guilt

Scale (Janda & Bazemore, 2011), which consists of 10 statements, and respondents were asked to use a five-point scale to report how much they would agree with each (1 being 'Strongly disagree' to 5 'Strongly agree').

Although intersectionality was an important factor in this study, it was not included in the theoretical model. Instead, intersectional categories, which include four cross-classifications of gender and marital status (married men, married women, unmarried men and unmarried women) were used as a moderator. The values of the moderator variable were used simply as groups or contexts for the theoretical model, so the above mediation model was estimated for each of the four intersectional groups. The statistical significance of the coefficients suggests that the model was supported for two of the intersectional groups, married men and unmarried women. Results for the other non-significant groups were not reported.

In the next example (Price et al., 2019), the membership of an intersectional group is not a moderator but a predictor, although the study follows a similar strategy of including and analysing each intersectional group separately. As the title of their paper suggests, the aim of their study was to examine the effect of 'identity-based victimization' (IBV) on mental health and academic performance among adolescents in the US. Intersectionality is relevant to this study because the victims' intersectional attributes (gender, race and sexual orientation) are believed to be the causes of their experiences of discrimination or bullying. The authors argued that, unlike other studies, most of which 'focus on *attributions* of discrimination', their study focused on the 'endorsed identities' so that they could study 'patterns of adversity associated with self-identified social identities' (2019, p. 187). In other words, rather than relying on the adolescents' own *subjective* explanation for the connection between their intersectional identities and experiences of discrimination, their study is more 'objective' in the sense of directly analysing the connections between self-endorsed intersectional identities and being victims of discrimination. Put briefly, experiences of being a victim of discrimination are a mediator between intersectional identities and mental health or academic performance, represented as a general model below:

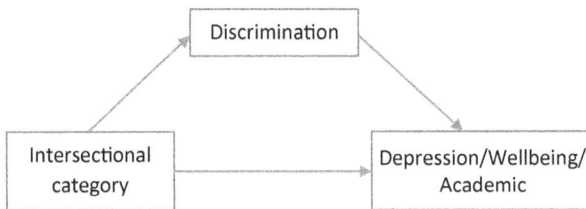

Figure 8.10   A generalized mediation model of Price et al. (2019) Used with permission.

Source: Price, M., et al. (2019). The intersectionality of identity-based victimization in Adolescence: A person-centered examination of mental health and academic achievement in a U.S. high school. *Journal of Adolescence*, 76,1.

Data were collected through the administration of a survey on a sample of an entire high school, with the valid sample size n = 946. 'Discrimination was assessed using the Everyday Discrimination Scale-Short Version (EDS)', a six-item scale (ibid.: 189). Identity-based bullying (IBB) 'was measured using an item derived from the Boston Youth Survey ... "In the past 12 months have you ever been bullied or assaulted because of any of those reasons?"', with the binary options (yes or no). Of the three response variables, 'Depression was assessed using the depression subscale of the Revised Child Anxiety and Depression Scale (RCADS), which includes 10 symptoms of depression (e.g., "I feel sad or empty")'; 'Wellbeing was evaluated using the 10-item Mental Health Inventory Wellbeing subscale (example item: "I am a happy person")' and 'academic achievement represented cumulative grade point averages (GPA) measured on a 4.0 scale' (ibid.).

For socio-demographic variables that are relevant to intersectionality, gender was measured with three categories: Cisgender boy, Cisgender girl and Gender expansive (transgender and other). Sexual orientation is binary (Heterosexual or LGBQ); so is race (White or Colour). Therefore, there are $3 \times 2 \times 2 = 12$ intersectional categories. Although this is not a large number, the authors conducted a cluster analysis to reduce the number of intersectional categories. After considering the possible solutions, they accepted the solution of the following three clusters (intersectional groups): LGBTQ Youth, Heterosexual Youth of Colour, and Heterosexual White Youth (ibid.: 190). The researchers reduced the number of intersectional groups by entirely relying on statistical outputs. Whilst the number of intersectional groups has been reduced from 12 to 3, which makes the subsequent analyses more manageable, most of the other potentially important intersectional groups are not treated as distinctive groups anymore; for example, gender was left out of the analysis. Moreover, neither gender nor race is visible anymore in the now bigger category 'LGBTQ Youth', leaving one to wonder how some theoretically important intersectional groups, such as 'expansive gender, LGBQ+, and of colour', would be identified and analysed. The authors explained that they chose this solution of cluster analysis because it 'has both adequate statistical fit and yields interpretable clusters with qualitative distinctions' (ibid.: 190). As a result, theoretical concerns with specific intersectional categories did not guide statistical analyses. Among the intersectional categories, 'Heterosexual White' was selected as the reference category for comparisons with 'Heterosexual Colour' and 'LGBTQ', respectively, and each of the three response variables was modelled separately; therefore, the authors presented six specific mediation models (ibid.: 192), one for each intersectional category.

The other two example studies are more complicated than the previous two in the sense that they treat intersectionality as both a predictor and a moderator. In their study, Williams and Lewis (2019) were concerned with depression among Black women in the US. They thought that a key cause or predictor of depression was 'gendered racial microaggression', which was defined as '"subtle and everyday verbal, behavioural, and environmental expressions of oppression based on the intersection of one's race and gender" (Lewis et al., 2013, p. 51)' (2019, p. 369). Whilst this is not entirely about intersectional attributes, the intersectionality of gender and race was believed to be the source of experiencing oppression in daily life. In between these two variables was the coping strategy as a mediator, which obviously makes sense as different Black women were expected to differ in terms of how they cope with microaggressions. Their coping strategies could be broadly classified as 'engagement strategies (e.g. confronting the stressor directly, problem-focused coping) and disengagement strategies (e.g. disengaging from the stressor, avoidance)' (ibid.). Their theory was that it was 'disengaging coping' that made Black women more likely to suffer from depression. Additionally, they adopted the notions of '*private* regard (i.e., how positively or negatively an individual feels about *their own* identity) and *public* regard (i.e., how positively or negatively an individual feels that *other people* feel about their identity)' (ibid., emphases added), which they included as a moderator in their model. As it is also based on intersectional identities, intersectionality is included and analysed here as a moderator as well. Putting these together, their theoretical model is as follows (Williams and Lewis, 2019, p. 372, Figure 1; the dotted line in their figure was removed as it is redundant):

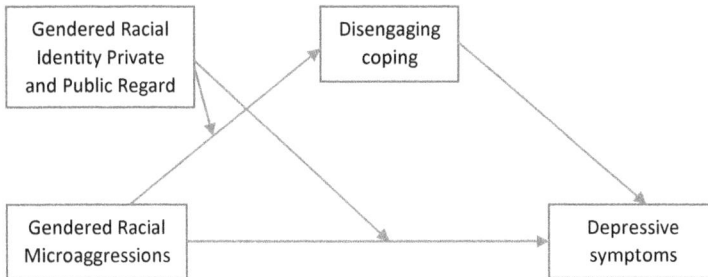

Figure 8.11 Williams and Lewis's (2019) model of mediation and moderation

Gendered racial microaggressions were measured with the Gendered Racial Microaggressions Scale (GRMS; Lewis & Neville, 2015), a 26-item measure assessing nonverbal, verbal and behavioural negative racial and gender slights, with each item being a six-point Likert scale from 0 (never) to 5 (once a week or more). Gendered racial identity was measured with a modified version of the private and public regard subscales of the Multidimensional Inventory of Black Identity (MIBI-Regard; Sellers et al., 1997). Coping was measured by using the Brief Coping with Problems Experienced Inventory (Brief COPE; Carver, 1997), a 28-item scale. Finally, depression was measured with the seven-item depression subscale of the Depression Anxiety Stress Scale (DASS-21; Lovibond & Lovibond, 1995) (ibid., p. 373). Their analysis included two other factors, spirituality and social support, which, however, were not shown in the conceptual model.

How was intersectionality represented in this study? On the one hand, the authors claimed that they 'applied an intersectional framework' and 'utilized intersectional measures' (ibid.: 371). On the other hand, note that only one intersectional group – Black women – was studied here. It is very likely that the authors assumed that this particular intersectional group was the most vulnerable to microaggressions and consequently depression, but it is impossible to know whether this is true without comparing it with the other intersectional groups. Although intersectionality was included and studied with two variables based on intersectional identities, the focus on one intersectional group alone has seriously restricted the study's ability to demonstrate any intersectional effect.

Our last example is the most sophisticated as it not only includes both mediation and moderation but also considers potential confounders in order to make their causal arguments more defendable. In their paper, Bauer and Scheim claimed that their aim was 'to push quantitative intersectionality methodology beyond consideration of heterogeneity in outcomes, toward identification of causal processes that drive intersectional inequities' (2019, p. 237). Extending Bauer's early work (2014), they made a distinction between 'descriptive intersectionality' and 'analytic intersectionality'. The key difference between the two is that the former focuses on heterogeneous outcomes alone whilst the latter focuses on both heterogeneous *processes and outcomes*. If the focus is on the outcomes alone, it is sufficient to compare the heterogeneous outcomes across the intersectional categories; such analysis of intersectionality is descriptive but less rigorous although easier to conduct in practice. If the aim is to study both the outcomes and the processes, then a stronger case is to be made for the causal relationships between the variables, which consequently is much more rigorous as well as challenging to carry out in practice. Drawing on the 'potential outcomes' or 'counterfactual' approach, Bauer and Scheim offered a step-by-step strategy for 'analytic intersectionality' and illustrated this with 'an example of inequalities in current psychological distress across ethno-racial and sexual/gender minority intersectional groups, mediated by past-year experiences of day-to-day discrimination' (ibid.). Their theoretical model can thus be represented with the following diagram (Figure 8.12a):

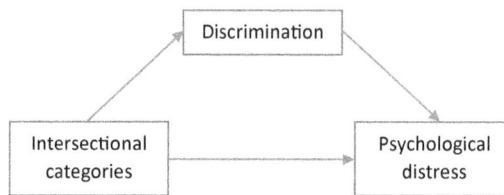

Discrimination

Intersectional categories → Psychological distress

Figure 8.12a   Bauer and Scheim's model without moderation

This is a typical example of a model of mediation, in which intersectional categories have both direct and indirect effects (through discrimination) on psychological distress. However, this is not the diagram presented in their paper (Figure 1, Bauer and Scheim, 2019, p. 238). As shown below, the model they presented (Figure 8.12b) includes two additional moderation effects:

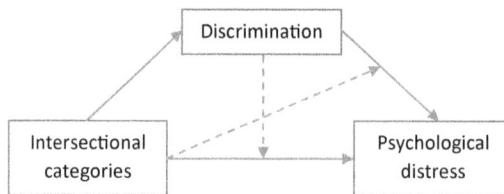

Discrimination

Intersectional categories → Psychological distress

Figure 8.12b   Bauer and Scheim's model with moderators

The two broken arrows indicate that intersectional categories and discrimination moderate each other's effect on psychological distress; in other words, the two variables interact with each other even though intersectional categories appear to possess more causal power over discrimination. Such theoretical formulation is potentially ambiguous or even confusing, as it is difficult to distinguish mediating effects from moderating effects. For example, how could 'Intersectional categories' cause 'Discrimination' and moderate its causal effect on 'Psychological distress' at the same time? The mediating effect means causal sequence, but the moderating effect means association alone with no causal sequence, and the two should not exist for the same pair of variables at the same time. Additionally, if 'Discrimination' moderates the effects of 'Intersectional categories' on 'Psychological distress', then the relationship between 'Discrimination' and 'Intersectional categories' becomes a loop or an association rather than a causal sequence.

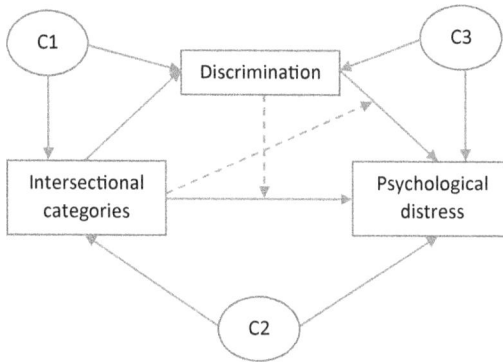

Figure 8.12c   Bauer and Scheim's model with moderators and confounders

Furthermore, as they adopted the potential outcomes approach, they needed to consider at least one potential confounder for each mediating relationship (Figure 8.12c, in which the position of the second confounder is rearranged and the shapes and names are modified):

For empirical research, they employed a commercial company to conduct an online survey with a quota sampling scheme on 2583 participants, aged 18 to 88 in the US and Canada, and 2542 participants with non-missing data were included in the analyses. Psychological distress and discrimination were measured as continuous variables with specialized scales. The potential confounders include age, sex assigned at birth, immigration history and disability, which were treated as covariates in the statistical models, but there was little discussion over how each of them may confound a particular causal relationship. Essentially, causal effects were estimated with regression models. Whilst it is sensible to assume that intersectional categories temporally precede discrimination and psychological distress, it is, however, too strong to assume that discrimination necessarily comes before psychological distress – it is possible or even likely that the causal connection goes in the opposite direction: those who suffer from anxiety or depression may be discriminated against at work or in social circles.

There are 12 intersectional groups, which are the product of six ethno-racial categories (White, Indigenous, Latin American/Hispanic, Middle Eastern, Black or Asian) and two sexual or gender minority categories (SGM versus heterosexual and cisgender, or non-SGM). They did not show the sample size for each intersectional group. Given the relatively large number of intersectional groups, Bauer and Scheim needed to find an efficient way to present their results. The causal effects of the intersectional categories were demonstrated in a few ways, including the systematic comparisons of each pair of the 12 groups, the comparisons between the reference group (White and non-SGM, which is supposed to be the most advantageous group) and each of the other groups, in terms of both direct and indirect effects on the outcome variable. They broke down the total effect of an intersectional category on the outcome into three components: the direct effect, the indirect effect and the mediated interaction (or moderation) effect, although they did not find anything statistically significant for the last.

8.6 Reflections and extensions

How useful are models of mediation and moderation for analysing intersectionality? In principle, both types of models are useful but for slightly different reasons. An important question researchers must consider first is which model they would use in order to demonstrate the effects of intersectionality in the most sensible and powerful manner. A major benefit of using mediation models is to specify *the position of intersectional attributes in an overall structural model*, something other methods introduced previously could not do. However, as mentioned previously, the nature of intersectional attributes means that it would be extremely rare for intersectional attributes to be mediators between two or more other variables, because most intersectional attributes come with birth, making it nearly impossible for other variables to precede these attributes. This explains why none of the examples presented in the previous section included intersectionality as a mediator. In models of mediation, intersectionality is most likely the predictor of other variables.

Another important observation is that most models in existing studies are very simple, with variables representing intersectional attributes being usually treated or combined into a single variable. This is so because only sex and race were included as the intersectional attributes, which are assumed to come simultaneously at a person's birth and stay mostly constant as they are for the rest of life. For many situations it may be safe to keep this assumption, but it may become necessary to expand the categories of intersectionality so that attributes taken at later time points in life could be included in the study. For example, a distinction between 'sex assigned at birth' and 'self-identified gender' may be useful. Moreover, intersectional studies could expand their scope of analysis by including a few attributes that people take on later in life, such as education, marital status, social class, etc. When these variables are included as *theoretically important* variables rather than simply 'controls' or 'covariates', it would become necessary to consider the structural relations among them so that intersectionality is no longer an initial predictor in a mediation model. Models with more predictors and mediators and therefore longer causal chains should be constructed with the support of more sophisticated theories. This relates to the nature of the data as well – currently almost all mediation models with intersectionality have been constructed with cross-sectional data. Studies analysing longitudinal data could have the opportunity to map out more clearly the temporal as well as the logical relationships between intersectional attributes and other variables of concern.

Unlike mediation, moderation could demonstrate that the additional information about a variable (intersectional attribute), which is not a part of the structural model, would change a relationship of interest. It is important to note that *moderation could be either specific or general*. Specific moderation refers to the moderating effect of a particular variable on a particular coefficient in the mediation model; that is, the moderation is a part of the overall structural model. In contrast, general moderation refers to the moderating effect of a particular variable on the proposed structural model, in which the moderator is not included in the conceptual model; essentially, the values of the moderator are taken as labels of groups or contexts in which the proposed structural model is estimated repeatedly. Intersectional attributes could be included as a moderator in either way, depending on the researcher's objectives. However, more care is needed in the 'specific moderation' scenario because it could be very confusing if a variable of intersectionality is both a mediator and a moderator at the same time. It is clearer to treat a particular variable as either a mediator or a moderator, but not both, in the same model.

A question relevant to both mediation and moderation is whether the researcher simply wants to demonstrate any statistically significant differences between intersectional groups in terms of an important outcome or has the ambition of making a case for the causal effect of intersectional attributes. Clearly, most researchers would like to make a case for causation but remain wary of the strong conditions for doing so. In making a case for causation, mediators are clearly more explicit than moderators, which on the other hand means that researchers must be more careful when setting up the structural relations. For this purpose, the principles and tools of structural equation models (SEM) could be useful. These models require the researcher to clearly specify the causal relations among the variables and take measurement errors into account at the same time. There is an additional benefit of using SEM to study intersectionality: SEM could incorporate concepts that are difficult to track empirically, such as racism and sexism. As Green et al. pointed out:

> Measuring racism or sexism purely through racial groups or gender may be far too simple to detect the underlying power structures they seek to measure. SEMs would allow issues such as racism or sexism to be specified as unobservable latent variables. These latent constructs could then be measured using multiple variables to account for their multiple causes/dimensions. A further strength would be that causal pathways could also be explicitly specified and tested, allowing for the evaluation of particular pathways (or theories) through which inequalities are produced. (2017, p. 216)

Most SEMs do not routinely include moderators, but mediators and moderators could work together while playing different functions; for example, mediation models are better at mapping out causal structures while models with moderators could demonstrate 'causal heterogeneity' (how a particular causal structure works in different settings or for different sub-populations).

8.7 Suggested readings and questions for discussion

One thing that I have done repeatedly in this book is urged the reader to consider whether the basic ideas of a method are in line with the general principles of intersectionality. In this light, it is very important for the reader to think carefully whether analysing mediation and moderation will serve the purpose of intersectionality. As demonstrated in this chapter, a key difference between the methods introduced in this chapter and the ones in previous chapters is that the explanatory variables (or predictors) are not simply analysed as mutually influencing each other; in mediation and moderation, the focus of analysis is on the structural positions of these variables. So, discuss the following question with your peers: As a theoretical perspective, what kind of structural relations, if any, would intersectionality expect the intersectional attributes or systems to have? Essentially, this means we must ensure that mediation and moderation fit the purposes of intersectionality before we employ them in our empirical investigations. The answers you and your peers offer may vary according to the nature of intersectional attributes or systems; therefore, it would be useful to answer the question with different types of attributes or systems. In other words, the structural position that a particular attribute takes must be meaningful in relation to its meaning and how it works.

To learn more about the technical details of mediation and moderation, in my view the most accessible text for learning the mediation models is David MacKinnon's (2008) *Introduction to statistical mediation analysis*. Although it is an introduction, the later chapters cover some relatively advanced topics, and although the title includes only mediation, it covers moderation as well in some chapters. A major merit of this book is its clear explanations of the concepts and assumptions underlying the important models. Perhaps a noticeable shortcoming is that it does not actually show how the reader could replicate the estimation of the example models. In this sense, Paul Jose's *Doing statistical mediation and moderation* (2013) may be a good complement, although this does not mean it is easy for the reader to follow the examples and computer codes in this book. A more widely used text is Andrew Hayes's (2022) *Introduction to mediation, moderation, and conditional process analysis: A regression-based approach*, currently in its fourth edition. It is popular because Hayes clearly listed the most important models with corresponding computer codes he produced by himself, using the most user-friendly computer program SPSS and the most widely used free language R.

All these texts follow the conventional linear-regression approach that most researchers are familiar with and feel confident using. However, this approach has been perceived as less rigorous than the counterfactual (or potential outcome) approach, which Tylor VanderWeele adopted in his book *Explanation in causal inference: Methods for mediation and interaction* (2015), which is more advanced than the other texts both conceptually and technically. If the reader has the appetite for learning about this approach, I recommend Judea Pearl's *Causal inference in statistics: A primer* (2016) and *Counterfactuals and causal inference: Methods and principles for social research* by Stephen Morgan and Christopher Winship (2014), which are both conceptually clear and technically rigorous. Judea Pearl is also one of the leading figures in the recent development of Directed Acyclic Diagrams (DAGs), and he published *The book of why: The new science of cause and effect* (with Dana Mackenzie, 2018), which is an excellent introduction.

As mentioned in the later sections, mediation and moderation could be studied as special cases of path models, and more generally, structural equation models (SEMs). SEM has become an independent research area with its own journals, conferences, computer programs, etc. For starters, I would recommend *A first course in structural equation modelling* by Tenko Raykov and George Marcoulides (2006), Tiffany Whittaker and Randall Schumacker's *A beginner's guide to structural equation modelling* (fifth edition, 2022) and Rex Kline's *Principles and practice of structural equation modelling* (4th edition, 2016).

9

MIXED-METHODS RESEARCH DESIGN

9.1 Overview and objectives

Research methods and designs are supposed to work closely and logically in order to achieve research objectives and answer research questions. In the second and the third chapters we touched on research design in general terms and in relation to either theorizing intersectionality or understanding intersectionality with qualitative information. The other chapters focus on more specialized methods, which should not mean that these methods could be used without considering a particular research design in which these methods are used. For example, all statistical methods require quantitative data collected usually from sample surveys; thus, a whole series of research design issues must be addressed when conducting these surveys, including defining the target population, drawing a representative sample, designing the instruments of measurement in a questionnaire, choosing a mode of data collection, etc. Researchers using set-theoretic methods are particularly urged to carefully consider the selection of the cases in order to understand different causal solutions and pathways.

The overall objective of this chapter is to introduce and evaluate, systematically and explicitly, ways of employing two or more methods together in a single research project on intersectionality. We will consider a few questions about 'mixed-methods design' and how it could serve our purpose of analysing intersectionality. First, to obtain a solid grounding for subsequent discussions, we must be clear about what 'a mixed-methods design' means and why it is useful and important to 'mix' two or more different methods. Then we will move on to the question of how mixed-methods research design may benefit the study of intersectionality. Most researchers would agree that mixed-methods research design is desirable, yet how this should and could be done remains an unsettled matter as there is no consensus among researchers as to how diverse methods should be mixed or integrated, not merely but often in terms of combining qualitative and quantitative methods. In the context of studying intersectionality, the question is particularly pertinent – researchers must justify a rationale for employing two or more types of data and methods to analyse the intersection of multiple attributes. It is therefore necessary and useful to consider the connection between mixed-methods research design and the analysis of intersectionality in both their general spirits and specific ways of doing so in practice. Without attempting to create a 'standard' procedure for mixing methods, this chapter demonstrates the importance of a clear and sensible logic of mixing methods with some examples of published studies.

9.2 Mixed-methods research design: Key questions and answers

Intuitively, the idea of making use of two or more different research methods in a single study sounds both appealing and straightforward: if each method serves a specific purpose of the study, then it is certainly logical as well as beneficial to employ all available methods. In practice, things are more complicated than that. Although the practice of using different research methods in a single study already existed many years ago, to intentionally apply different types of research methods as a research design in the social sciences was recognized only about three decades ago when major textbooks and peer-reviewed journals were published. Unsurprisingly, the increasing popularity of mixed-methods design has come with competing views of what it means and how researchers should go about conducting it in practice. Perhaps the most widely shared understanding of mixed-methods research is simply the use of a qualitative method and a quantitative method in the same research project. After reviewing the major perspectives and definitions, Creswell and Clark offer their definition by specifying what the researcher does (2018, p. 5):

- Collects and analyses both qualitative and quantitative data rigorously in response to research questions and hypotheses.
- Integrates (or mixes or combines) the two forms of data and their results.
- Organizes these procedures into specific research designs that provide the logic and procedures for conducting the study, and
- Frames these procedures within theory and philosophy.

Other methodologists have offered somehow different definitions (Flick, 2018; Morgan, 2014; Tashakkori et al., 2020), but most researchers would accept the above as a serviceable definition and most disagreements are around minor issues. Here, it is more important and useful for us to consider a series of questions about mixed-methods research by taking the above definition as a reference. Answering these questions will clarify our understanding and dismiss some myths as well.

9.2.1 What are we mixing?

The answer to this question appears to be obvious: according to the above definition, mixed-methods research means mixing qualitative and quantitative data. Strictly speaking, this is not entirely correct – the term is 'mixed *methods*', not 'mixed *data*'. Clearly, both data and methods are mixed – if both qualitative and quantitative data are collected, then both qualitative and quantitative methods must be used for collecting and analysing the data. This may not be always true, however, because the data may not always correspond to the methods used. For example, various forms of textual data such as newspaper articles, emails, blogs, etc. are qualitative, but both qualitative and quantitative methods could be used for collecting and analysing such data. The opposite might be true as well: the data are both qualitative and quantitative whilst the method is entirely quantitative, for example, when qualitative data are transformed into quantitative information. Thus, the widely held assumption that mixed-methods research is always about mixing something qualitative with something quantitative does not always stand; sometimes, it may be beneficial to mix two quantitative or qualitative methods, and some data or methods are beyond the qualitative vs quantitative divide.

9.2.2 Why are we mixing?

The definition by Creswell and Clark (2018) describes what the researcher should do when using mixed methods, but why do researchers want to mix different data and methods? Later in their book they listed several situations in which mixed-methods research is required, which implies that mixed-methods research is *not always required or even desirable*. It is therefore important to state clearly that *the use and the benefits of mixed methods should not be assumed*; quite the opposite, *the reasons for using mixed methods must be explained and justified*. A key assumption of mixed-methods research is the complementarity of qualitative and quantitative methods, which in turn relies on other assumptions. For example, it is commonly asserted that qualitative methods offer depth while, in contrast, quantitative methods offer breadth; put in a different way, qualitative methods are restricted to a small number of cases, while quantitative methods are superficial although they enjoy a larger scale. Clearly, this comes from the idea that deeper understandings come only from qualitative descriptions of a small number of cases, and they cannot come from numbers or statistical models. In fact, words can be very superficial, whilst numbers and statistical models could lead to deep insights that we did not realize before looking at the numbers and models.

Another assumption (or misconception) is that qualitative data and methods represent the complexity of social reality while quantitative ones do not. This implies that data and methods should match the complexity of social reality rather than make complex social phenomena simpler for analysis and understanding. This is a misconception because many methods and models of complexity are highly quantitative and mathematical. All in all, whilst mixing qualitative and quantitative data and methods is certainly an option for social researchers, the potential benefits of doing so should not be assumed, and researchers should not take the pros and cons of qualitative vs qualitative methods for granted.

9.2.3 Mixing or integrating?

In their definition, Creswell and Clark used three verbs: mix, integrate, combine. They made it clear that the key difference lies in 'mix' and 'integrate': 'Integration, or the bringing together of the quantitative and qualitative data and results, is the centerpiece of mixed methods research' (2018, p. xxiv). Mixed-methods research should not simply mean 'mixing' one qualitative method with another quantitative method in a single study; instead, it should require the logic and the rationale of *connecting* any data and methods that are suitable for the research purposes and questions. It is not clear what one is actually doing when mixing two or more things other than putting them together; to integrate, in contrast, suggests that different things are related to one another for a desirable benefit so that they form a coherent or organic whole. Integration of different data and methods is certainly more desirable than mixing them, but it is more challenging as well – it is not enough to simply use different data and methods and assume that the benefits are obvious and come out automatically. But, how to integrate rather than simply mix different data and methods is 'the most confusing and troubling to researchers' (ibid.), because there are few well 'standard' or 'default' procedures for integrating different data and methods which researchers could follow, as their choice will depend on a number of factors, including the research question, the theoretical perspective, the availability of data, the academic background of the researcher. Regardless, the researcher must answer the questions Bryman asked:

> how far do mixed methods researchers analyze, interpret, and write up their research in such a way that the quantitative and qualitative components are mutually illuminating? … The key issue is whether in a mixed methods project, the end product is more than the sum of the individual quantitative and qualitative parts. … if the quantitative component follows the qualitative one, is there some attempt to embellish the quantitative findings so that the qualitative element is not solely a springboard for hypotheses to be tested using a quantitative approach? (2007, p. 8)

In the end, Bryman suggested that 'the mixed methods research should ask a simple question: Has my understanding of my quantitative/qualitative findings been substantially enhanced by virtue of the fact that I also have qualitative/quantitative findings, and have I demonstrated that enrichment?' (ibid.: 20) He drew the researcher's attention to the distinction between integration and triangulation: to integrate different data and methods is not simply to 'triangulate' because

> [m]ixed methods research is not necessarily just an exercise in testing findings against each other. Instead, it is about forging an overall or negotiated account of the findings that brings together both components of the conversation or debate. The challenge is to find ways of fashioning such accounts when we do not have established templates or even rules of thumb for doing so. (Ibid.: 21)

Since then, methodologists of mixed methods have suggested some generic 'templates', which we shall discuss below.

9.2.4 How should we mix or integrate different data and methods?

To satisfy the demand for specific 'recipes' of mixed-methods design, some methodologists have offered options of specific mixed-methods designs. Creswell and Clark proposed three 'core mixed methods designs' (2018, Chapter 3): the convergent design, the explanatory sequential design and the exploratory sequential design. Morgan (2014) introduced four basic designs by considering which part comes first and which is the core, which are very similar to the three proposed by Creswell and Clark. Researchers need to consider three questions when deciding on which one of these is the most appropriate for accomplishing their objectives: the integration of data, the temporal sequence of data collection and the priority of method.

For a convergent design, the temporal sequence of collecting and analysing qualitative and quantitative data is not a significant concern, and neither method is more important than the other, but it is important to compare and contrast the two sets of data in order to discover how they confirm or disagree with each other. Essentially, the convergent design is similar to triangulating different sources of evidence, aiming to examine and evaluate how agreeable they are; presumably, higher agreeability lends stronger support to a conclusion. The challenge is how to make it sensible to compare data of different types so that the consistency between them could be assessed. For example, some official statistics show that the correlation between the financial status of a family and the probability of experiencing domestic violence is very weak and insignificant, which, however, is at odds with what female victims of domestic violence have reported. How could these findings 'converge' to anything? At the moment, we are short of clear ideas for determining when different data have 'converged'.

An exploratory sequential design starts with collecting qualitative data in order to explore and discover which issues are important and set up the context for subsequent quantitative data collection and analysis. This design is particularly useful when little is known about the targeted phenomenon and when quantitative information is important for assessing any effects. Some uncertainties are worth mentioning. Perhaps the most important is the assumption that the qualitative study in the first stage could be meaningfully translated into a useful form of quantitative analysis in the second stage. However, this may not be the case for certain topics or populations; for example, the study in the first stage may have found that poverty is an important factor for children's mental disorders, but it is a great challenge to carry out a quantitative follow-up study to learn how many children in poverty have suffered from mental disorders, because it is no easy matter to define and measure poverty and mental illness, especially among children.

An explanatory sequential design starts with quantitative data collection and analysis in order to map out the overall association among a large number of cases; then qualitative research follows to identify the causes or causal pathways that account for the overall association. The quantitative analysis establishes the target of the subsequent explanatory work. The pathway analysis advocated by Nicholas Weller and Jeb Barnes (2014) fits the bill perfectly. Initially, quantitative information establishes a relationship between an explanatory variable $X1$ and an outcome Y, controlling for other factors $X2$. The strategy is 'to combine the existing quantitative large-N studies with process-tracing case studies' (ibid.: 3). Quantitative data and findings help the researcher 'gain perspective on cases vis-à-vis the broader population' (ibid.: 5). Then comes the question of how this relationship occurs, so the next objective is to find the causal pathways leading from $X1$ to Y. Weller and Barnes laid out some analytic requisites for pathway analysis to be successful. First, the study 'must establish a robust relationship between $X1$ and Y that is likely to represent a causal relationship' (ibid.: 22). 'Second, large-N datasets are needed that help understand (a) the functional form of the relationship between $X1$ and Y; (b) the values of $X1$ and Y (and relevant controls) in specific cases; and/or (c) the expected magnitude and direction of the relationship between $X1$ and Y in individual cases' (ibid.: 23). They listed four steps in the process of selecting cases (ibid.: 59–67):

1.   Assessing the requisites for pathway analysis
2.   Reviewing the literature on the X1/Y relationship
3.   Visualize key variation
4.   Selecting cases

Clearly, this is a very thoughtful design with detailed explanations for why and how the initial quantitative description is connected to the later qualitative exploration. However, it is worth drawing the reader's attention to a few assumptions in such design. First, the statistical relationship between X1 and Y is believed to be the outcome of certain causal processes, which the researcher must justify by drawing on other sources of information. Second, for which cases the supposed causal relationship is valid, which relates to the notion of 'causal homogeneity' or 'causal diversity', needs to be answered carefully with empirical evidence. If every case has its own causal pathway from X1 to Y and there are many cases, then the empirical work of demonstrating every one of them could be overwhelming. On the other hand, a study may be criticized for assuming a 'universal causal pathway' if only one causal pathway is reported. This research design seems to be more effective when the number of cases is relatively small so that the researcher could know each case well enough. If the number of cases is very large, then it could be very difficult to make out any clear pattern in the relationship. Third, this design is stronger at helping researchers select cases by making use of quantitative information about the context and the targeted population than showing how any pathway could be discovered in the second stage.

9.2.5 Research designs beyond the qualitative vs quantitative divide

All mixed-methods research designs introduced above assume that only two methods are used, one being qualitative and the other quantitative. It is therefore important to point out that those are not the only ways to conduct a mixed-methods study. Researchers should be open and prepared to use all available sources of evidence and methods to answer the research questions. For example, one could use two quantitative methods if both sample survey data and historical time series are available. Similarly, one could use two qualitative methods in the same study as well, such as interviews plus document analysis.

For some designs, it may not be very meaningful to distinguish the qualitative from the quantitative as the two are inherent aspects of the research process. Such research designs are genuinely 'integrated' mixed-methods designs, because different data and methods are connected components of an organic whole. One example of such a design is the Qualitative Comparative Analysis (QCA) and set-theoretic analysis introduced in Chapter 5, which add the methodological discipline of quantitative analysis to qualitative analysis in order to maximize the rigour of research and reveal the causal complexity and inductive sensitivity of qualitative analysis to quantitative analysis. The membership of a case in a particular set, which is qualitative, is quantified (calibrated). Later, the causal solutions are qualitative in nature, but they are assessed with statistics such as consistency and coverage.

Another example of inherently mixed-methods research design is social network analysis. Usually, the number of cases (or nodes) is small so that the relations among each pair can be clearly represented with a map-like diagram. In selecting the cases, the researcher must learn as much as possible by making use of qualitative contextual data. The subsequent analysis of the network becomes quantitative as several aspects of the network are measured with quantitative indicators, including the number of ties, centrality, betweenness, strength of ties, etc. Furthermore, quantitative data about the cases such as age, social class, etc. could be added to the network analysis. Eventually, these quantitative analyses will lead to qualitative interpretations of the structural positions, the ties, and the overall structural features of the network, and the quantitative results will be able to be compared qualitatively.

A further example is the quantitative analysis of textual data (newspaper articles, blogs, emails, novels, legal documents). In contrast to QCA or social network analysis, the benefits of using the quantitative methods to analyse texts become most compelling when the number of cases (texts) is very large, such as hundreds or even thousands. These data are clearly qualitative in nature, but several quantitative analyses could be conducted. Initially, if the total number of texts is very large, the researcher could draw a sample of them, either randomly or purposefully. Then, the sampled texts could be transformed into quantitative data. Here, some transformations could be more natural and less subjective because they readily come from the qualitative data, such as the number of words, the page number of an article in a newspaper, the number of receipts of an email, the number of clicks or likes of a blog or video. Further quantitative information such as word counts can be collected as well.

Finally, Cultural Consensus Modelling (CCM) is another example of analysing qualitative data with quantitative methods, which assesses how much people share certain cultural beliefs across several communities or countries (Romney, 1999; Romney et al. 1986; Weller, 1987, 2007). CCM aims to tease out the similarities and differences among the communities or countries in order to learn how much their norms and values have been accepted by their members. Ulijaszek (2013, p. 272) offered an updated and brief introduction to the method and an example. According to him, researchers using CCM need to take the following three steps:

1. identify the significant issues relating to the topic of enquiry, which can be carried out by literature review, interview, questionnaire, or focus groups; clearly, this part of the analysis is mostly qualitative;
2. determine the values attributed to those issues, which involves quantification of attitudes and beliefs about issues salient to the topic in hand; this part is quantitative because the attitudes and beliefs of the values will be measured with quantitative instruments so that their consistency could be measured later on, a process inherently similar to psychological instruments;
3. determine cultural competence and cultural consensus within the group or groups under investigation, which involves statistical manipulation using factor analysis; this part is mostly quantitative with qualitative interpretations of the results.

9.3 Mixed-methods research design and intersectionality

9.3.1 Does intersectionality require mixed-methods research design?

This question assumes a clear answer to another question: what kind of research does intersectionality as an analytical and theoretical framework require? This is a very important question not only because prominent advocates of intersectionality have emphasized much more the theoretical principles than the methodologies but also because it is a general principle of good research to guide empirical research with theories. Creswell and Clark stated that 'the use of theory and conceptual framework in mixed methods research' as a particular research design depends on such a principle (2018, p. xxv). Yet no widely accepted methodological principles and procedures have been established for either intersectionality or mixed-methods research, making it very difficult to connect the two without entailing criticisms. Here, I shall highlight a number of ways in which mixed-methods research may (or may not) serve the purposes of intersectionality and illustrate how these have been done in the practice of research in the next section.

To start with, some researchers have evaluated the pros and cons of mixed-methods designs for studying intersectionality. For example, Griffin and Museus (2011) identified a few respective advantages of quantitative and qualitative methods for the study of intersectionality. More specifically, quantitative methods could offer the following three benefits: (1) Category Comparison: to identify inequities that exist at the intersections of multiple social identities or groupings; (2) Category Deconstruction: to disaggregate quantitative data to analyse subgroups within a particular category to generate a more complex picture of reality than is presented when the entire racial category is examined; (3) Generalizability Assessment: to quantify the findings of a qualitative inquiry into the experiences of a person or persons who are situated at the intersection of social identities or groupings to assess whether those findings are generalizable to the larger population at that intersection. And qualitative methods could offer two benefits: (1) Voice Excavation: to excavate the unique voices of those who are situated at the intersections of multiple social identities and groupings, which can illuminate their unique experiences and realities that might otherwise remain unheard; and (2) Disparity Explanation: to answer questions regarding why particular groups at social identity intersections suffer from disparities in areas such as psychosocial well-being, moral and civic development, or postgraduate educational and occupational success. Similarly, Grace (2014) suggested four dimensions along which researchers could enhance the rigour in mixed-methods research in intersectionality, including the timing of data collection, the weighting of quantitative and qualitative data, when and how the different data types are mixed in the study, and the way in which the study is informed by the theoretical framework and its assumptions. All are very similar to the factors that Creswell and others have asked researchers to consider when mixing or integrating qualitative and quantitative methods. Grace and his colleagues illustrated their suggestion with a specific study (Grace et al., 2014), which we shall discuss in the next section.

On the other hand, we cannot assume that most, let alone all, researchers of intersectionality accept or require mixed-methods research design. In answering the question 'What research problems require mixed methods?' (2018, pp. 7–12), Creswell and Clark believed that they were sufficiently comprehensive with the following seven possible situations:

- to obtain more complete and corroborated results
- to explain initial results
- to first explore before administering instruments
- to enhance an experimental study with a qualitative method
- to describe and compare different types of cases
- to involve participants in the study
- to develop, implement, and evaluate a program.

This list was not created with the purpose of studying any particular topic in mind. For the study of intersectionality, one could say that whilst all seven situations are suitable, none fits the spirits of intersectionality particularly well. More specific discussions are needed in order to make a stronger case for applying mixed-methods research to the study of intersectionality.

One way to move forward is to identify the barriers that prevent researchers from applying mixed-methods research to better understand and explain intersectionality. If mixed-methods research is defined as the simultaneous and integrated use of both qualitative and quantitative methods in a single study, then a barrier to adopting a mixed-methods research design in intersectionality is the 'incompatibility' between quantitative methods and the key demands of intersectionality. Nobody has argued against the general compatibility of qualitative methods with intersectionality, while some limitations of quantitative methods are acknowledged. Therefore, once the barrier to applying quantitative methods in intersectionality is removed, nothing will prevent researchers from applying mixed-methods research to the analysis of intersectionality. So, let's try to remove this barrier.

9.3.2 The rigidity of demographic categories

How to characterize and theorize demographic categories such as sex, sexuality, gender, race, ethnicity, nationality, etc. has been a thorny issue in the study of intersectionality. Initially, intersectionality became a prominent issue because the intersections of some of these categories revealed previously ignored but marginalized groups, most notably but certainly not limited to Black women. Had the classification of sex, race and other attributes remained binary, the research on intersectionality would have been very straightforward. More recently, some prominent scholars of intersectionality have berated the existing classification of demographic attributes with several interrelated problems. First, the existing categories of demographic attributes are not inclusive enough, leaving people of certain attributes excluded; the continuing expansion of the categories of gender and sexuality is perhaps the most obvious example. Second, the boundaries and the meanings of demographic attributes are not fixed but rather fluid. Third, the categories employed in a typical social survey questionnaire may not be consistent with how members of some marginalized groups interpret them. Fourth, demographic variables should not have been taken seriously as explanatory variables in and of themselves for the marginalization of some intersectional groups (Bowleg, 2008, p. 322). The study by Harper (2011) paid particular attention to these problems. Through a large-scale longitudinal survey on university students, she made a few important observations: only about one-third of the students described themselves as being of one race; students' identities shifted over time – one-third marking only one race when they entered college, whereas more than half (56%) marked two or more races during their senior year (Harper, 2007). Therefore, their identities were not as static as assumed, and their understanding of certain categories varied with family backgrounds.

Whilst these are undeniably important and serious issues, it is not hopelessly hard for quantitative research instruments and methods to be adapted to accommodate them. More categories could be added to demographic variables to make them more inclusive. And if the temporal change of the chosen categories is a significant concern, then longitudinal data should be collected given available resources, or retrospective data could be collected in a cross-sectional survey. The issues of unfixed or inconsistent classifications are not insurmountable either. Pilots could be conducted to determine the boundaries and meanings of demographic attributes. The new categories or meanings could be incorporated in the design of subsequent quantitative instruments.

9.3.3 The complexity of intersectional categories

It is certainly more challenging to study the intersectional categories than to study one of them at a time. As McCall (2005, p. 1790) pointed out, a full commitment to intersectionality significantly complicates quantitative analysis because intersectionality calls upon us to study multiple groups along multiple axes, and the more categories we seek to include, the more challenging it is to measure individual and interactive effects. This is a challenge that both qualitative and quantitative researchers must face, and it is difficult to think of any reason for which quantitative researchers are in a less favourable position in this regard. In fact, quantitative methods are more powerful of systematically dealing with the large number of intersectional categories than qualitative methods, as demonstrated in previous chapters. Another criticism of quantitative methods is that they 'seek to disentangle categories in order to address their impacts and interactions'; therefore, 'they fail to appreciate one of intersectionality's central messages that race, gender, and class oppressions create a *synthetic* experience that can't be understood by decompositional analysis of the interplay between discrete factors (Fernandes, 1997; Hancock, 2013)' (Bailey et al., 2019, p. 4). This implies that all quantitative analysis is decompositional rather than synthetic, or only qualitative methods can analyse synthetic experiences. There is no need to probe into the meanings of 'decompositional' and 'synthetic'; it is, however, wise to refrain from making sweeping claims and explore what quantitative methods can do or how they can be adapted for a particular task. As a general principle, it is also wise to make our analysis simple and clear rather than complex and ambivalent.

9.3.4 The voices of the marginalized

As far back as the mid-1960s, Howard Becker had already claimed that, ideologically, sociologists would always 'take the side of the underdog' (1967). Intersectionality has taken one step further by aiming to discover which 'underdogs' have been mistreated and how. Some become 'underdogs' because they happen to be in the intersections of several suppressing social forces. It is perplexing, however, how the commitment to helping the 'underdogs' is connected to qualitative or quantitative methods. For example, some have stated that 'qualitative methods interrogate the boundarymaking process, often focusing on the experiences of those detrimentally affected by the interactions of multiple factors … place the perspectives of multiple marginalized groups at the center of research' (Bailey et al., 2019, p. 4). By mentioning qualitative methods alone, these researchers clearly imply that quantitative studies do not or cannot do these things, yet again it is difficult to imagine what will prevent quantitative researchers from doing these. As demonstrated in some of the previous chapters, quantitative research is in no weaker position to tackle these issues. It is a myth that only qualitative methods such as interviews and focus groups are able to study experiences and only words could describe and explain the experiences of the 'underdogs'. In fact, quantitative research has accumulated an enormous amount of expertise and knowledge of studying people's experiences, feelings, attitudes and behaviours.

9.3.5 The commitment to enhance social justice

Of the most widely quoted words of Karl Marx is his eleventh thesis on Feuerbach: 'The philosophers have only *interpreted* the world, in various ways, the point, however, is to *change* it' (1978[1888], p. 145, emphasis original). Although never openly stated, intersectionality is one of the few endeavours that have taken Marx's advice seriously; the only difference is that the suppressed was not the working class anymore but a variety of groups with certain intersectional attributes. Inspired by Crenshaw and Hill Collins, many researchers of intersectionality have repeatedly pointed out that intersectionality is much more than simply an analytical or theoretical framework for academic research; perhaps more importantly, it is a commitment to enhance social justice by liberating the marginalized. In this sense, it is insufficient, or so it is argued, for researchers to publish papers and books about intersectionality; rather, they are expected to create new knowledge, democratic institutions, identities and practices (Chun et al., 2013, p. 924). The researchers who employ research methods to examine intersections but fail to commit themselves to social justice and equality are not actually doing *genuine* research on intersectionality (Alexander-Floyd, 2012). If so, it should be useful to make a distinction between two forms of intersectionality: the 'academic intersectionality' whose mission is much more modest, simply to apply the analytical framework of intersectionality for academic research, and 'practical intersectionality' as a political campaign, which aims to mobilize collective political actions that change the existing political institutions and liberate the subordinated from marginalization and suppression. It would be ideal if a researcher could do both. Clearly, this is a much bigger issue that this book cannot address; for the concern of this chapter, the key point is that the commitment to social justice does not require or necessarily endorse any particular research methods or designs. Therefore, there should be no good reason for stopping quantitative methods from joining qualitative ones to analyse intersectionality with mixed-methods research designs.

9.4 Examples of mixed-methods research on intersectionality

What has been presented and discussed is what they are, examples; there are other mixed-methods research designs that researchers of intersectionality may find useful. Each study is selected to show at least one distinctive feature so that the reader could learn some innovative ideas of how to mix and integrate different research methods for studying intersectionality.

9.4.1 Embedding qualitative research in quantitative research longitudinally

Across many countries and for many years, HIV (human immunodeficiency virus) has been a major public health issue. Researchers have learnt that sexual intercourse among gay and bisexual men and men who have sex with men is responsible for some of the transmission of the virus. Men who have sex with men must adapt their sexual behaviours in order to avoid getting infected, and these coping strategies are referred to as 'seroadaptations'. How effective they are, however, remains very uncertain, something a study tried to find out (Grace et al., 2014). Grace (2014) also offered his advice on how mixed-methods research designs could serve the purposes of intersectionality, using the study of his team as an illustration.

This study was conducted at a community sexual health clinic in Vancouver, Canada. From June 2011 to January 2012, they recruited men who satisfied the following eligibility criteria: '(1) self-disclosed that they had had sex with men at the time of their recent HIV test, (2) were 19 years of age or older, (3) had recently received a negative HIV test result using a point-of-care HIV test and/or a pooled nucleic acid amplification test for HIV at our study recruitment site, (4) spoke and read English, (5) intended to reside in the Greater Vancouver area for the next 12 months and (6) were able to sign and fully comprehend the study consent form' (Grace et al., 2014, p. 318). The rationale for including some of these is very clear; for example, the fourth criterion on English was to ensure the participants were able to communicate with the researchers without any language barriers, and the second criterion on age and the sixth on consent were for ethical reasons. The study required the participants to be available for at least 12 months, which is why the fifth criterion was included. The first criterion is clearly the most important, representing the nature of the targeted population. The reason for including the third criterion is not obvious, and the authors did not provide an explanation; presumably, it might be too big a medical or ethical responsibility to involve those who tested HIV positive in their study. The intersectional nature of the targeted population is not entirely clear because the relevant intersectional attributes certainly include sex (men vs women) and sexuality (heterosexual vs LGBTQIA+), but other attributes, such as HIV status (positive or negative), age, use of adaptive methods, etc., could be relevant as well. The sample is not a random sample, and the sample size (166) is not large.

The most innovative feature of this study lies in the way qualitative methods were embedded in the quantitative ones in a longitudinal manner. Over a period of 12 months, all participants were asked to complete one self-administered questionnaire online and to provide social network data in an interview. The quantitative data comprised the responses collected from the online survey and the social network interview, which were longitudinal because they were collected at four time points (7 days, 14 days, 30 days, 180 days and 360 days). Qualitative data was longitudinal as well but repeated at only two time points, one right after the first round of the online survey and social network interview, and the other at about the same time as the last round (see Grace 2014, p. 14, for a diagram of the whole process). The qualitative data collection was 'embedded' or 'nested' in the quantitative data collection in the sense that participants of the qualitative data collection were drawn as a sub-sample from the entire sample – 33 participants who reported to have had at least one instance of condomless anal sex with another man were selected to participate in the two rounds of qualitative in-depth interviews. The quantitative and social network data allow the researchers to see the whole picture of the profiles and the social relations of the participants, and the qualitative data and analysis would let them learn the details of adaptive behaviours among the most vulnerable group. Such design allowed the researchers to link the qualitative interviews with the quantitative and social network data; therefore, they could interpret one part of the results in the context of the other. Finally, the longitudinal nature of both the qualitative and the quantitative data allowed the researchers to detect and explain significant changes of the participants' behaviours.

This is one of the mixed-methods studies that focus on only one intersectional group, running the risk of losing sight of other intersectional groups, which may not necessarily be a weakness if there is a strong case for focusing on this particular group. In this study, the researchers did seem to assume that it was alright to focus on men who have sex with men while ignoring other intersectional groups, because they were the most vulnerable to HIV infection. This may not be the case for other studies, particularly when the comparison of all relevant intersectional groups will lead to stronger arguments for the effect of inter-sectional attributes. The researchers focused on the qualitative results without presenting the quantitative results, perhaps due to the small sample size, which is unfortunate, as the readers would not be able to see the benefit of letting different data analyses illuminate each other.

9.4.2 Incorporating participants' qualitative input into quantitative data collection

If a well-designed mixed-methods study should have a clear rationale for connecting different research methods coherently and logically, then it is not enough simply to use these methods side by side in the same study. This example to be introduced illustrates a sensible way to achieve this by incorporating the participants' qualitative input into the subsequent quan-titative study so that the limitations of quantitative research will be minimized. This design is particularly effective from the perspective of intersectionality when the researchers solicit input from the intersectional groups who are deemed as having been disadvantaged. The substantive issue that Heather Metcalf (2016) and her colleagues (2018) aim to tackle is the lack of diversity among people who learn and later take a career in subjects of STEM (science, technology, engineering and medicine). This is a lose–lose situation – the students lose their opportunities to find employment in many well-paid industries, and the industries lose many potentially capable employees. It is therefore important to identify the barriers to widening the participation by certain groups in these subjects. They have found the existing research problematic in multiple ways, including masking 'the experiences of women of colour', drop-ping 'the responses of indigenous participants' and merging 'racial groups in problematic ways', and rarely enquiring 'about lesbian, gay, bisexual, trans, queer/questioning, and others (LGBTQIA+) or disabled scientists or engineers' (Metcalf et al. 2018, p. 581). In short, in order to achieve the required level of statistical significance, previous studies ignored many inter-sectional groups by maintaining a sufficiently large sample size. As a result, the categories of survey instruments do not represent those of the intersectional groups, a problem that

Metcalf and her colleagues particularly aim to rectify. This does not mean, however, that they should abandon the method of collecting large-scale quantitative data.

Following the general approach of 'critical mixed-methodology', their study

> looks deeply at our survey design and the purpose and context surrounding each survey item and element—reflects on the construction of variables and whether they adequately capture the experiences and identities of our participants, and understands the potential interpretations and consequences of those interpretations for respondents, communities, policy making, and future research (Metcalf, 2016). (Metcalf et al., 2018, p. 584)

Clearly, there is no better way to incorporate the experiences and identities of the participants than to invite them to contribute to the design of the research instruments. They refer to their strategy as 'creating inclusion through survey design'. More specifically, they take two actions. The first step is to conduct a pilot study to collect qualitative feedback from the participants to their initial design of survey instruments: 'before launching our survey broadly across our membership, we piloted it with the traditional categories, plus those shown in the research and practice as most comprehensive, and open-ended response options for pilot participants to add any options that might be missing' (ibid., p. 592). This feedback will certainly make the categories (or response options) in their instruments much more inclusive than those included in the previous study. A risk remains, however, that the pilot, due to its small scale, may still have missed some important categories or options. To minimize such a risk, they provided 'space for participants to comment directly on the response options available' in the full survey (ibid.); that is, they were literally collecting both qualitative and quantitative data at the same time. The subsequent analyses of these data would be an integration of qualitative and quantitative methods as well, as both parts relate to the same group of participants.

It is important to realize that the researchers of the above study enjoyed the autonomy of designing their own research instruments, a luxury that many individual researchers and students do not have; rather, most will have to use existing secondary data. Metcalf and her colleagues mentioned this situation in their paper and gave other researchers the following advice: 'Even using preexisting, national-level data, where we do not have any influence over the survey design and implementation, taking a critical intersectionality approach allows us to ask these questions analytically' (2018, p. 587). Whilst it remains vague as to how researchers take 'a critical intersectionality approach' or 'ask these questions analytically', the low level of inclusiveness in existing survey instruments is a much bigger issue that should be addressed first. The lack of awareness of intersectionality among survey designers is clearly an issue, but even for those who are well aware of the importance of including marginalized groups, they must cope with some technical difficulties, including the sample size required for achieving a certain level of statistical significance for all intersectional groups, and the related issue of the sparseness of data for some statistical methods and models. It may also be a tricky issue to analyse qualitative responses to survey instruments alongside quantitative data, as the qualitative responses tend to come from only a small number of participants and vary significantly from one participant to another.

9.4.3 Embedding RCTs and quantitative surveys in longitudinal focus groups

Stigma has been claimed as the biggest barrier to tackling mental illness. To overcome it, the World Psychiatric Association (WPA) embarked on an International Programme to Fight the Stigma and Discrimination because of Schizophrenia in 1996. Norman Sartorius, the former Director of WHO's Mental Health division, published an article in *Nature* in 2011, with the title 'Short-Lived Campaigns are Not Enough'. To discover how certain intersectional groups experience and cope with stigmas of mental illness, a team of Canadian researchers launched an ambitious '4-year, multi-site (Calgary, Vancouver, and Toronto) mixed-methods intervention study that evaluated the effectiveness of interventions in reducing self and social mental health stigma among Asian men' (Morrow et al., 2020: abstract). As a part of this large study, they studied Asian men's experiences of stigma and mental illness in Vancouver. Whilst this suggests that the primary intersectional attributes that the researchers were interested in are ethnicity and gender, the study also examined the mediating effects of 'age, immigration experiences, sexual and gender identities, racism and racialization processes, normative expectations about masculinity, and material inequality' (ibid., p. 1306). The key objective of the research project was to move beyond existing studies by exploring and revealing the heterogeneity of the experiences of stigma and mental illness across different social groups.

The research design involved both interventions through randomized controlled trials (RCTs), questionnaire surveys, which is the quantitative part of the study, and focus groups conducted before and after the RCTs, which is the qualitative part. The researchers conducted 10 pre-intervention focus groups. Then they carried out RCTs on three groups with respective treatment, including Acceptance and Commitment Therapy (ACT), Contact-Based Empowerment Education (CEE) and the combination of ACT + CEE, plus a fourth group as control. Quantitative data were collected through a questionnaire survey, capturing the participants' self-reports of stigma, psychological flexibility, valued life domains, mindfulness and empowerment readiness. Finally, seven post-intervention focus groups were conducted. The qualitative data included not only the transcripts of the focus groups but also observations and logs by participants. Presumably, the idea behind such a design was to assess the effectiveness of the interventions, which, however, is not the focus of the published report. The benefit of mixing qualitative and qualitative data remains obscured as well – the findings are exclusively qualitative, with the descriptive statistics of the participants the only quantitative results.

This study has revealed an important tension in designing mixed-methods research and following the principles of intersectionality at the same time. This was first reflected in how the participants identified themselves and the organization of the focus groups. When organizing focus groups, the common practice is to put participants of the same attributes in a group so that they feel comfortable with sharing their experiences, which clearly assumes that the attributes are clearly defined. In the spirit of intersectionality, however, the attributes are not supposed to be taken as 'fixed', at least not rigid. Although the targeted population of this study was 'Asian men', the researchers 'relied on self-identification and did not police participants' gender or ethno-racial identities in recruitment processes' (ibid., p. 1307). Given the number of regions and nationalities in Asia and the possible variety of male identities, there would be a large number of cross-classified categories of 'Asian men'. The published paper may not have the space for reporting all of the self-identified categories, but in the end the researchers did not 'assign men on the basis of their particular ethnic identity, age, or language' but 'formed mixed groups', which allowed them 'to observe interactions among intergenerational and multi-ethnic groups of participants' (1308). A similar tension exists between the intervention and the within-group heterogeneity. Essentially, any intervention assumes the homogeneity of the intervention's effect on the studied units; otherwise, the study should have been redesigned with different units. However, this may be inconsistent with the fundamental ideas of intersectionality, such as the fluidity and the social construction of identity. In order to make their study truly intersectional, the researchers

> created opportunities for observation and data collection focused on the ways in which masculinity was constructed by participants in relation to breadwinner status, age, and other lived experiences and structural inequities. While the interventions targeted stigma, our qualitative data collection focused on within group differences. We attended to the ways in which men described their experiences of stigma and connected these to their migration experiences, including employment and class status, age, and masculinity. (Ibid., p. 1307)

A challenge worth serious attention from researchers of intersectionality is that the research targets, the eligibility criteria of the participants and the relations under study all become so uncertain, varied and diversified that it becomes very difficult to organize clear and well-defined research activities. Finally, another merit of this study in light of intersectionality, as the authors claimed, is 'This diversity within our research team, and our commitment to team interpretation of the data, allowed us to engage in more nuanced and complex theorizations of ideas like culture and filial piety' (ibid.). This is intersectionality applied to the researchers. It is certainly beneficial to the study if the intersectional backgrounds of the research team members happen to be relevant to the objectives or the targeted population. Note, however, that additional effort is required in order to reconcile and manage the heterogeneous views and preferences among the members.

By now it should have become clear to the reader that while some innovative attempts have been made to connect mixed-methods research to intersectionality, this research strategy still has a long way to go in coming up with designs that are consistent with the spirit of intersectionality and the requirements of rigorous academic principles at the same time.

9.5 Suggested readings and questions for discussion

A lot of work is needed for mixed-methods research and research on intersectionality to dovetail each other in a way that both sides would find desirable. There is a shortage of texts on the subject of mixed-methods research design serving the purposes and principles of intersectionality, which reflects the discrepancy between the lively development of theoretical and conceptual discussions and the lack of progression on the methodological front. There is no shortage of texts on mixed-methods research design for social science research in general, such as those mentioned in this chapter. Among these, the one by Creswell and Clark is perhaps the most widely known. Creswell also published a shorter version, *A concise introduction to mixed methods research* (2021), which students new to the field may find more accessible. Some authors have emphasized 'integrating' rather than 'mixing' research methods; see, for example, Bazeley (2018), Morgan (2014), Plowright (2011), etc. Still more texts have introduced and discussed more specific research designs; for example, some methodologists have particularly promoted the use of case studies in combination with large-scale quantitative analysis, particularly regression models, including Goertz (2017), Seawright (2016), and Weller and Barnes (2014). The strategies introduced and discussed in these texts may still sound quite generic, and the reader may find the examples or cases more useful.

This means that the reader must also think hard about how a particular strategy of integration could guide their individual research project and how the design in another study may be applied in their study. As none of these texts was written for the study of intersectionality, the reader can only find inspiration in published papers, some of which have been introduced and discussed in this chapter. This is both a challenge and an opportunity to creatively use multiple methods, on the one hand, and accomplish the objectives of intersectionality at the same time. It is worth starting with the following question: what kind of research design will best serve the purpose of a study on intersectionality? Answer this question in the context of your study without feeling any pressure of using mixed-methods designs; that is, if you are confident that you could achieve your research objectives with a single-method design, there would be no need to mix different methods.

Finally, a situation that this chapter did not include is when you find multiple studies on the same issue of intersectionality that used different methods, which raises the hope of conducting mixed-methods research across not one but several studies. How should this new type of mix-methods studies be conducted? Meta-analysis is a set of statistical methods that allow researchers to compare, evaluate and synthesize results from multiple independent studies in order to generate an overall estimate of effect size, which is widely used in medical and quantitative studies. For meta-analysis, integration and synthesis are possible because most pieces of information about the studies, such as sample sizes, are comparable. As far as I know, there is no corresponding 'meta-analysis' for qualitative and mixed-methods studies. Clearly, the challenge is to determine in what sense the results from different studies using different methods and designs are comparable and therefore it would be meaningful to synthesize them into a more concise summary. If it is safe to assume that the number of studies on intersectionality using a variety of methods and designs will increase rapidly in the coming decades, then researchers need ways of distilling useful information from these studies.

10

REFLECTIONS AND CONCLUSIONS

10.1 Overview and objectives

We have reached the end of this book, but not the journey of exploring the use of existing research methods for studying intersectionality empirically. As with many other social science concepts and theories, once intersectionality has been established as a widely used perspective and idea, researchers need to work on the clarity of its meaning, specify its classifications and sub-types, and either use existing methods or invent new ones so that new empirical discoveries can be made, which in turn will enhance further research activities. Despite its unusually strong inclination to go beyond academic research and grow into a social justice campaign, intersectionality can only maintain its momentum and popularity with the support of rigorous and unbiased empirical studies. Anyone serious about intersectionality must consider how to improve the quality of empirical investigations on intersectionality. In spite of the desire for developing research methods that are 'customized' for the purposes and principles of intersectionality, so far no such methods have been invented, because the idea of intersectionality became widely used when many methods had already been invented and developed, making it unnecessary and perhaps even unwise to 'reinvent the wheel'. What researchers of intersectionality should do is use these methods innovatively and professionally. This is why I think books like this one are worth writing and reading. What I have tried to do in this book is show how some of the existing methods could be employed for the purpose of demonstrating the effects of intersectionality. In this final chapter, I would like to stand back from the technicalities and share my personal experiences and thoughts on a few general issues with the reader, including the relationship between the research and the researcher, the relationship between academic research and political campaign, and some of the research methods that were not discussed, at least not extensively in this book. In the end, I would like to summarize my way of studying intersectionality empirically as a generic approach that, I hope, will guide future empirical investigations on this very important social phenomenon.

10.2 Reflections on personal experiences

Social scientists disagree with each other on many matters. One of them is the role of the researcher in research. At one end is the desire to make social science research as 'objective' and 'hard' as possible so that it could become as useful and respectable as natural sciences; for example, there has been a suggestion for *Making Social Science Matter* because it has failed (Flyvbjerg, 2001) and a call for *Making Social Sciences More Scientific* (Taagepera, 2008). For researchers in this camp, their backgrounds, identities and experiences should not intervene in the research process and therefore have nothing to do with the quality of research. In contrast, as long as they can keep themselves employed, many academics in the social sciences can afford paying little attention to such calls. In fact, some of them have moved in the opposite direction; for example, one notable sign of making social science research even more subjective and 'soft' is the increasing popularity of autoethnography (Adams et al., 2021; Poulos, 2021). For those in this camp, since the researchers' identities and experiences unavoidably affect how the research is conducted and how the results are interpreted, it would be desirable to take them into account or even capitalize on them. This is clearly a crude representation of the current situation – there are some moderate variations in between these two extreme views, but such division among social scientists will continue to exist for a long time.

For the study of intersectionality, who the researcher is, especially in relation to those under study, seems to be a particularly important question, which is somewhat puzzling given the caveat that intersectionality is not about identity or identity politics. Some even have demanded that 'The intersectional researcher must begin by examining their positionality within the hierarchies of focus and avoid identifying as an objective observer outside the frame of investigation' (Fehrenbacher & Patel, 2020, p. 150). To reflect on personal status and experiences is a guiding principle for almost all qualitative research, but it appears to be especially important for intersectionality. Accordingly, a reflective section on the researcher's identity is something essential that must be included in a paper about intersectionality, such as some of the studies cited in the previous chapters. When writing about their identities, most authors say that they are in a more advantageous position than those they were studying, which is not at all surprising as, by definition, those under study must have suffered from a certain form of disadvantage or discrimination whilst the researcher enjoys a decent job. A series of questions then arises: Does the discrepancy between the researcher's social position and that of those under study compromise the researcher's ability to understand those they are studying? Would the quality of research have been higher were those under study able to study themselves? Since this is not actually feasible, how could the reflection by the academic researcher improve the quality of research?

Without getting into controversy over these questions, I feel obliged to share reflections on whether, and if so how, my personal identities and experiences may have affected the writing of this book. Despite the fact that this is a book about research methods, it is about research methods used in the study of intersectionality, so I do not think that I can escape from such an obligation; otherwise, this book would have to bear the risk of being criticized as 'incomplete' or 'not genuine' if some reflections on the author's personal status and experience were missing, which is why I promised in the Preface to offer reflections on how my identities and backgrounds have influenced my writing.

If pressed, I would use the following words to describe my identities: male, middle-aged, married (husband), father, well-educated (PhD from a good university), (legal) immigrant (in four countries), (visible) ethnic minority (in Western societies), middle-class (both income and lifestyle), experienced lecturer and researcher (for more than 20 years), author of several books and many articles, etc. Do any of these have anything to do with the writing of this book? Honestly, my answer is mostly negative. Perhaps the only relevant identity is that I am a university lecturer, which is not particularly helpful because instead of this book I could have written other books and articles. A more important confession I need to make is that I have accepted the idea that my personal experiences and feelings should not 'contaminate' 'scientific' research. I put the two words in quotation marks because I know other academics would not take them seriously or would interpret them in very different ways. It has become part of my unconsciousness that *what we should care about is the science, not the scientist*. I cannot recall exactly where I got this idea from, but that shows the power of 'educational culture' – ideas become inculcated in people's minds without even being explicitly stated.

Colleagues and fellow researchers would associate such a way of thinking with negative labels, including 'positivistic', 'naïve', 'superficial', 'objectifying', 'insensible', etc. Especially considering intersectionality, they would tell me off for staying in the ivory tower without caring about the disadvantaged, the suppressed or the discriminated, which is particularly unacceptable for a sociologist. To quantify views, emotions and experiences, to measure and model relations and processes with mathematics and statistics, to focus on aggregate patterns rather than individual idiosyncrasies – these are all interpreted as traits of a rigid, mechanical and superficial mode of social science research. These academic orientations could be directly linked to the intersectionality of the personal identities of the researcher. Recently, I met two senior female academics on two separate occasions, respectively, and both were very surprised to learn that I work on loneliness and analyse qualitative data. One of them even said, 'That's not something for someone like you to work on!'. Clearly, they found me surprisingly (perhaps a bit frustratingly as well) different from the image of a male Chinese academic who churns out statistics on a computer on a daily basis. I do not find such a stigmatized image particularly offensive – although I do not have a reliable source of evidence, I believe it is true that most social scientists of Chinese origin working in Western countries use quantitative methods. What I do find offensive is the implication that Chinese male academics are incapable of studying more subtle issues and that statistical analysis is mechanical and superficial.

In addition to the academic stereotype of Chinese academics in Western countries, another implication is that they are not really well positioned to study intersectionality because they are economically better off than other minority groups in Western societies. It is true that the average level of education and income among the Chinese in any Western country is higher than most other racial or ethnic minority groups, even higher than that of White people; for example, according to the American Community Survey 2021 (United States Census Bureau, retrieved 1 March, 2023), the median household income among the Chinese (including Taiwanese) is around 100,000 dollars, which is the second highest to (only lower than that of Indians) and much higher than that of White people (75 thousand) and of African Americans (less than 47,000). In 2018, the percentage of college (university) graduates among Asian and Pacific Islanders was the highest in the US, more than 56%, much higher than that among White people (35%) and Black people (25%) (Statistica, accessed 1 March 2023). For a sociologist writing about intersectionality, this comes not as something to be proud of but to feel qualms about. Fortunately, I did have some experience of disadvantage and discrimination. My childhood was mostly spent in poverty – my dad had to ride his bike for long hours to purchase some potatoes, and I remember waiting in a very long queue simply to buy some cabbages. In the first year I became a lecturer in China, I volunteered to stay in one of the poorest villages near my university for half a year, where it was hard to find clean drinking water and scrambled eggs were a luxury. In the US and the UK, both myself and my family members were harassed or attacked by both White and Black youngsters. There is no need to add more incidents to the list, because it does not matter. Perhaps it is incredible for advocates of intersectionality that the above unpleasant experiences failed to make me a sociologist of poverty, immigration, race and ethnicity or any other issue connected to my intersectional identities and experiences, but many White men stood in solidarity with Black women in the past, so why do I have to experience suppression and discrimination to conduct research on intersectionality? The fact that intersectionality was initiated by Black female academics and many researchers of intersectionality come from disadvantaged minority groups should not mean that one has to come from such backgrounds in order to offer valuable contributions to the study of intersectionality.

10.3 Politicizing academic research?

Another disagreement among social scientists, which is related to the one above, is whether social science research should be politicized. Of the three widely recognized 'founding fathers' of sociology, Emile Durkheim and Max Weber take a stand clearly opposite to that of Karl Marx. It is very important to note that whilst Durkheim and Weber asked social scientists to avoid letting their political views influence their academic research, they did *not* mean that social scientists should not involve themselves in political parties or actions; in fact, both Durkheim and Weber participated in political activities (see their respective biographies, Fournier, 2012; Radkau, 2009). Still, there was a significant divide between them and Karl Marx, although the three did not have the chance to openly discuss their differences on this matter. It is sensible to imagine that Durkheim and Weber would not go as far as Marx to turn their theories into a political ideology and set up a political party with the mission of putting the ideology into action. As mentioned before, it should be fair to expect most enthusiastic advocates of intersectionality to be on the side of Marx. In fact, they are worried about the 'depoliticalization' of intersectionality. For example, May (2015, p. 19) cautioned against the 'flattening' of intersectionality, one symptom of which is depoliticizing its approach. According to May, intersectionality is and ought to be a form of social action with a 'problem-solving capacity, one that is contextual, concerned with eradicating inequity' (ibid.).

On the one hand, the urge to go beyond the ivory tower and eradicate intersectional injustice is certainly understandable. It is morally honourable to ensure that the experiences and views of all minority groups in a society be heard and respected. Intersectionality expands such a moral and humane effort from minority groups defined by one dimension to multiple dimensions. In this sense, intersectionality benefits from an overall historical trend, at least in Western societies if not the whole world, of tolerating, caring and protecting any groups who are subject to injustice, discrimination, exclusion or disadvantages. On the other hand, it is important to make it clear to all researchers whether their work still deserves the badge of honour 'intersectionality' if their work describes and explains how intersectionality works without the capacity or even the intention of directly participating in political actions. Personally, I have unconsciously and 'naively' absorbed the idea that academic research should not be about the researcher; instead, it should be about something more general and universal. If I were forced to choose, I would stand on the side of Durkheim and Weber, not the side of Karl Marx. Again, this may sound incomprehensible considering that I read many of Marx's works in China, and I even published a paper on the social theories embedded in *The Communist Manifesto* right after graduation. Perhaps my choice will become more sensible if we recall what happened to the countries in which Marx's economic and political theories were adopted as political ideologies and actions were taken to accomplish it.

More generally, perhaps this reflects a general trend across the whole higher education sector in many parts of the world: academic research is expected to deliver 'value for money' or 'value for problem-solving', and money or power starts to carry academic value. Some researchers of intersectionality have made it absolutely clear that they needed 'explicit and user-friendly methods that can effectively translate intersectional theory into practical approaches that can be understood by decision-makers and policy researchers' (Hankivsky et al., 2014, p. 120). For some social problems we may be able to do this, but for others the causal chains may be very long or take a very long time to evolve, and there may be unexpected twists and turns. A challenge to today's social scientists is to know when to stop being short-termly pragmatic.

10.4 Two further challenges to empirical research on intersectionality

In the development of intersectionality as a general principle or approach, discursive discussions have outweighed empirical investigations, and in empirical investigations qualitative studies have outweighed quantitative analyses. It is encouraging to see, however, that academic research has become more and more balanced. If the reader has read the previous chapters, it should be clear by now that currently no single method could offer comprehensive as well as effective analysis of intersectionality without limitations. A core challenge is to systematically examine the effects of possible intersectional categories on the interested form of disadvantage. Expanding the discussion on this issue, this section reveals and considers two further challenges to the empirical study of intersectionality.

10.4.1 Drawing a representative sample of intersectional groups

All the methods introduced so far, whether they are qualitative or quantitative, are specific methods for analysing existing data, information or evidence. But these data, information or evidence are often not produced for the purpose of representing intersectional discrimination or interlocking systems (racism, sexism, etc.). In this sense, the methods introduced in this book will soon reach their limits. It is therefore important to consider how research design can help studying intersectionality, not simply relying on past cases or existing datasets that were not designed for studying intersectionality. It is highly desirable and even essential for researchers to think ahead of the most effective way of conducting an empirical research project in light of the spirit of intersectionality. As a specific example, much academic attention and effort has been invested in dealing with the large number of possible intersectional categories. The existing strategies appear to be struggling because they react to this challenge *after the data have already been collected*. To meet up the challenge more effectively, researchers must consider the way in which data are to be collected so that sufficient data will be available for comparing and analysing all intersectional groups. Otherwise, no matter how large the overall sample size is, it remains highly likely that data for some intersectional groups could be extremely sparse due to the 'natural' lack of diversity in social reality.

To illustrate, suppose the available resources mean that our sample size should be 1000 and we are interested in only two intersectional attributes, race and gender. For the sake of making the illustration simple, let's say each variable is binary – which is not to deny that neither is binary in social reality – that is, White and Non-White for race and Man and Woman for gender. Also, suppose we know that the distribution for each variable in the population is the following: 50% Women and 50% Men, and 80% White and 20% Non-White. To make our sample represent the structure of the population, we would be happy if the sample distribution was about the same as the population distribution for each variable, as the table below represents:

Table 10.1a An even sample distribution across race and gender

	White	Non-White	Total
Men	400	100	500
Women	400	100	500
Total	800	200	1000

Note that this is one of the many possible sample distributions, and we would be very lucky if our sample were to end up with such distribution. It is possible that the distribution of our sample might be extremely uneven, as represented in the following table:

Table 10.1b An uneven sample distribution across race and gender

	White	Non-White	Total
Male	300	200	500
Female	500	0	500
Total	800	200	1000

Comparing the numbers in the two tables, the reader can see that the marginal distributions remain the same – the cases are evenly split for gender and the split is 80/20 for race. However, our sample may have no female non-White participants, an important intersectional group we want to study. The distribution of an actual sample may not be as extreme as the above, of course, but the extreme situation works as a clear example for making an important point: to collect useful information for the purpose of studying intersectionality, the conventional sampling method of assessing the *representativeness of a sample by one factor* runs the risk of ending up with no or little data for the intersectional groups we want to study. It is therefore imperative to ensure that the sample structure will represent the population structure for all the intersectional groups under study at the outset of the sampling process. This could be seen as an undesirable consequence of 'one-dimensional thinking' in empirical research. Further research from sampling specialists is needed in order to design a sampling procedure for the purposes of intersectionality.

10.4.2 Linking power structures to individual attributes

Intersectionality does not merely aim to demonstrate the connection between intersectional attributes and a certain form of disadvantages or discrimination. Categories such as sex or race are *imperfect proxies* for experiences of discrimination and marginalization that result from inequality based on membership in a specific sex or racial category (Ridgeway, 2011). Being a member of a specific racial or sex group does not in and of itself result in inequality; instead, membership in a particular category is embedded in *systems* that facilitate or restrict access to power and resources (ibid.). As Bowleg and Bauer (2016, p. 337) bluntly put it, 'No attention to power, no intersectionality'. Many of the categories of intersectional identities are based on power inequities, but categories such as race and income are often conflated with racism or classism which may not be accurate for certain cases (Bauer, 2014; Else-Quest & Hyde, 2016). As a result, some researchers endorse an anti-categorical approach to intersectionality (Knudsen, 2006). This interpretation of intersectionality theory is difficult to reconcile with empirical research, either quantitative or qualitative, because empirical researchers must start with and rely on certain stable categories in data collection and analysis, although this may be particularly the case for quantitative analysis.

Measuring and modelling intersectional discriminations based on multiple aspects of 'who you are' without simultaneously theorizing the power and oppression is useful but not enough. In that vein, we need to focus on not just the identities (e.g. ethnicity, immigration) but also the power-related experiences of them (e.g. sexism, White supremacy) (Moradi and Grzanka, 2017). It is against the spirit of intersectionality to identify only individual attributes as 'risk factors' for the discriminations and disenfranchisements that individuals suffer from. It is not even sufficient to simply describe the connection between intersectional categories and the occurrence of discrimination, because that does not explain the connection. Intersectionality as a theoretical and an ideological approach demands sensible explanations for how power structures and hierarchies and related social processes produce the undesirable social experiences of individuals with those intersectional identities. But how these systems work is a question that cannot be addressed by analysis of individual attributes. How do we empirically analyse intersectional attributes and power at the same time? What kind of evidence do we need for demonstrating that certain intersectional disadvantage is caused by power mechanisms? Without well-constructed empirical investigations, there will be only assertions, not convincing answers.

Unfortunately, another disconnection between the theoretical principles of intersectionality and empirical investigations is the absence of established methods for linking the interlocking power structures and individual intersectional attributes. There have been some ongoing debates within intersectionality research regarding the distinction between study of categories of identity and structures of power (Cho et al., 2013). It is a great challenge to research intersectionality to incorporate these power structures and processes empirically; at the moment, most studies describe the association between intersectional attributes and disadvantages without explaining the association by resorting to power relations. Methods introduced in this book can only present evidence for disadvantage, unable to demonstrate that power relations are responsible for such disadvantage. Perhaps this means that genuine intersectionality research is beyond empirical research? On the one hand, we do not have to be pessimistic about this question – social scientists and methodologists have either discovered or created methods for tackling even more complicated issues. On the other hand, we do need to be more imaginative of using and modifying existing methods to serve the purposes of intersectionality. Without getting into the details, one option is to learn from a longstanding debate between so-called 'risk factor epidemiology' and 'eco-epidemiology' (Susser & Susser, 1996a, 1996b). The risk factor approach is concerned with studying the determinants of disease in individual cases, which is similar to the conventional statistical models. In contrast, eco-epidemiology broadens our assessment of the determinants of health through incorporating the wider 'ecology' individuals operate their lives within; if we see each intersectional power structure and location as 'an ecology', then we could follow the same logic used in eco-epidemiology.

10.5 Further methods and issues for future research

Other than the research methods introduced in the previous chapters, there are a few more recent or advanced methods that have been developed for analysing intersectionality. I have not introduced them until now because, despite their technical sophistication, discussions over their usefulness to analysing intersectionality are still ongoing; more importantly, as I shall try to explain below, how consistent they are with the tenets of intersectionality and whether they will necessarily deliver distinctive insights remain unknown. In social science research, technical sophistication is worth pursuing only when it serves theoretical and substantive purposes.

10.5.1 Measuring intersectional discrimination

All of the research methods and ideas of design introduced in this book focus on how to most sensibly and effectively connect intersectional positions to a particular form of disadvantage. In doing so, they take it for granted that the target of analysis (or the response variable) is defined clearly and measured accurately. Indeed, despite its various forms, the experienced disadvantage is simply the presence of an unfortunate life experience, such as being made redundant, possessing a serious illness, being denied the access to certain opportunities (e.g. promotion) or services (e.g. healthcare), etc. Even in sophisticated quantitative analysis, these situations are usually represented with a variable of several simple values.

In contrast to these context-specific indicators of intersectional injustice, some quantitative researchers (for example, Richman & Zucker, 2019) have called for a certain kind of universal measures of intersectional inequality or injustice so that data collected with these measures could be compared and analysed together with intersectional attributes or positions. Ayden Scheim and Greta Bauer (2019) published their Intersectional Discrimination Index (InDI) for intercategorical intersectionality research, with the aim to measure the experience of intersectional discrimination in general. The term 'intercategorical intersectionality' comes from Leslie McCall's (2005) distinction of this kind of intersectionality from 'intracategorical intersectionality'. In this book, we have always focused on the former. The latter term refers to disadvantaged experiences *within* a particular intersectional group, such as Black women LGBTQIA+, without an intention to compare it with other intersectional groups. The importance of this particular intersectional group is sometimes assumed, but the researcher has an obligation of making a case for such an assumption. Although a useful distinction, it is not our major concern here. Scheim and Bauer have tried to make their index more sensitive to different contexts by creating three sub-indexes. These are Anticipated Discrimination (InDI-A), Day-to-Day Discrimination (InDI-D) and the Major (InDI-M) discrimination. They made it clear that all three do not require attribution by the participant to particular grounds, meaning that the participants are not expected to assign their intersectional identities as a significant course of the discrimination they experienced, as there are some controversies on whether such attribution is reliable and will make the analysis unnecessarily complicated. The items included cover a wide range of forms of discrimination, such as lack of access to health services, being harassed in public, being physically attacked, difficulty in finding a job or accommodation, being unfriendly treated such as being laughed at, etc. The indexes enjoyed strong construct validity and test–retest reliability in the US and Canada.

The major merit of this index is that it has included the most common forms of discrimination – although the items can never be exhaustive, and they could certainly be modified later when it becomes necessary. Consequently, data collected with the use of this index could give us an overall measure of how much the participants think they have been discriminated against. The use of more than 10 items has a statistical advantage as well – they will allow researchers to take measurement errors into their analysis.

That said, the merit could be a source of concern as well. It is assumed that all experiences of intersectional discrimination share some common elements. Some will certainly ask whether it is truly a good idea to measure the experiences of discrimination with a single index such as InDI. Implicit in the index is the assumption that the overall experience is more important than each specific form of discrimination, and all forms of discrimination are equally important. The index is only useful when these assumptions are accepted. Perhaps no less important is the assumption that it is meaningful and beneficial for the index to be used across different contexts and intersectional groups so that we can compare these groups with the data of this index. Researchers need to consider the trade-off of comparable vs group-specific analysis.

10.5.2 Discovering intersectional clusters

Besides multilevel models, some researchers have resorted to statistical methods for classifying cases into a smaller number of groups in order to deal with the problem of an overwhelmingly large number of intersectional groups. These methods include cluster analysis and latent variable methods. In a recent systematic review of 16 studies, Bauer and her colleagues (2022) found that eight used latent class analysis, two latent profile analysis and six clustering analysis. These methods aim to discover groups of individuals based on analysis of relations among multiple variables; in the end, they will produce new categories reflecting meaningful patterns of multiple attributes.

A brief description of these methods at the conceptual level may be needed here. The idea of cluster analysis is to measure the distances between the cases under study and then put the cases into a number of 'clusters' based on the distances. The distances will be calculated with data of a few selected variables; obviously, it is important for the researcher to decide on which variables are to be selected. Cases within a particular cluster are expected to be much more similar among themselves than cases of different clusters. But this is not always clear-cut, as this could be achieved with different solutions. Besides a statistical rule for determining the number of 'optimal' clusters, researchers are expected to make a decision based on theories or substantive knowledge of the cases. In short, the number of clusters finally chosen should be both statistically sound and substantively meaningful. In contrast to cluster analysis, in which not only the variables used but the clusters are all assumed to be observable, latent class and profile analyses assume that the clusters are 'latent' (unobservable) entities that are responsible for the observed variables. Latent class analysis assumes that these clusters have 'categorical' values, while latent profile analysis assumes that the clusters' values are 'metrical'.

To illustrate, let's discuss the study by Price and her colleagues (2019) that was mentioned in the chapter on mixed-methods research. The researchers aim to study the effects of discrimination and identity-based bullying (IBB) on academic performance and mental health among high school adolescents. Here, we are particularly interested in how they classify the adolescents based on their self-reported identities. They included three variables related to identity, and each has only two or three values: gender (cisgender boy, cisgender girl and gender expansive), sexual orientation (heterosexual, LGBTQ) and race (White and Colour). A note is in order: clearly, these values were limited to these numbers in this particular study, not reflecting the diverse categories in people's real experiences. Therefore, there are $3 \times 2 \times 2 = 12$ possible intersectional groups, which is not particularly large. The researchers claimed that one of their objectives was to discover whether there were 'distinguishable identity categories', not really to reduce the number of intersectional groups to a more manageable one. After applying the 'two-step clustering method', they decided to accept the solution of three clusters: 'LGBTQ', 'Heterosexual Colour' and 'Heterosexual White'. The reader may notice immediately that gender is not part of the story anymore, and race does not matter for the LGBTQ group. These three 'intersectional clusters' were then compared in terms of academic performance and mental health.

It is important to note a few important issues that are beyond this particular study. First, the three intersectional groups were identified statistically rather than identified based on theoretical or substantive interests or judgements, although they were 'found' meaningful after the analysis was completed. This is clearly fine if the study is essentially exploratory; however, if the researcher has a strong theoretical or substantive reason for focusing on a certain intersectional group, then studies like this will be desirable. Second, the analysis in this study has become actually less nuanced, not more nuanced as the researchers planned to do, because the number of intersectional groups has been substantially decreased. The authors did not explain or make it clear whether they applied clustering methods in order to make the number of intersectional groups more manageable or discover any pattern of identity-based intersectionality that was 'hidden' among the possible intersectional groups, or both; it is advisable that future studies make this clear. Finally and relatedly, the relationship between intersectional identities and the response variables (academic performance and mental health) was analysed with the newly discovered intersectional groups rather than the original ones. Whilst this was the researchers' plan, there exists a risk that the results produced with these new groups may have obscured more detailed findings had the original groups been analysed. Given the total number of intersectional groups is not overwhelming in this case (12 rather than hundreds), it is both wise and feasible to conduct separate analysis on the original and the new groups and compare them before reaching any final conclusion.

10.5.3 Demonstrating the causal effect of intersectionality

For researchers and methodologists of intersectionality, the ultimate challenge is to demonstrate how intersectionality works. At the moment, what the vast majority of studies on intersectionality have demonstrated is the association rather than the causation between intersectional positions and a particular form of disadvantage. As research on other topics, it is certainly tempting to jump from the association to a causal argument, but researchers must learn to *refrain from automatically attributing any disadvantage to intersectional positions without demonstrating any convincing logic of analysis or evidence*. To move forward cautiously, it may help to put intersectionality in a form of probabilistic causal theory, which could be stated as the following: *the interlocking of power systems such as sexism, racism, etc. causes those with intersectional attributes (or located in intersectional positions) disproportionately more vulnerable to discrimination, disadvantage or any other unfortunate life events and experiences*. It is my hope that other researchers find this formulation generally acceptable, although they may modify the exact wording. Such specific formulation of intersectionality as a theory is essential for the development of intersectionality because we need it to bridge the general principles of intersectionality and empirical investigations. Then we must meet the challenge of enhancing the rigour of our empirical investigations on intersectionality while remaining loyal and respectful to the basic tenets of intersectionality. This probabilistic causal theory of intersectionality remains quite general and therefore requires further specification. Here I wish to draw the reader's attention to several issues that we need to address in order to move the study of intersectionality forward.

To start with the explanatory variable, what does 'the interlocking of power systems' mean? And how should we study it empirically? After searching and reading the existing literature, I have not come to any clear and convincing answers. I do not think this is because the answers are obvious – they are certainly not; on the contrary, the questions are in fact very difficult to answer. At the moment, empirical research on intersectionality studies intersectional attributes or identities, assuming that they represent the effect of the interlocking power systems, but if we take the causal theory of intersectionality seriously, we must operationalize this key concept in order to collect and analyse empirical evidence for demonstrating its effects. No matter how interesting or powerful a concept may sound, it remains powerless before its effect is demonstrated with convincing evidence. This concept is particularly challenging because it contains other concepts (sexism, racism, etc.) that need to be operationalized. If any of these 'isms' could be defined as a set of social norms and institutional rules that grant one group of people (White people, men, etc.) the power to take advantage of another group of people (Black people, women, etc.), then researchers need to identify these social norms and institutional rules first. Then they need to demonstrate how these norms and rules 'interlock' with each other. A metaphor may help make a theory clear and interesting, but the theory must be specified with an accurate language in order to avoid any confusion, ambiguity and inconsistency.

Correspondingly, how intersectional attributes and identities should be operationalized and analysed in empirical research requires further serious consideration. Here, intersectionality has posed a few specific challenges to empirical research, including the different classifications of identities by participants and researchers, the temporal changes of the participants' classifications, and the ambiguities or fuzziness of classifications. Researchers, either qualitative or quantitative, must pay serious attention to the meaning of categories used for describing attributes and positions, and be prepared and open to the contingent scenarios and processes that produce differential forms of social injustice. Fortunately, these are mostly technical issues, not insurmountable difficulties.

Similarly, further work is required for operationalizing and measuring the response variable. So far, almost all studies have focused on a particular incidence of discrimination or disadvantage, such as being made redundant or suffering from a disease. However, as illustrated above, recently some researchers have proposed indexes to measure 'intersectional disadvantage' as a general life experience. This requires researchers to consider which kind of intersectional disadvantage they should focus on in a particular study. In addition, as other important social science concepts have been studied, it is useful as well as necessary to establish a systematic taxonomy of intersectionality disadvantage by considering dimensions such as time, place, national and cultural contexts, etc.

It is only after these conceptual and operational issues have been carefully considered and addressed that we could move on to the task of establishing any causal relationship between the two sides empirically. To achieve this, it is worth noting that the probabilistic causal theory stated above implies a causal relationship at two levels: 'interlocking power systems' is clearly a phenomenon at the societal level, intersectional attributes or positions are at the individual level, and 'intersectional disadvantage' could be studied at either the individual or the societal level. These causal relations could be represented by making use of 'Coleman's Boat' (Coleman, 1990, p. 702).

Seen in this light, research on intersectionality has experienced three phases. Initially, as described in the cases of lawsuits in the first two chapters, the research was conducted on the experiences of some individuals – more specifically, Black female employees. Then in the next phase, some prominent Black feminists realized the importance of this issue and raised it to the societal level, developing and promoting a distinctive approach to thinking about intersectionality as a pattern and a consequence of power relations. After this approach became widely accepted and established, the increasing demand for studying intersectionality empirically resulted in research returning to the individual level, due to the fact that most empirical data are at the individual level.

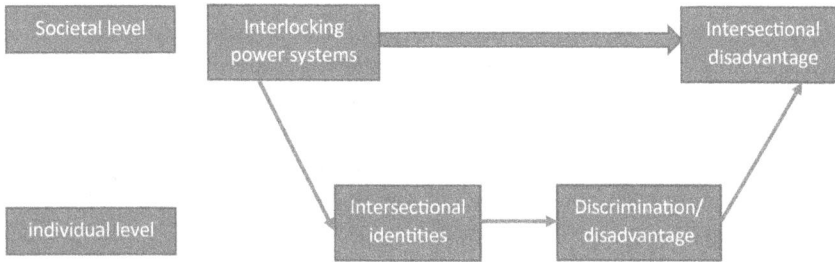

Figure 10.1 Intersectionality at individual and societal levels

To enhance the power and influence of intersectionality as a causal social theory, research-ers first need to collect data at both individual and societal levels so that analyses linking the two levels could be conducted. At the same time, researchers should make the best use of recent developments in the methods for analysing causal relations, such as directed acyclic graphs (DAGs; Pearl, 2016; Pearl & Mackenzie, 2018), propensity score matching (Bai & Clark, 2018; Guo & Fraser, 2014; Leite, 2017), natural experiments (Dunning, 2012), process tracing (Beach & Pedersen, 2019; Bennett, 2014), etc. In short, the causal relations in the theory of intersectionality should be demonstrated rather than merely asserted.

10.6 A generic approach to intersectionality

The best way to end this book, I think, is to offer a generic approach to intersectionality that embodies the lessons we have learnt and guides future endeavours at the same time. It is an approach, not a method, in the sense that it concerns the important questions research-ers need to consider without giving 'standard' answers or providing techniques. Answers to these important questions and the related reflections will establish and clarify the rationale of intersectionality as a way of thinking about and doing intersectionality. The approach is 'generic' in the sense that it identifies the research on intersectionality as a general task of demonstrating the intersectional effects of multiple factors on a specific outcome so as to open up a space in which as many existing research designs and methods as available could be applied. Without aiming to offer a rigid step-by-step procedure, the rationale behind this approach and its key elements will provide researchers with a flexible but useful framework for planning, designing and conducting their analysis of intersectionality.

First of all, specify the exact nature and form of discrimination, disadvantage, marginali-zation or any other unfortunate life event or experience. In short, what is the outcome to be analysed and explained? Given that intersectionality has been motivated by a strong sense of revealing and rectifying the misfortunates experienced by a particular group of people, it is imperative to be absolutely clear about the unfortunate event or experience, because the process of defining and measuring the outcome will shape or even determine the subsequent research activities. In practice, researchers usually recognize a particular case or form of inter-sectional injustice with both the outcome and the intersectional group at the same time; for example, Black LGBTQIA+ women suffer from little access to effective health services. Analytically, however, it is important and useful to examine them separately as the nature, form and measurements of the outcome will instruct us as to what kind of evidence we need to demonstrate its presence. What does each of the key concepts mean? Is it directly observable or latent so that we have to use proxy indicators to collect evidence about it? How are the meanings of key concepts constructed in a particular social context? How does the meaning of each key term vary from one group to another in that particular social context? Is it a transient or long-term experience? Is it specific to a particular context or a general experience across different contexts and with different elements? In the end, researchers need to obtain good knowledge of the meanings of the outcome and its possible values.

The next analytical step and task is to select the intersectional attributes, determine the values (or categories), and learn about the meanings of both the attributes and their values. In doing these, researchers need to strike a balance between theoretical importance and analytical feasibility. It is good practice to start by explaining 'ideally' – that is, without considering practical and technical constraints – how many and which intersectional attributes should be included in the analysis; if it turns out that it is not feasible to include so many attributes, the researcher needs to offer an explanation for how the 'final' attributes are selected. Note that if the above two-level theoretical model (Figure 10.1) is accepted, then the selection of these attributes is not the end of the story on the explanatory side; the researcher should consider and try to identify any evidence for 'the interlocking power systems' behind the selected attributes. As pointed out above, currently this remains a weakness of research on intersectionality, so the researcher has to be creative in discovering these power systems and making a sensible link of them to the attributes at the individual level.

Once the attributes have been selected, the distinction between inter-categorical or intra-categorical intersectionality study (McCall, 2005) comes into consideration. While this might seem to be a matter of choice, I hope the reader would agree with me that the *inter-categorical approach should take priority*, because directly jumping to an intra-categorical study on intersectionality without first examining other intersectional categories carries the risk that the importance or complexity of a particular intersectional category may not stand. Even when there exists a strong and valid reason for concentrating on one particular intra-category, its salience can only be demonstrated when being compared with other intersectional categories in terms of the unfortunate outcome. It is therefore always wise, perhaps even imperative, to examine all possible intersectional categories before focusing on any one or more of them. The researcher should make a complete list of all possible intersectional categories as cross-classifications of the selected attributes' values and consider whether any of them are meaningless or irrelevant; for example, the cross-classifications involving young people and widowhood does not make much sense. The reader may recall that this is a kind of work that QCA and set-theoretic methods take seriously. The systematic examination of all possible intersectional categories should be an essential step that all studies of intersectionality must take.

Now we come to the moment of connecting the above two steps together in a logical manner. Clearly, there are many ways of making the connection, and the previous chapters have introduced some of them. A few important points are worth adding here. In discussions on the logic of research design, there is a distinction between two types of studies, 'effects of causes' vs 'causes of effects', which appears to be useful for research on intersectionality as well. The first focuses on the effects (or the outcome) of a selection of causes; that is, the concern is not with the causes as there is no question about which causes are selected and why – rather, the concern is with how many effects the causes have made. In the context of intersectionality, the researcher aims to determine how disadvantaged some social groups are given their intersectional attributes or positions. In contrast, other studies are more concerned with the causes given a particular outcome. For intersectionality, this means that the researcher is more interested in discovering which intersectional groups have suffered from a particular form of disadvantage and why. Clearly, it may not be always clear and easy to distinguish these two types of studies in practice, but they could alert the researcher to the focus of study.

When connecting intersectional positions and a particular disadvantage, it is also advisable to avoid being orthodox regarding the intersectional effect. In other words, while we certainly accept the importance of paying serious attention to intersectionality, whether a set of specific intersectional attributes turns out to be responsible for a particular outcome should be taken as an empirical question, not an a priori condition. Even enthusiastic advocates of intersectionality should be prepared to accept the possibility that in some special circumstances there may be little variation within a single dimension, making it unnecessary to bring in another dimension.

It is also important for researchers to be prepared for exploring and considering different causal pathways in connecting intersectional attributes and the unfortunate outcome. It is indeed simplistic to argue or even assume a 'one-to-one' causal relationship between certain intersectional positions and the experience of an unfortunate life event, while in fact the causal process could go in the opposite direction, and it is even possible that the causal process is a loop. Researchers therefore need to consider different 'causal scenarios', and it helps to map them out with diagrams and then analyse them with the ideas and principles of DAGs mentioned above. This involves identifying which factors are mediators and which are moderators, and determining and removing potential biases due to confounders. Another thing that even enthusiastic advocates of intersectionality should be prepared to accept is that intersectional positions may not always turn out to be the most important factor for the interested disadvantage once we have considered all the mediators, moderators or contexts.

Finally, without implying that this will make the generic approach 'complete', it is important to bring time into our consideration, which has been rarely been taken into account so far. It was briefly mentioned previously that some researchers have noticed the potential temporal change of intersectional attributes. On the one hand, we certainly need to consider such a change. On the other hand, it is difficult to imagine that the socio-demographic attributes of a large population are unstable throughout people's lives. It may be more reasonable to examine how durable people's unfortunate experiences are, which actually represents an additional aspect of intersectional injustice. Again, it would be better to treat these as empirical questions waiting for reliable evidence to confirm, rather than as conditions to be taken for granted. As far as I am aware, methods for studying time-dependent data such as longitudinal analysis, survival analysis, event history analysis, sequence analysis and processual sociology have not been used in the study of intersectionality, which should offer additional help with the enterprise of research on intersectionality.

REFERENCES

Acker, J. (2011). Theorizing gender, race, and class in organizations. In E. L. Jeannes, D. Knights, & P. Y. Martin (Eds.), *Handbook of gender, work, and organization* (pp. 65–80). Wiley & Sons.

Adams, T. E., Jones, S. H., & Ellis, C. (2021). *Handbook of autoethnography* (2nd ed.). Routledge.

Agresti, A. (2012). *Categorical data analysis* (3rd ed.). Wiley.

Agresti, A. (2018). *An introduction to categorical data analysis* (3rd ed.). Wiley.

Agresti, A., & Finlay, B. (2018). *Statistical methods for the social sciences* (5th ed.). Pearson.

Agresti, A., & Franklin, C. (2014). *Statistics: The art & science of learning from data* (3rd ed.). Pearson.

Alexander-Floyd, N. G. (2012). Disappearing acts: Reclaiming intersectionality in the social sciences in a post-Black feminist era. *Feminist Formations, 24*(1), 1–25.

Appleton, D. R., French, J. M., & Vanderpump, M. P. J. (1996). Ignoring a covariate: An example of Simpson's paradox. *The American Statistician, 50*, 340–341.

Atkinson, P., & Delamont, S. (2010). *Sage qualitative research methods* (four-volume set). Sage Publications.

Axelsson Fisk, S., Mulinari, S., Wemrell, M., Leckie, G., Perez Vicente, R., & Merlo, J. (2018). Chronic Obstructive Pulmonary Disease in Sweden: An intersectional multilevel analysis of individual heterogeneity and discriminatory accuracy. *Social Science & Medicine: Population Health, 4*, 334–346.

Bai, H., & Clark, M. H. (2018). *Propensity score methods and applications*. Sage Publications.

Bailey, J., Steeves, V., Burkell, J., Shade, L. R., Ruparelia, R., & Regan, P. (2019). Getting at equality: Research methods informed by the lessons of intersectionality. *International Journal of Qualitative Methods, 18*, 1609406919846753.

Bauer, G. R. (2014). Incorporating intersectionality theory into population health research methodology: challenges and the potential to advance health equity. *Social Science & Medicine, 110*, 10–17.

Bauer, G. R., Mahendran, M., Walwyn, C., & Shokoohi, M. (2022). Latent variable and clustering methods in intersectionality research: Systematic review of methods applications. *Social Psychiatry and Psychiatric Epidemiology, 57*, 221–237.

Bauer, G. R., & Scheim, A. I. (2019). Methods for analytic intercategorical intersectionality in quantitative research: Discrimination as a mediator of health inequalities. *Social Science & Medicine, 226*, 236–245.

Bazeley, P. (2018). *Integrating analyses in mixed methods research*. Sage Publications.

Beach, D., & Pedersen, R. B. (2019). *Process-tracing methods: Foundations and guidelines.* University of Michigan Press.

Beale, F. (1970). Double jeopardy: To be black and female. In T. Cade (Ed.), *The black woman: An anthology* (pp. 90–100). New American Library.

Becker, H. S. (1967). 'Whose side are we on?' *Social Problems, 14,* 239–247.

Bennett, A. (2014). *Process tracing: From metaphor to analytic tool.* Cambridge University Press.

Berger, M. T., & Guidroz, K. (Eds.) (2009). *The intersectional approach: Transforming the academy through race, class, and gender.* University of North Carolina Press.

Boudon, R. (2001). 'Sociology that matters', inaugural lecture, European Academy of Sociology, 26 October 2001, Swedish Cultural Center.

Bowleg, L. (2008). When Black + Woman + Lesbian ≠ Black Lesbian Woman: The methodological challenges of qualitative and quantitative intersectionality research. *Sex Roles, 59,* 312–325.

Bowleg, L., & Bauer, G. (2016). Invited reflection: Quantifying intersectionality. *Psychology of Women Quarterly, 40*(3), 337–341.

Brady, H., & Collier, D. (2010). *Rethinking social inquiry: Diverse tools, shared standards* (2nd ed.). Rowman & Littlefield.

Browne, I., & Misra, J. (2003). The intersection of gender and race in the labor market. *Annual Review of Sociology, 29,* 487–513.

Bryman, A. (2007). Barriers to integrating quantitative and qualitative research. *Journal of Mixed Methods Research, 1*(1), 8–22.

Cade, T. (Ed.) (1970). *The black woman: An anthology.* New American Library.

Carbado, D. W. (2013). Colorblind intersectionality. *Signs, 38,* 811–845.

Carver, C. S. (1997). You want to measure coping but your protocol's too long: Consider the brief COPE. *International Journal of Behavioral Medicine, 4,* 92–100.

Cherkaoui, M., Demeulenaere, P., & Boudon, R. (2003). *The European tradition in qualitative research.* Sage Publications.

Cho, S., Crenshaw, K. W., & McCall, L. (2013). Toward a field of intersectionality studies: Theory, applications, and praxis. *Signs, 38,* 785–810.

Chun, J. J., Lipsitz, G., & Shin, Y. (2013). Intersectionality as a social movement strategy: Asian immigrant women advocates. *Signs, 38*(4), 917–940.

Cohen, J., Cohen, P., West, S. G., & Aiken, L. S. (2003). *Applied multiple regression/correlation analysis for the behavioural sciences* (3rd ed.). Lawrence Erlbaum.

Cole, E. R. (2009). Intersectionality and research in psychology. *American Psychologist, 64*(3), 170–180.

Coleman, J. (1990). *The foundation of social theory.* Harvard University Press.

Collier, D. (2014). Comment: QCA should set aside the algorithms. *Sociological Methodology, 44*(1), 122–126.

Collins, P. H. (2015). Intersectionality's definitional dilemmas. *Annual Review of Sociology, 41,* 1–20.

Collins, P. H. (2019). *Intersectionality as critical social theory.* Duke University Press.

Collins, P. (2020). Intersectionality as Critical Social Theory. In P. Kivisto (Ed.), *The Cambridge handbook of social theory* (pp. 120–142). Cambridge: Cambridge University Press. doi:10.1017/9781316677452.008.

Collins, P. H., & Bilge, S. (2020). *Intersectionality: Key concepts* (2nd ed.). Polity.

Combahee River Collective. (1977). A black feminist statement. In C. Moraga & G. Anzaldúa (Eds.) (1983), *This bridge called my back: writings by radical women of color* (pp. 210–218). Kitchen Table: Women of Color Press.

Cooper, A. J. (1892 [1988]). *A voice from the south*. Oxford University Press.

Crenshaw, K. (1989). Demarginalizing the intersection of race and sex: A Black feminist critique of antidiscrimination doctrine, feminist theory and antiracist politics. *University of Chicago Legal Forum, 1*(8), 139–167.

Crenshaw, K. (1991). Mapping the margins: Intersectionality, identity politics, and violence against women of color. *Stanford Law Review, 43*, 1241–1299.

Crenshaw, K. (2015, September 24). Why intersectionality can't wait. *Washington Post*.

Creswell, John W. (2021). *A concise introduction to mixed methods research* (2nd ed.). Sage Publications.

Creswell, J. W., & Clark, V. L. P. (2018). *Designing and conducting mixed methods research* (3rd ed.). Sage Publications.

Cruz, R. V. (2022). The role of sex guilt as a mediating variable in the association of relationship and sexual satisfaction: An intersectional approach. *Sexuality & Culture, 26*, 616–639.

De Meur, G., Rihoux, B., & Yamansaki, S. (2009). Addressing the critiques of QCA. In B. Rihoux and C. C. Ragin (Eds.), *Configurational comparative methods: Qualitative Comparative Analysis (QCA) and related techniques*. Sage Publications.

Demeulenaere, P. (Ed.). (2011). *Analytical sociology and social mechanisms*. Cambridge University Press.

Denzin, N. K., & Lincoln, Y. S. (2023). *The Sage handbook of qualitative research* (6th ed.). Sage Publications.

Dhamoon, R. K. (2011). Considerations on mainstreaming intersectionality. *Political Research Quarterly, 64*(1), 230–243.

Dill, B. T., & Zambrana, R. (Eds.). (2009). *Emerging intersections: Race, class, and gender in theory, policy, and practice*. Rutgers University Press.

Dunning, T. (2012). *Natural experiments in the social sciences: A design-based approach*. Cambridge University Press.

Else-Quest, N. M., & Hyde, J. S. (2016). Intersectionality in quantitative psychological research II: Methods and techniques. *Psychology of Women Quarterly, 40*(2), 155–170.

Esposito, J., & Evans-Winters, V. (2022). *Introduction to intersectional qualitative research*. Sage Publications.

Evans, C. (2019). Adding interactions to models of intersectional health inequalities: Comparing multilevel and conventional methods. *Social Science & Medicine, 221*, 95–105. https://doi.org/10.1016/j.socscimed.2018.11.036.

Evans, C. R. (2015). Innovative approaches to investigating social determinants of health – social networks, environmental effects and intersectionality. Doctoral dissertation. Chan School of Public Health, Harvard T.H. Accessed at https://dash.harvard.edu/handle/1/23205168.

Evans, C., Leckie, G., & Merlo, J. (2020). Multilevel versus single-level regression for the analysis of multilevel information: The case of quantitative intersectional analysis. *Social Science & Medicine, 245*, 112499. https://doi.org/10.1016/j.socscimed.2019.112499.

Evans, C. R., Williams, D. R., Onnela, J. P., & Subramanian, S. V. (2018). A multilevel approach to modeling health inequalities at the intersection of multiple social identities. *Social Science & Medicine, 203,* 64–73.

Evans, E., & Lépinard, E. (2019). *Intersectionality in feminist and queer movements: Confronting privileges.* Routledge.

Fehrenbacher, A. E., & Patel, D. (2020). Translating the theory of intersectionality into quantitative and mixed methods for empirical gender transformative research on health. *Culture, Health & Sexuality, 22*(suppl. 1), 145–160.

Finch, R. W. H., Bolin, J. E., & Kelley, K. (2019). *Multilevel modelling using R* (2nd ed.). Chapman & Hall/CRC.

Flick, U. (2018). *Doing triangulation and mixed methods.* Sage Publications.

Flyvbjerg, B. (2001). *Making social science matter: Why social inquiry fails and how it can succeed again.* Cambridge University Press.

Fournier, M. (2012). *Emile Durkheim: A biography.* Polity.

Garson, G. D. (2019). *Multilevel modeling: Applications in STATA, IBM, SPSS, SAS, R, & HLM.* Sage Publications.

Gates, H. L., Jr. (1988). Foreword: In her own write. In A. J. Cooper (1892[1988]), *A voice from the south* (pp. vii–xxii). Oxford University Press.

Gelman, A., & Hill, J. (2007). *Data analysis using regression and multilevel/hierarchical models.* Cambridge University Press.

Gerring, J. (2011). *Social science methodology: A unified framework* (2nd ed.). Cambridge University Press.

Goertz, G. (2017). *Multimethod research, causal mechanisms, and case studies: An integrated approach.* Princeton University Press.

Goldstein, H. (2011). *Multilevel statistical models* (4th ed.). Wiley.

Goldthorpe, J. (2016). *Sociology as a population science.* Cambridge University Press.

Goldthorpe, J. H. (2000). Current issues in comparative macrosociology. In *On sociology: Numbers, narratives, and the integration of research and theory* (pp. 45–64). Oxford University Press.

Grace, D. (2014). *Intersectionality-informed mixed method research: A primer.* The Institute for Intersectionality Research & Policy, SFU.

Grace, D., Chown, S., Jollimore, J., Parry, R., Kwag, M., Steinberg, M., Trussler, T., Rekart, M., & Gilbert, M. (2014). HIV-negative gay men's accounts of using context-dependent seroadaptive strategies. *Culture, Health and Sexuality, 16*(3), 316–330.

Green, M. A., Evans, C. R., & Subramanian, S. V. (2017). Can intersectionality theory enrich population health research? *Social Science & Medicine, 178,* 214–216.

Griffin, K. A., & Museus, S. D. (2011). Application of mixed-methods approaches to higher education and intersectional analyses. *New Directions for Institutional Research, 151,* 15–26.

Grusky, D. (2019). *Social stratification: Class, race, gender in sociological perspective* (4th ed.). Routledge.

Grzanka, P. R. (2014). *Intersectionality: A foundations and frontiers reader.* Routledge.

Gueta, K. (2017). A qualitative study of barriers and facilitators in treating drug use among Israeli mothers: An intersectional perspective. *Social Science & Medicine, 187,* 155–163.

Guo, S., & Fraser, M. W. (2014). *Propensity score analysis: Statistical methods and applications.* Sage Publications.

Hancock, A.-M. (2016). *Intersectionality: An intellectual history*. Oxford University Press.

Hankivsky, O., Grace, D., Hunting, G., Geisbrecht, M., Fridkin, A., Rudrum, R. ... & Clark, N. (2014). An intersectionality-based policy analysis framework: Critical reflections on a methodology for advancing equity. *International Journal for Equity in Health, 13,* 119–135.

Harper, C. E. (2007). Count me in: A mixed-methods analysis of the theoretical, methodological, and practical implications of accounting for multiracial backgrounds in higher education. Unpublished doctoral dissertation, University of California, Los Angeles.

Harper, C. E. (2011). Identity, intersectionality, and mixed-methods approaches. *New Directions for Institutional Research, 151,* 103–115.

Hayes, A. F. (2022). *Introduction to mediation, moderation, and conditional process analysis: A regression-based approach* (3rd ed.). Guilford Press.

Heck, R. H., Thomas, S. L., & Tabata, L. N. (2022). *Multilevel and longitudinal modelling with IBM SPSS*. Routledge.

Hedström, P. (2005). *Dissecting the social: On the principles of analytical sociology*. Cambridge University Press.

Hedström, P., & Bearman, P. (Eds.). (2009). *The Oxford handbook of analytical sociology*. Oxford University Press.

Hedström, P., & Swedberg, R. (Eds.) (1998). *Social mechanisms: An analytical approach to social theory*. Cambridge University Press.

Horowitz, I. (1995). *The decomposition of sociology*. Oxford University Press.

House, J. (2019). The culminating crisis of American sociology and its role in social science and public policy: An autobiographical, multimethod, reflexive respective. *Annual Review of Sociology, 45,* 1–26.

Hox, J., Moerbeek, M., & van de Schoot, R. (2017). *Multilevel analysis: Techniques and applications* (3rd ed.). Routledge.

Ickert, C., Senthilselvan, A., & Jhangri, G. S. (2021). Multilevel modeling of health inequalities at the intersection of multiple social identities in Canada. *The Sociological Quarterly*. https://doi.org/10.1080/00380253.2020.1868956.

Jaccard, J. (1998). *Interaction effects in factorial analysis of variance*. Sage.

Jaccard, J. (2001). *Interaction effects in logistic regression*. Sage.

Jaccard, J., Turrisi, R., & Wan, C. (1990). *Interaction effects in multiple regression*. Sage.

Jaccard, J., & Wan, C. (1996). *LISREL analyses of interaction effects in multiple regression*. Sage.

Janda, L. H., & Bazemore, S. D. (2011). The revised Mosher Sex-Guilt Scale: Its psychometric properties and a proposed ten-item version. *Journal of Sex Research, 48*(4), 392–396.

Joas, H., & Knöbl, W. (2009). *Social theory: Twenty introductory lectures*. Cambridge University Press.

Jones, K., Johnston, R., & Manley, D. (2016). Uncovering interactions in multivariate contingency tables: a multi-level modelling exploratory approach. *Methodology Innovation, 9,* 1–17.

Jose, P. E. (2013). *Doing statistical mediation and moderation*. Guilford Press.

Kaufman, R. L. (2019). *Interaction effects in linear and generalized linear models: Examples and applications using Stata*. Sage.

Keister, L. A., & Southgate, D. E. (2022). *Inequality: A contemporary approach to race, class, and gender* (2nd ed.). Cambridge University Press.

Kline, R. (2016). *Principles and practice of structural equation modelling* (4th ed.). Guilford Press.

Knapp, G. A. (2005). Race, class, gender: Reclaiming baggage in fast travelling theories. *European Journal of Women's Studies, 12*(3), 249–265.

Knudsen, S. V. (2006). Intersectionality: A theoretical inspiration in the analysis of minority cultures and identities in textbooks. *Caught in the Web or Lost in the Textbook, 53*, 61–76.

Kreft, I., & de Leeuw, J. (1998). *Introducing multilevel modelling*. Sage Publications.

Lawrance, K. & Byers, E. S. (1995). Sexual satisfaction in long-term heterosexual relationships: The interpersonal exchange model of sexual satisfaction. *Personal Relationships, 2*, 267–285.

Leite, W. L. (2017). *Practical propensity score methods using R*. Sage Publications.

Lewis, J. A., & Neville, H. A. (2015). Construction and initial validation of the Gendered Racial Microaggressions Scale for Black Women. *Journal of Counseling Psychology, 62*(2), 289–302.

Lieberson, S. (1987). *Making it count: The improvement of social research and theory*. University of California Press.

Lieberson, S. (1991). Small N's and big conclusions: An examination of the reasoning in comparative studies based on a small number of cases. *Social Forces, 70*, 307–320.

Lieberson, S. (1994). More on the uneasy case for using mill-type methods in small-n comparative studies. *Social Forces, 72*, 1225–1237.

Lieberson, S. (2001). A review of fuzzy-set social science by Charles C. Ragin. *Contemporary Sociology, 30*, 331–334.

Lieberson, S. (2004). Comments on the use and utility of QCA. *Qualitative Methods, 2*, 13–14.

Lovibond, P. F., & Lovibond, S. H. (1995). The structure of negative emotional states: comparison of the Depression Anxiety Stress Scales (DASS) with the Beck Depression and Anxiety Inventories. *Behavior Research and Therapy, 33*(3), 335–343.

Lucas, S. R., & Szatrowski, A. (2014). Qualitative comparative analysis in critical perspective. *Sociological Methodology, 44*(1), 1–79.

Luke, D. A. (2020). *Multilevel modelling* (2nd ed.). Sage Publications.

Lykke, N. (2011). Intersectionality analysis: Black box or useful critical feminist thinking technology? In H. Lutz, M. T. Herrera Vivar, & L. Supik (Eds.), *Framing intersectionality: Debates on a multi-faceted concept in gender studies* (pp. 207–220). Ashgate.

Lynch, M. (1996). Class, race, gender and criminology: Structured choices and the life course. In M. D. Schwartz & D. Milovanovic (Eds.), *Race, gender, and class in criminology: The intersection* (pp. 3–28). New York, NY: Garland.

MacKinnon, D. (2008). *Introduction to statistical mediation analysis*. Taylor & Francis.

Mahoney, J., Goertz, G., & Ragin, C. C. (2013). Causal methods and counterfactuals. In Stephen L. Morgan (Ed.), *Handbook of causal analysis for social research*. Springer.

Manzo, G. (Ed.). (2014). *Analytical sociology: Actions and networks*. Wiley.

Marx, K. (1978[1888]). Theses on Feuerbach. In Robert C. Tucker (Ed.), *The Marx–Engels Reader* (2nd ed., pp. 143–145). W. W. Norton & Company.

May, V. M. (2015). *Pursuing intersectionality, unsettling dominant imaginaries*. Routledge.

McCall, L. (2005). The complexity of intersectionality. *Signs: The Journal of Women in Culture and Society, 30*, 1711–1800.

Medina-Perucha, L., Scott, J., Chapman, S., Barnett, J., Dack, C., & Family, H. (2019). A qualitative study on intersectional stigma and sexual health among women on opioid substitution treatment in England: Implications for research, policy and practice. *Social Science & Medicine, 222*, 315–322.

Merlo, J. (2003). Multilevel analytical approaches in social epidemiology: Measures of health variation compared with traditional measures of association. *Journal of Epidemiology and Community Health, 57*, 550–552.

Merlo, J. (2018). Multilevel Analysis of Individual Heterogeneity and Discriminatory Accuracy (MAIHDA) within an intersectional framework. *Social Science & Medicine, 203*, 74–80.

Merlo, J., Asplund, K., Lynch, J., Rastam, L., & Dobson, A. (2004). Population effects on individual systolic blood pressure: A multilevel analysis of the World Health Organization MONICA Project. *American Journal Epidemiology, 159*, 1168–1179.

Merlo, J., Chaix, B., Ohlsson, H., Beckman, A., Johnell, K., Hjerpe, P., et al. (2006). A brief conceptual tutorial of multilevel analysis in social epidemiology: Using measures of clustering in multilevel logistic regression to investigate contextual phenomena. *Journal Epidemiology Community Health, 60*, 290–297.

Merlo, J., Chaix, B., Yang, M., Lynch, J., & Rastam, L. (2005). A brief conceptual tutorial of multilevel analysis in social epidemiology: Linking the statistical concept of clustering to the idea of contextual phenomenon. *Journal Epidemiology Community Health, 59*, 443–449.

Merton, R. K. (1967). *On theoretical sociology: Five essays, old and new*. The Free Press.

Metcalf, H. (2016). Broadening the study of participation in the life sciences: How critical theoretical and mixed-methodological approaches can enhance efforts to broaden participation. *CBE-Life Sciences Education, 15*, rm3. https://doi.org/10.1187/cbe.16-01-0064.

Metcalf, H., Russell, D., & Hill, C. (2018). Broadening the science of broadening participation in stem through critical mixed methodologies and intersectionality frameworks. *American Behavioral Scientist, 62*(5), 580–599.

Misra, J., Curington, C. V., & Green, V. M. (2021). Methods of intersectional research. *Sociological Spectrum, 41*(1), 9–28.

Moradi, B., & Grzanka, P. R. (2017). Using intersectionality responsibly: Toward critical epistemology, structural analysis, and social justice activism. *Journal of Counselling Psychology, 64*, 500–513.

Moraga, C., & Anzaldúa, G. (Eds.) (1983). *This bridge called my back: Writings by radical women of color*. Kitchen Table: Women of Color Press.

Morgan, D. L. (2014). *Integrating qualitative & quantitative methods: A pragmatic approach*. Sage Publications.

Morgan, S., & Winship, C. (2014). *Counterfactuals and causal inference: Methods and principles for social research*. Cambridge University Press.

Morrow, M., Bryson, S., Lal, R., et al. (2020). Intersectionality as an analytic framework for understanding the experiences of mental health stigma among racialized men. *International Journal of Mental Health Addiction, 18*, 1304–1317.

Nash, J. C. (2008). Re-thinking intersectionality. *Feminist Review, 89*, 1–15.

Oana, E., Schneider, C. Q., & Thomann, E. (2021). *Qualitative comparative analysis using R: A beginner's guide*. Cambridge University Press.

Pearl, J. (2016). *Causal inference in statistics: A primer*. Wiley.

Pearl, J., & Mackenzie, D. (2018). *The book of why: The new science of cause and effect*. Penguin.

Pew Research Center (2022). More than twice as many Americans support than oppose the #MeToo movement, September.

Plowright, D. (2011). *Using mixed methods: Frameworks for an integrated methodology*. Sage Publications.

Poulos, C. N. (2021). *Essentials of autoethnography*. American Psychological Association.

Powell, M. E. (1996). The claims of women of color under Title VII: the Interaction of Race and Gender, 26 Golden Gate U. L. Rev. http://digitalcommons.law.ggu.edu/ggulrev/vol26/iss2/6

Price, M., Polk, W., Hill, N. E., Liang, B., & Perella, J. (2019). The intersectionality of identity-based victimization in adolescence: A person-centred examination of mental health and academic achievement in a U.S. high school. *Journal of Adolescence, 76*, 185–196.

Rabe-Hesketh, S., & Skrondal, A. (2021). *Multilevel and longitudinal modeling using Stata* (4th ed.). Stata Press.

Radkau, J. (2009). *Max Weber: A biography*. Polity.

Ragin, C. (2000). *Fuzzy-Set social science*. University of Chicago Press.

Ragin, C. (2008). *Redesigning social inquiry: Fuzzy sets and beyond*. University of London Press.

Ragin, C., & Fiss, P. (2016). *Intersectional inequality: Race, class, test scores and poverty*. University of Chicago Press.

Raudenbush, S. W., & Bryk, A. S. (2001). *Hierarchical linear models: Applications and data analysis methods* (2nd ed.). Sage Publications.

Raykov, T., & Marcoulides, G. (2006). *A first course in structural equation modelling*. Psychology Press.

Richman, L. S., & Zucker, A. N. (2019). Quantifying intersectionality: An important advancement for health inequality research. *Social Science & Medicine, 226*, 246–248.

Ridgeway, C. (2011). *Framed by gender: How gender inequality persists in the modern world*. Oxford Scholarship Online.

Rodriguez, J. K., Holvino, E., Fletcher, J. K., & Nkomo, S. M. (2016). The theory and praxis of intersectionality in work and organisations: Where do we go from here? *Gender, Work, and Organization, 23*(3), 201–222.

Romney, A. K. (1999). Culture consensus as a statistical model. *Current Anthropology, 40*(Suppl.), S103–S115.

Romney, A. K., Weller, S. C., & Batchelder, W. H. (1986). Culture as consensus: A theory of culture and informant accuracy. *American Anthropology, 88*, 313–338.

Rosenthal, L., Overstreet, N. M., Khukhlovich, A., Brown, B. E., Godfrey, C.-J., & Albritton, T. (2020). Content of, sources of, and responses to sexual stereotypes of Black and Latinx women and men in the United States: A qualitative intersectional exploration. *Journal of Social Issues, 76*(4), 921–948.

Rosenthal, R., & Rosnow, R. L. (2008). *Essentials of behavioural research: Methods and data analysis* (3rd ed.). McGraw Hill.

Rosnow, R. L., & Rosenthal, R. (1989). Definition and interpretation of interaction effects. *Psychological Bulletin, 105*, 143–146.

Rosnow, R. L., & Rosenthal, R. (1991). If you're looking at the cell means, you're not looking at the interaction (unless all main effects are zero). *Psychological Bulletin, 110*, 574–576.

Scheim, A., & Bauer, G. R. (2019). The intersectional discrimination index: Development and validation of measures of self-reported enacted and anticipated discrimination for intercategorical analysis. *Social Science & Medicine, 226*, 225–235.

Schneider, C. Q., & Wagemann, C. (2012). *Set-theoretic methods for the social sciences: A guide to qualitative comparative analysis*. Cambridge University Press.

Schulman, K. A., Berlin, J. A., Harless, W., Kerner, J. F., Sistrunk, S., Gersh, B. J., Dube, R., Taleghani, C. K., Burke, J. E., Williams, S., Eisenberg, J. M., Ayers, W., & Escarce, J. J. (1999). The effect of race and sex on physicians' recommendations for cardiac catheterization. *New England Journal of Medicine, 340*, 618–626.

Seawright, J. (2016). *Multi-method social science: Combining qualitative and quantitative tools*. Princeton University Press.

Sellers, R. M., Rowley, S. A. J., Chavous, T. M., Shelton, J. N., & Smith, M. (1997). Multidimensional inventory of Black identity: Preliminary investigation of reliability and construct validity. *Journal of Personality and Social Psychology, 73*, 805–815.

Shoben, E. W. (1980). Compound discrimination: The interaction of race and sex in employment discrimination. 55 *NYU Law Review, 793*, 803–804.

Skocpol, T. (1979). *States and social revolutions: A comparative analysis of France, Russia and China*. Cambridge University Press.

Snijders, T. A. B., & Bosker, R. J. (2011). *Multilevel analysis: An introduction to basic and advanced multilevel modelling* (2nd ed.). Sage Publications.

Soldatic, K., & Grech, S. (2016). *Disability and colonialism: (Dis)encounters and anxious intersectionalities*. Routledge.

St. Pierre, E. A., & Roulston, K. (2006). The state of qualitative inquiry: A contested science. *International Journal of Qualitative Studies in Education, 19*(6), 673–684.

Steinbugler, A. C., Press, J. E., & Dias, J. J. (2006). Gender, race, and affirmative action: Operationalizing intersectionality in survey research. *Gender & Society, 20*(6), 805–825.

Stinchcombe, A. L. (1968). *Constructing social theories*. University of Chicago Press.

Susser, M., & Susser, E. (1996a). Choosing a future for epidemiology: I. Eras and paradigms. *American Journal of Public Health, 86*, 668–673.

Susser, M., & Susser, E. (1996b). Choosing a future for epidemiology: II. From black box to Chinese boxes and eco-epidemiology. *American Journal of Public Health, 86*, 674–677.

Taagepera, R. (2008). *Making social sciences more scientific: The need for predictive models*. Oxford University Press.

Tashakkori, A., Johnson, R. B., & Teddlie, C. (2020). *Foundations of mixed methods research: Integrating quantitative and qualitative approaches in the social and behavioural sciences* (2nd ed.). Sage Publications.

Tunbridge, W. M. G., Evered, D. C., Hall, R., Appleton, D. R., Brewis, M., Clark, F., Grimley, Evans, J., Young, E., Bird, T., & Smith, P. A. (1977). The spectrum of thyroid disease in a community: The Whickham survey. *Clinical Endocrinology, 7*, 481–493.

Trahan, A. (2011). Qualitative research and intersectionality. *Critical Criminology, 19*, 1–14.

Ulijaszek, S. (2013). Cultural consensus modelling of disease. In C. Banwell, S. Ulijaszek, & J. Dixon (Eds.), *When culture impacts health: Global lessons for effective health research* (pp. 269–278). Elsevier.

United Nations (UN). (2000). *Gender and racial discrimination: Report of the Expert Group Meeting*. www.un.org/womenwatch/daw/csw/genrac/report.htm (accessed 8 October 2022).

Vanderpump, M. P., Tunbridge, W. M., French, J. M., Appleton, D., Bates, D., Clark, F., Grimley Evans, J., Hasan, D. M., Rodgers, H., Tunbridge, F., et al. (1995). The incidence of thyroid disorders in the community: a twenty-year follow-up of the Whickham Survey. *Clinical Endocrinology, 43*(1), 55–68.

VanderWeele, T. (2015). *Explanation in causal inference: Methods for mediation and interaction.* Oxford University Press.

Wang, X., & Sobel, M. E. (2013). New perspectives on causal mediation analysis. In S. L. Morgan (Ed.), *Handbook of causal analysis for social research* (pp. 215–242). Springer.

Washington, M. H. (1988). Introduction. In A. J. Cooper (1892[1988]), *A voice from the south* (pp. xxvii–liv). Oxford University Press.

Weller, N., & Barnes, J. (2014). *Finding pathways: Mixed-method research for studying causal mechanisms.* Cambridge University Press.

Weller, S. C. (1987). Shared knowledge, intracultural variation, and knowledge aggregation. *American Behavioural Scientist, 31*, 178–193.

Weller, S. C. (2007). Cultural consensus theory: Applications and frequently asked questions. *Field Methods, 19*, 339–368.

Wemrell, M., Mulinari, S., & Merlo, J. (2017). An intersectional approach to multilevel analysis of individual heterogeneity (MAIH) and discriminatory accuracy. *Social Science & Medicine, 178*, 217–219.

Whittaker, T., & Schumacker, R. (2022). *A beginner's guide to structural equation modelling* (5th ed.). Routledge.

Williams, M. G., & Lewis, J. A. (2019). Gendered racial microaggressions and depressive symptoms among Black women: A moderated mediation model. *Psychology of Women Quarterly, 43*(3), 368–380.

Yang, K. (2010). *Making sense of statistical methods in social research.* Sage Publications.

Young, C. (2020). Interlocking systems of oppression and privilege impact African Australian health and well-being in greater Melbourne: A qualitative intersectional analysis. *Journal of Social Issues, 76*(4), 880–898.

Yuval-Davis, N. (2006). Intersectionality and feminist politics. *European Journal of Women's Studies, 13*(3), 193–209.

INDEX

www.ingramcontent.com/pod-product-compliance
Lightning Source LLC
Chambersburg PA
CBHW081145020426
42333CB00021B/2670